CREATING LEARNING COMMUNITIES

CREATING LEARNING COMMUNITIES

A Practical Guide to Winning Support, Organizing for Change, and Implementing Programs

Nancy S. Shapiro
Jodi H. Levine

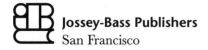

Jossey-Bass Publishers
San Francisco

Jossey-Bass books and products are available through most bookstores. To contact Jossey-Bass directly, call (888) 378-2537, fax to (800) 605-2665, or visit our website at www.josseybass.com.

Substantial discounts on bulk quantities of Jossey-Bass books are available to corporations, professional associations, and other organizations. For details and discount information, contact the special sales department at Jossey-Bass.

Manufactured in the United States of America.

Library of Congress Cataloging-in-Publication Data

Shapiro, Nancy Sherman.
    Creating learning communities : a practical guide to winning support, organizing for change, and implementing programs / Nancy S. Shapiro, Jodi H. Levine. — 1st ed.
      p.   cm. — (The Jossey-Bass higher and adult education series)
    Includes bibliographical references (p.   ) and index.
    ISBN 0-7879-4462-9
    1. College teaching—United States.   2. Group work in education—United States.   3. Educational change—United States.   I. Levine, Jodi H. II. Title. III. Series.
    LB2331.S473   1999
    378.1'25'0973—dc21

99-33625

FIRST EDITION
PB Printing 10 9 8 7 6 5 4 3 2

THE JOSSEY-BASS

HIGHER AND ADULT EDUCATION SERIES

For Ira, Susanna, and Brian
—N.S.S.

And for our students and our teachers
—J.H.L.

CONTENTS

PREFACE

Learning communities represent a major transformation in how campuses think about teaching and learning. They are characterized by a "variety of approaches that link or cluster classes during a given term, often around an interdisciplinary theme, that enroll a common cohort of students. This represents an intentional restructuring of students' time, credit and learning experiences to foster more explicit intellectual connections between students, between students and their faculty, and between disciplines" (MacGregor, Smith, Tinto, and Levine, 1999). These communities vary from minimal arrangements of linked or clustered classes, to team-taught interdisciplinary programs, to more elaborate models with designated residence halls, in-house advising, and the ambiance of a small college on a large research campus. In between is an array of alternatives that include faculty collaboration, interdisciplinary themes, focused writing classes, experiential learning, and undergraduate research.

A practical guide to learning communities would not be practical if it did not guide practitioners through the questions most often associated with the work. What are learning communities? More important, what do effective learning communities look like? How are they implemented? What does success look like?

Before campuses invest in the human, fiscal, and physical resources required to implement effective learning communities, they need to understand not only what learning communities are but why they are an appropriate and logical response to what is known about student success. The results of several major and influential longitudinal studies of higher education have confirmed what a number of educators have intuitively recognized for a long time: that success in college is directly connected to student-faculty interaction, student involvement in cocurricular activities, and, most important, peer influences and interaction. Yet in the face of this evidence, most campuses persist in using time-worn and isolated disciplinary and course structures.

The learning community model offers one of the most complete and targeted responses to the growing concerns about the climate of higher education. They are one promising way to create the kind of learning environment that colleges and universities need.

This book was written for several audiences. It is for college administrators and faculty who are considering bringing a learning community model onto their campuses and for those who already have some form of a learning community but are curious about other models. It contains valuable information for those who want to be prepared when their president, provost, or dean asks them to take on the challenge of building and sustaining learning communities on their campuses or in their colleges. We wrote it for faculty who on many campuses are likely to initiate the process of forming a learning community.

This book grew out of our own experiences as first-time directors of learning communities at the University of Maryland, College Park, and Temple University. In it we answer some of the questions that we posed to ourselves when we accepted the task of creating learning communities: What are learning communities? How do they differ from and complement other ways of organizing the undergraduate experience? How do we get started thinking about learning communities, and who needs to be at the table? How do we involve faculty, and why is it important to keep faculty involved from the beginning? How will we recruit students into the programs and keep them there? How can we create incentives for a traditional campus to think differently about organizing for learning? How much will it cost in both time and money? And how will we know it is worth the investment? How, in practical terms, do we get from here to there? And how will we know when we have arrived?

We examine in the chapters that follow the critical pieces that need to be in place from the beginning and suggest how to build campus consensus around the concept of learning communities. We refer to multiple examples but have not tried to create a comprehensive catalogue of learning communities. Instead, we have tried to balance the lessons learned from the experiences of our respective institutions with selected examples from other universities and colleges. Periodic reflections on our own work allow us to describe the two learning communities programs we know best, warts and all—and sometimes the warts offer the most instructive insights.

The careful reader will hear three voices in this book: Nancy Shapiro's voice, describing the College Park Scholars at the University of Maryland; Jodi Levine's voice describing Temple University's Learning Communities; and our combined voice, drawing generalizations from the literature and the experiences of learning communities programs across the country. In several places we use our programs as case studies because they allow us to tell stories from different points of view: the Temple University Learning Communities—open to all students, serving a primarily urban commuter population, designed around linked courses and operating on a relatively lean budget; and the University of Maryland College Park Scholars—a living, learning honors program that is intended to recruit students with very strong academic credentials and supported through a substantial campus commitment of money and full-time tenured faculty. Our two programs are different enough to bring balance to our examples, yet together they demonstrate how robust and powerful the learning communities concept must be to thrive in such different environments.

Although we have drawn the preponderance of our examples from research universities, we strongly support and reference learning communities on all types of campuses. We include examples from commuter campuses (Queens College, Indiana University, Purdue University Indianapolis) and residential campuses (University of Missouri-Columbia, University of Wisconsin), and from both four- and two-year institutions (LaGuardia Community College, Delta, William Rainey Harper, and Diablo Valley Colleges).

As the universe of learning community leaders and practitioners grows, it becomes increasingly difficult to catalogue the established and developing learning communities programs. (The Washington Center for Improving the Quality of Undergraduate Education, which many consider the premier clearinghouse for information on learning communities, maintains a partial listing of curricular learning communities: http://192.211.16.13/katlinks/washcntr/learncom/index.html.) This community contains many voices representing a variety of approaches to learning communities designed to meet the needs of diverse student, faculty, and institutional cultures. Although we endeavored to capture many of these voices in this book, we recognize that many of our examples come from institutions similar to our own.

Our attention to research universities stems in part, as we describe in Chapter One, from the response to the urgently felt need to redirect the energy and attention at large research universities toward the importance of undergraduate education. Of course, research universities are not the only campuses that have moved in the direction of forming learning communities, but they are the campuses where there is the greatest resistance, the most groundwork to be done, and the most obvious challenge to the prevailing cultural norms. Many small liberal arts colleges, comprehensive universities, and community colleges have success-fully integrated learning communities into their campus cultures for many different reasons, but in this book we chose to address the most challenging targets: those with the potential to affect the broadest band of students, presuming that smaller colleges and comprehensive universities could adapt insights from lessons learned to their own environments.

We start with a question, "Why learning communities?" Chapter One offers definitions and characteristics of learning communities and explores the answer to this question through a review of several prominent longitudinal research studies and policy reports that advocate the very types of learning environments and outcomes that learning communities seek to create. Chapter Two continues to address this question through a discussion of the historical influences and contemporary settings for learning communities' work. This chapter also describes models and approaches to learning communities.

Chapter Three is the first of three chapters describing the types of transformative change necessary for learning communities to take root and flourish. It begins with a general discussion of learning communities and the change process and concludes with practical advice on resources, primarily human and fiscal. Chapter Four addresses learning communities and curriculum—the essence of learning communities. Changing faculty roles and reward structures are the focus of Chapter Five.

Students and faculty are the central players in learning communities, but building learning communities requires administrative partnerships that extend beyond the classroom across the campus. These partnerships are discussed in Chapter Six. Chapter Seven deals with the logistics of establishing learning communities: planning, the registration process, marketing strategies, and building community.

Chapters Eight and Nine address evaluation and assessment. In Chapter Eight, we discuss developing a research plan, defining research questions, using collaborative approaches to research, and sharing results. Chapter Nine reviews different types of evidence describing the impact of learning communities on students, faculty, and the institution. Chapter Nine summarizes the supporting evidence that answers the question we raise at the beginning of this book: "Why learning communities?" We are convinced that learning communities significantly enrich the educational experience and success of undergraduate students and contribute to a climate for reconsidering the nature of pedagogy and scholarship.

We conclude with an examination of the issues we have raised and offer some personal reflections on our own experiences with learning communities: What do we know now that we wish we knew then? What lessons could not be taught but rather had to be learned through trial and error? What knowledge have we acquired along the way? and What one piece of advice would we offer to beginners? Chapter Ten contains our responses.

Our experiences—both as directors of learning communities and as researchers and authors of a book describing learning communities—have convinced us that although there may be no silver bullet solution to the significant challenges facing institutions of higher education in the upcoming decade, learning communities contribute significantly to the main undergraduate mission of a campus, encouraging the intellectual maturation, personal growth, and character development of students.

Acknowledgments

We are indebted to many people who have encouraged and supported us in this enterprise, and we gratefully acknowledge their generosity of time, wisdom, and spirit. Our enthusiasm for learning communities and the energy behind this book come from the faculty, the student affairs practitioners, and the campus administrators who have embraced the concepts we describe here and who have turned theories into realities, to the great good fortune of our students and our campuses.

The book was inspired by two programs, College Park Scholars and Temple University Learning Communities, which themselves were inspired in part by two special faculty-administrators: Ira Berlin, professor of history at the University of Maryland, College Park, and Dan Tompkins, faculty fellow for learning communities at Temple University. To our learning communities partners on our campuses: Thank you for allowing us to make your experiences such an integral part of this book.

The list of individuals we wish to thank would fill pages. Our learning communities colleagues at campuses across the country were generous in sharing their experiences by responding to our countless e-mail and telephone requests for more information. Numerous faculty, administrators, and reviewers from many different campuses and associations contributed to the diversity of examples and overall texture of the book. We especially thank Dennis Baron, Barbara Cambridge, Michael Colson, James Degnan, John Gardner, Barbara Holland, Brit Kirwan, Arthur Levine, Jean MacGregor, Katherine McAdams, Mahlon Straszheim, and William Zeller. We are also grateful to Gale Erlandson and David Brightman, supportive editors who helped us shape the project in ways that gave us a clear sense of direction and audience.

Nancy Shapiro wishes to thank her colleagues across the University of Maryland campus, especially the faculty and staff of the College Park Scholars Program whose ideas and energy have created an extraordinary community of learners. Coauthoring this book with Jodi has been a wonderful journey of discovery, reflection, and exploration; we learned from each other as we traded anecdotes and perspectives. Finally, there would be no book without the constant support, deep patience, and blind faith of my family and friends. My children, Susanna and Brian—one just finished with college and one getting ready for the adventure—have given my work with learning communities a special focus. My husband, Ira, has shared every aspect of my work, and to him I owe my deepest gratitude.

Jodi Levine wishes to thank her colleagues at Temple University for their patience, encouragement, and support throughout the writing of this book. Special thanks to my graduate students Brian Foley and Erin Gehringer for their research and proofreading assistance. I thank my dear friend Karen Carter for once again working her magic. I am especially grateful to my coauthor, Nancy. Thank you for inviting me to join you in writing this book. For over a year we formed our own learning community: sharing lessons learned, building a network of support, and integrating our unique ways of knowing and writing. Finally, I thank my family and friends. From start to finish, you were loving and supportive—sharing my excitement for this project and helping me remain focused on the task at hand.

July 1999

Nancy S. Shapiro
College Park, Maryland

Jodi H. Levine
Philadelphia, Pennsylvania

THE AUTHORS

Nancy S. Shapiro, founding director of the College Park Scholars Program, University of Maryland, designed and developed the first interdisciplinary living-learning programs at the university. She has had extensive experience in undergraduate education reform, including research, teaching, and administrative leadership roles in composition and rhetoric, writing across the curriculum, faculty development, and general education. She was the principal investigator for the grant from Funds for the Improvement of Post Secondary Education that created the Discovery Projects undergraduate research curriculum at the University of Maryland. Her publications include a coauthored book, *Scenarios for Teaching Writing* (National Council of Teachers of English, 1996), articles and reviews on a variety of undergraduate education topics, including learning communities, and an edited collection of essays on K–16 statewide initiatives, *Metropolitan Universities.* She is the director of the K–16 Partnership for Teaching and Learning for the University System of Maryland and works with the thirteen system institutions to foster critical partnerships and learning communities to improve the quality of teaching and learning for Maryland's teachers and students from kindergarten through college.

Jodi H. Levine is director of first-year programs at Temple University, Philadelphia. In this role, she directs the university's learning communities, freshman seminar, and supplemental instruction initiatives. She is responsible for the Academic Resource Center, a support unit for students who have not yet declared majors and students preparing for allied health programs. Levine has published and presented on a variety of issues relating to designing, implementing, sustaining, and evaluating learning communities. She recently edited *Learning Communities: New Structures, New Partnerships for Learning* (National Resource Center for the First-Year Experience and Students in Transition at the University of South Carolina, 1999).

CREATING LEARNING COMMUNITIES

CHAPTER ONE

INTRODUCTION

Why Learning Communities?

In 1993 the Wingspread Group, a blue-ribbon study group on higher education, issued a strongly worded challenge to the higher education community, beginning its report with these words:

> A disturbing and dangerous mismatch exists between what American society needs of higher education and what it is receiving. Nowhere is the mismatch more dangerous than in the quality of undergraduate preparation. . . . What does our society need from higher education? It needs stronger, more vital forms of community. It needs an informed and involved citizenry. It needs graduates able to assume leadership roles in American life. . . . Above all, it needs a commitment to the idea that all Americans have an opportunity to develop their talents to the fullest. Higher education is not meeting these imperatives [pp. 1–4].

That report, among others (Boyer, 1987; Astin, 1993; Coles, 1993), challenged many of the constituencies within the higher education community to rethink priorities while studying the complex political and societal forces that bear on their institutions. Many of these shaping influences are external to the university: an increasingly diverse student population, a technological transformation that is fostering an entrepreneurial for-profit industry around higher education, and a movement to make postsecondary education more universal. Yet one of the most pressing issues lies directly within our locus of control: a growing public dissatisfaction with the attention that faculty give to undergraduate learning. As postsecondary education becomes more necessary and more universal, the public is becoming increasingly skeptical of the quality of a four-year liberal arts education and the effectiveness of instructional approaches. The public and employers are concerned that students are not learning what they should in college: clear communication skills, critical thinking skills, and a developed sense of civic responsibility.

Students who come to colleges and universities today reflect a greater diversity of experience, ethnicity, expectations, and preparedness than ever before, and institutions need to be ready to face the challenges these students bring with them. New teaching and learning technologies are forcing a redefinition of the college experience, and campuses have been responding to the calls for change by restructuring, reorganizing, and reengineering. College administrators are beginning to talk the language of the business community: strategic planning, consumer-oriented programs, entrepreneurial activity, and bottom-line productivity, sometimes defined as increased enrollment, retention, and student achievement. The question thus becomes, How do we address the pragmatic realities facing higher education today without losing sight of our undergraduate teaching mission? One answer is learning communities.

Learning communities have arrived at a critical moment. Although they are not new (in fact, they are among the oldest and most revered models of education), they are experiencing a renaissance, particularly as they respond to the combination of internal and external pressures to better meet the needs of undergraduates and expectations of their parents ("consumers," to extend the business community metaphor).

What Is a Learning Community?

There is no proprietary definition of a learning community, in spite of all the essays, monographs, and other volumes that attempt to construct the essential definition. A common definition is this one:

> Any one of a variety of curricular structures that link together several existing courses—or actually restructure the material entirely—so that students have opportunities for deeper understanding and integration of the material they are learning, and more interaction with one another and their teachers as fellow participants in the learning enterprise [Gabelnick, MacGregor, Matthews, and Smith, 1990, p. 19].

Although many learning communities supporters subscribe to this definition, others prefer a broader description that describes the curricular as well as cocurricular potential of learning communities. For example, Alexander Astin, who recommended organizing students into learning communities to overcome feelings of isolation common on large campuses, offered a definition that recognized that learning occurs in a variety of settings:

> Such communities can be organized along curricular lines, common career interests, avocational interests, residential living areas, and so on. These can be used to build a sense of group identity, cohesiveness, and uniqueness; to encourage continuity and the integration of diverse curricular and co-curricular experiences; and to counteract the isolation that many students feel [Astin, 1985, p. 161].

The debate over what a learning community is will not end with this book. It is a lively and active discussion out of which emerge a core set of assumptions, beliefs, and values as to what constitutes a learning community. Our contribution to this debate, in terms of defining the "what" of learning communities, is to advance the notion that learning communities initiatives share basic characteristics:

- Organizing students and faculty into smaller groups
- Encouraging integration of the curriculum
- Helping students establish academic and social support networks
- Providing a setting for students to be socialized to the expectations of college
- Bringing faculty together in more meaningful ways
- Focusing faculty and students on learning outcomes
- Providing a setting for community-based delivery of academic support programs
- Offering a critical lens for examining the first-year experience

First, learning communities break students and faculty into groups that tend to be smaller than other units on campus (MacGregor, Smith, Matthews, and Gabelnick, 1997). This is accomplished through coenrollment in a defined set of curricular offerings, an essential, organizational characteristic of learning communities. Since learning communities are an effective way to bring students and faculty together in more intimate groups, many campuses promote smallness as a defining characteristic of their learning communities program. At Temple University, a large campus with a significant number of commuting students, the learning communities program adopted this motto: "Create a small college atmosphere at a large university." The University of Maryland promotes its College Park Scholars Program as "making the big store small."

Second, learning communities encourage integration of the curriculum. Learning communities are an effective way to address fragmentation in the curriculum, particularly within general education (Goodsell Love, 1999). General education is the generic, umbrella term that includes the grounding in knowledge and skills that all college students are expected to take with them when they graduate. Schneider and Schoenberg (1998, p. 7) characterize general education as acquiring intellectual capacities and understanding multiple modes of inquiry, civic knowledge, and values. Learning communities are curricular structures that allow faculty to teach, and students to learn, in more interdisciplinary, intellectually stimulating, and challenging ways. Students begin to recognize individual courses as part of an integrated learning experience rather than as separately taught requirements for a degree.

Next, by bringing small groups of students together in the classroom, learning communities help students establish academic and social support networks inside and outside the classroom. One of the primary influences on student development during college is the peer group (Astin, 1993; Newcomb, 1962). By definition, "peer group"—whether defined from an individual or a collective perspective—includes the elements of identification, affiliation, and acceptance (Astin, 1993). If students are not affiliating with fellow students, they are likely associating with nonstudent groups who do not share the same attitudes, values, expectations, and practices regarding the student role.

Fourth, learning communities provide a setting for students to become socialized to what it means to be a college student. Student interaction with peers reinforces the attitudes, values, and behaviors necessary to succeed as a member of the peer group. An important characteristic of learning communities is that students learn from each other. During college, students begin to recognize peers as important partners in the learning process. They contact each other outside class for academic support and encouragement, and typically they form study groups. One side effect of students' greater involvement with each other through learning communities is improved class attendance. Learning communities faculty report that student attendance and participation are greater in learning communities than in non–learning communities classes. Learning communities introduce accountability to the classroom. Faculty report that as members in a cohort, students are more accountable to each other and their teachers and as a result are less likely to skip class or arrive unprepared (Goodsell Love, 1999).

In a study of the FIG (Freshman Interest Group) Program at the University of Washington, Tinto and Goodsell (1993) found that enrolling in FIGs helped students deal with the feelings of anonymity and detachment they tended to experience in large classes. Participants used the FIG as a forum for discussing their dissatisfaction with large lecture courses, and they reported that being a FIG member positively influenced their class attendance habits. One student thought that it was important to attend his FIG writing class because both the teacher and his peers would notice his absences (p. 108). According to another student, "A nice thing about FIGs is that since you know everyone, they really encourage you not to skip out. There's more encouragement not to miss classes. If you go to your first class, then there's everyone telling you to go to your second" (pp. 108–109).

Another characteristic of learning communities is that they bring faculty together in meaningful ways by encouraging greater faculty interaction as teachers and learners. Learning communities provide a context for faculty development and engage faculty in a highly supportive teaching environment. Coplanning is an important characteristic of learning communities. Faculty spend time talking with one another about their teaching: modes of instruction, course content, student work, assessment, and applications of technology. As a result, learning communities faculty often report more risk taking in their teaching. For example, when Temple University's learning communities faculty were interviewed as part of a case study of the program, one professor commented that teaching in a learning community helped him "reinvent his teaching methodology" and gave him an "impetus to think more innovatively" (Reumann-Moore, El-Haj, and Gold, 1997).

Sixth, learning communities typically focus faculty and students on learning outcomes. As curricular structures, learning communities move campuses from an emphasis on teaching to an emphasis on teaching and learning. As teaching teams, learning communities faculty discuss their goals for the community and for student success, including plans for assessing student learning. Goodsell Love (1999) described a cycle of learning that takes place when students and faculty are brought together in learning communities: "A dynamic chain of events is set in motion: a focus on student learning outcomes directs the need for continued faculty development, which in turn facilitates the creation of an arena that promotes effective student learning." Evidence of student learning and the methods for achieving and assessing student learning are then fed back into the program through ongoing faculty development.

Learning communities also provide a setting for community-based delivery of student support services, such as academic advising, career mentoring, and tutoring. Through these communities, academic support can be brought to students, alleviating the need for students to visit separate offices and units across the campus when questions or problems arise. Many learning communities promote a "one-stop shopping" model to help students connect with the administrative bureaucracy of a university. Orientation, registration, schedule changes, financial aid, housing assignments can all be handled administratively in a learning community. This approach introduces students to campus resources much earlier in their careers than in the past. For example, the University of Maryland's College Park Scholars brought in a representative from career development to do a resumé writing workshop to help second-semester freshmen participants write resumés in preparation for securing their required internships. Program participants who are familiar with the services offered by career counselors will be more likely to seek their assistance in the future.

The University of Oregon involves academic advisers in the instructional delivery of its FIG program. In addition to the discipline-based courses, Oregon's learning communities include a one-credit "College Experience" course taught by either academic advisers or faculty members. When faculty members teach the courses, advisers work with them to design and facilitate the academic planning unit (Bennett, 1999). This course helps learning communities students recognize the role and value of academic advising and other academic support services to their success.

Finally, learning communities become a critical lens for examining the first-year experience. Many campuses report that the process of developing and implementing learning communities led to other curricular or program reforms, including changes to orientation, placement testing, residence hall programming, academic advising, and student activities.

In the early stages of learning communities at Temple, program staff became active participants in the orientation and advising process for new students. They learned that the university was not meeting the academic advising and support needs of students who had not yet decided on a major. These students were the most at risk to leave after their first year and more likely to experience academic difficulties than their peers with declared majors. The university committed the resources to develop the Academic Resource Center, an academic advising and support program for students who have not yet chosen a major. The majority of new students advised by the Academic Resource Center are now enrolled in learning communities and first-year seminar courses that allow them to explore majors while satisfying general education requirements.

These characteristics—or essential elements—create an integrated teaching and learning experience for participants in learning communities. But regardless of the definition on which the foundation of a learning community initiative is based, learning communities are defined by the participants: those who put them together, those who live and learn in them, and those who mentor and teach in them. Perhaps the best way to understand the essence of the learning community experience is to listen to the voices of those participants.

The excerpts that follow are from essays written by students in Maryland's College Park Scholars learning communities as part of a writing contest in which they were asked to write an essay on what it means to be part of a community:

> The transition from a small private school to an immense and diverse university can be quite intimidating. To solve the problem of this transition, a sense of community is imperative. I expect to be part of a group much stronger and more close-knit than any other organization on campus. The manner in which the program groups their students makes it noteworthy. Since I will be living with students who have similar curricular interests, I expect that befriending them will be quite effortless [Abhishek Srinivas, entering freshman, Life Sciences Program, fall 1998].

> As the time with my old communities draws to an end and my new community awaits, I am excited and nervous. I am going to have to leave my comfort zone for a while until I find a brand new one at [the university]. I plan to give all I can to the community and take everything it is capable of giving me. This [learning community] program is a way to make a transition from high school to college. I know that by being in the program I will be exposed to a diversity of people and make friends quickly. I think this will help me become a smarter, more well rounded individual [Alfred Luberto, entering freshman, CPS Arts Program, fall 1998].

Why Are Learning Communities Important?

As many campuses work to determine what learning communities are, others are just beginning to ask why they are important. Several recent policy studies in higher education create a compelling case for the introduction of learning communities on college campuses. Three longitudinal research studies lay the foundation: Boyer's classic report for the Carnegie Commission on Undergraduate Education, *College: The Undergraduate Experience;* Alexander Astin's data-driven analysis, *What Matters in College;* and Pascarella and Terenzini's *How College Affects Students.* Five commissioned studies move the discussion forward with recommendations and action plans: *Involvement in Learning: Realizing the Potential of American Higher Education* (National Institute of Education, 1984), *Returning to Our Roots: The Student Experience* (Kellogg Commission, 1997); *Reinventing Undergraduate Education: A Blueprint for America's Research Universities* (Boyer Commission, 1998); *Powerful Partnerships: A Shared Responsibility for Learning* (Joint Task Force on Student Learning, American Association for Higher Education, American College

Personnel Association, National Association of Student Personnel Administrators, 1998), and *The Academy in Transition: Contemporary Understandings of Liberal Education* (Schneider and Shoenberg, 1998).

Longitudinal Studies

The longitudinal studies offer a descriptive picture of the state of higher education at the time the research was being conducted. The architects of these studies went beyond reporting their findings and presented implications that still have an impact on the thinking and planning in higher education.

College: The Undergraduate Experience in America (1987). In the late 1980s, the Carnegie Foundation for the Advancement of Teaching supported a study to evaluate the undergraduate experience in American colleges and universities. In the final report, Boyer presented an analysis of the problems, possibilities, and potential of American colleges and challenged the higher education community to seize the moment. Key findings of this report addressed a set of divisions or dichotomies: the discontinuity between K–12 schools and college, campuses' confusion over mission and goals, the division between the liberal arts curriculum and the career-oriented vocationalism that factors so largely in the minds of students and parents, the forced choices faculty must make between research and teaching and between loyalty to their discipline and loyalty to their institution, and the widening gap between the academic affairs community and the student affairs community that has come to be reflected in all aspects of governance of the institution.

These are mighty challenges, yet throughout the study, Boyer offers a consistent response to the sense of impending fragmentation: look to connections. Find a way to balance community and individualism (p. 66); create an institution where the curricular and the cocurricular are two aspects of a single mission (p. 195); design a curriculum that is rooted in an integrated core where students are introduced to the connections across disciplines as well as the essential knowledge within disciplines (p. 91).

Boyer's analysis had far-reaching implications. The Carnegie Commission report attacked problems head on and made clear recommendations for realigning undergraduate education in American colleges and universities, giving a boost to higher education reformers who were prepared to implement new models of undergraduate education. Some examples were included in the study, but the great contribution of this report was that it opened the door for these experimental models to enter the mainstream of American higher education.

What Matters in College (1993). Astin analyzed responses from more than twenty thousand students, twenty-five thousand faculty members, and two hundred institutions of higher education and presented a rich analytical framework to assess the impact of college on students. This study is unusual for many reasons, not the least of which is that Astin identified 190 institutional characteristics and described how each influenced student growth and development, maturity, values and beliefs, career aspirations, and overall satisfaction with college.

Astin's comprehensive study had these major findings:

Growth in general knowledge is associated with the number of courses taken that emphasize writing skills, science or scientific inquiry, and history or historical analysis.

Critical thinking skills are strongly correlated with the number of courses taken that emphasize the development of writing skills, enrolling in interdisciplinary courses, and active engagement by the students in discussion, debate, class presentations, and talking over career and vocational plans.

Overall academic development is influenced most by student-oriented faculty and peer socioeconomic status, as well as group projects (collaborative learning) and having papers critiqued by instructors.

Leadership skills and interpersonal skills are most closely correlated with student-to-student interaction and socializing with students from different racial and ethnic groups and the number of writing skills courses taken.

What is particularly interesting about this snapshot of a complex, multifaceted study is that learning communities build on all the most positive associations and create environments for learning that are clearly empirically grounded.

How College Affects Students (1991). In their comprehensive study of the impact of college on undergraduates, Pascarella and Terenzini reviewed more than three thousand studies addressing cognitive and affective outcomes. Cognitive outcomes are those associated with higher-order thinking: knowledge acquisition, problem solving, analytical thinking, and synthesis. Affective outcomes include values and personality, attitudes and prejudices, and maturity and self-esteem. After carefully assessing and evaluating differences among "elite" and non-"elite" institutions—historically black and single-sex colleges, commuter and residential schools, two-year versus four-year schools, and dozens of other comparisons—Pascarella and Terenzini arrived at the following conclusion:

To a certain extent, all of the preceding discussion boils down to the issue of psychological size. With few exceptions, institutional size by itself does not appear to be a salient determinant of student change. There is evidence, however, that size is indirectly influential through the kinds of interpersonal relations and experiences it promotes or discourages. A number of steps have already been proven effective in increasing student engagement and reducing the psychological size of larger institutions by affording opportunities for students to become involved with smaller groups of individuals . . . includ[ing] cluster colleges and other purposeful housing arrangements, architectural alterations, academic organizations, co-curricular activities, work-study . . . and so on [p. 654].

The recommendations that came from this exhaustive meta-analysis have significantly influenced the development and evolution of learning communities over the past decade. The breadth of this study strengthened the resolve of forward-thinking campuses to put their theories to the test in campus-based learning communities.

Policy Studies

These three grounded research studies built a solid base for subsequent policy analyses sponsored by independent foundations and nonprofit associations. The policy reports reviewed next describe a process of reinventing and transforming undergraduate education to create new types of learning environments. In several instances, the reports specifically recommend organizing students and faculty into small communities of learners.

Involvement in Learning: Realizing the Potential of American Higher Education (1984). One of the earliest studies that came out in favor of creating learning communities was issued in 1984 by the National Institute of Education (NIE), U.S. Department of Education), which charged a study group to examine conditions of excellence in American higher education. In the report, the group issued a warning that higher education was failing to realize its potential and outlined the basic understanding that excellence in higher education was centered on student learning (p. v). The rapid expansion of higher education, followed by a period of tightening resources, resulted in a gap between the expectations and realities of student learning, curricular coherence, facilities, faculty morale, and academic standards. Institutions were ignoring important information on student achievement and retention, and failing to meet national expectations for higher education.

The *Involvement in Learning* report described three critical conditions of excellence: student involvement, high expectations, and assessment. The authors considered student involvement the most important of these and listed frequent interactions with faculty and peers as one way that students can demonstrate commitment to learning. The authors cited research demonstrating that frequent interaction with teachers is more strongly related to student satisfaction with the courses and intellectual and social environment of college than any other measure of involvement.

In its recommendations for increasing student involvement, the study group advocated front-loading resources into more and improved services for first- and second-year students, including the following recommendation: "Every institution of higher education should strive to create learning communities, organized around specific intellectual themes or tasks" (p. 35).

Effective learning communities were characterized as having the following characteristics (p. 33):

- Offering a smaller unit than most other communities on campus
- Having a sense of purpose
- Providing a way to overcome the isolation of faculty members from one another and their students
- Encouraging faculty to relate to each other as both specialists and educators
- Encouraging continuity and integration in the curriculum
- Helping to build a send of group identity, cohesion, and specialness

This report recognized that learning communities increased opportunities for dialogue between students and teachers and promoted more active modes of learning. The authors added that learning community experiences were even more critical at larger institutions, where students have a great need for meaningful academic identifications.

Returning to Our Roots: The Student Experience (1997). In 1997 the Kellogg Commission challenged the National Association of State Universities and Land Grant Colleges to accept a new leadership role in American higher education. According to the report, public colleges and universities today face new challenges to their identity and existence at a time when these institutions are needed more than ever before. The commission catalogued the challenges, which still sound familiar: enrollment pressures, new competitors, funding difficulties and cost increases, eroding public trust, and limited institutional flexibility. The commission distilled their response to these challenges in one overriding directive,

"Leadership to put students first" (p. 7), and recommended that member institutions become genuine, student-centered learning communities.

The idea of learning communities described in the Kellogg Commission report reflects all the common understandings that permeate the discussion in this book: "In such a community, all activities and responsibilities are related. Students, staff, and faculty come to see themselves as engaged in a common enterprise. Above all, the quality of learning is nearly inseparable from the experience of functioning as an integral part of the community itself" (p. 9).

Powerful Partnerships (1998). Modeling the collaboration that is recommended in this task force report, the American Association of Higher Education, the American College Personnel Association, and the National Association of Student Personnel Administrators advocated for a new relationship between academic affairs and student affairs on college campuses. They challenged the higher education community to "share responsibility for learning." The task force offered ten learning principles and recommendations for collaborative action supported by empirically validated illustrations and examples:

1. Learning is fundamentally about making and maintaining connections.
2. Learning is enhanced by taking place in the context of a compelling situation that balances challenge and opportunity.
3. Learning is an active search for meaning by the learner.
4. Learning is developmental—a cumulative process involving the whole person.
5. Learning is done by individuals who are intrinsically tied to others as social beings.
6. Learning is strongly affected by the educational climate in which it takes place.
7. Learning requires frequent feedback if it is to be sustained.
8. Much learning takes place informally and incidentally.
9. Learning is grounded in particular contexts and individual experiences.
10. Learning involves the ability of individuals to monitor their own learning.

The recommendations that flow from these principles provide a blueprint for institutions that want to move forward with action plans, and the examples create a concrete touchstone that grounds this report in reality. For example, under principle 7, the task force recommended that students be

- Expected to meet high but achievable standards and provided timely information on their progress
- Engaged in a recurring process of correction and improvement
- Encouraged to take risks

One example cited is Iowa State's collaboration between the College of Design and the Department of Residence. Here, design students live together in the Design Exchange House, a learning community that includes a design studio where students create projects for classes and career portfolios and they receive continual feedback from peers and teachers.

The *Partnerships* document moves beyond the research studies of the early 1990s into policy recommendations for rethinking campus structures. Such recommendations would have been premature ten years before, but the campus climate has changed dramatically. Collaborations across divisions on a campus are no longer seen as threatening. In fact, the advocates of these collaborations make a strong case that for all the right reasons—idealistic (student learning) and pragmatic (budgetary)—these collaborations create a campus community where the whole is greater than the sum of the parts.

Contemporary Understandings of Liberal Education (1998). In an effort to assess and respond to contemporary challenges to traditional liberal education, Schneider and Shoenberg authored an American Association of Colleges and Universities discussion paper that charts a path to a new definition of liberal learning. Schneider and Shoenberg view the goals of liberal education as leading to the development of intellectual capacities rather than to specific, but limited subject matter content. A key strategy to acquiring these intellectual capacities is the dismantling of traditional disciplinary requirements for undergraduate general education and a move toward more interdisciplinary studies: "Multidisciplinary and integrative learning designed to create an awareness of relationships, tensions, and complementarities among ideas and epistemologies" (p. 11). They predict "new emphases on engaging the diversity of human communities and global cultures; the radiation of experiential learning and its close congener, service learning; cooperative and collaborative learning; interdisciplinarity; topically linked courses or 'learning communities'; undergraduate research; discovery approaches to science" (p. 6).

The first level of these intellectual capacities that Schneider and Shoenberg hold up as the new goals of liberal education are a reinterpretation of a competency model of teaching and learning, where success is not measured by what is required and taught but rather by what students know and can do at the end of their course of study. Students who can solve problems in creative ways, can write and speak fluently and persuasively, have gained a measure of self-knowledge grounded in values, and can move easily through the diverse human community have acquired a liberal education and the intellectual capacities that will carry them into the next phase of their lives.

Yet, according to Schneider and Shoenberg, old habits are hard to break. Institutions of higher education will have to take a hard look at their traditional organization, blurring the lines between general education and the major, re-warding faculty for collaborations, and recognizing their efforts in transforming curricula and teaching, in addition to traditional research. All these predictions are already taking place in learning communities, the real incubators of innovation on campuses across the country.

Reinventing Undergraduate Education (1998). In 1998 the Boyer Commission on Educating Undergraduates in the Research University took up the challenge of addressing what makes research universities unique in the constellation of American higher education—and answered that question with one word: *research.* Yet to the dismay of many, research opportunities are typically missing in the undergraduate curriculum. The commission set out to find good examples of undergraduate research experiences and make recommendations drawn from those best practices. It should not surprise anyone that the best examples of undergraduate research opportunities were found in learning communities. The commission wrote:

> What is needed now is a new model of undergraduate education at research universities that makes the baccalaureate experience an inseparable part of an integrated whole. Universities need to take advantage of the immense resources of their graduate and research programs to strengthen the quality of undergraduate education. . . . Research universities should foster a community of learners. Large universities must find ways to create a sense of place to help students develop small communities within the larger whole [p. 5].

Conclusion

America's college campuses are changing in response to both external and internal forces in widespread attempts to meet the challenges facing the higher education community. More students with differing degrees of preparation are enrolling in colleges and universities, and traditional models of higher education are no longer sufficient to respond to society's needs. Higher education is not immune from market forces, technological innovation, and an emerging globalization of access and resources. Learning communities have emerged as a practical, pedagogically sound concept for addressing the criticisms and challenges leveled at higher education today. Regardless of how we choose to define success in college—whether it is a statistical measure of persistence and retention, or gains in critical thinking and writing abilities that show up as positive outcomes on student learning assessments—we now have compelling evidence to suggest that creating learning communities on campuses leads to greater student success in college.

Why learning communities? Because they build on our knowledge of the undergraduate experience, reinvent undergraduate education, and expand on our contemporary understandings of liberal education to create a multidimensional student experience grounded on a foundation of what matters in college.

CHAPTER TWO

TYPES AND MODELS OF LEARNING COMMUNITIES

Maricopa Community Colleges uses an analogy to help visitors to its Web site, "Integrated Learning Garden," to understand the concept of learning communities: "We represent learning communities at the Maricopa Community Colleges as this garden of prickly pear cacti. They have special needs to survive the desert climate. But when nurtured, they flourish and bear beautiful fruit and flowers" (Maricopa Community Colleges Web site, 1998).

Many campuses are looking to learning communities as models of curricular reform that restructure the undergraduate experience in ways that promote greater student involvement in learning. They recognize that learning communities intentionally reorganize courses or restructure the curriculum completely so that students, together with their peers and teachers, can build more meaningful connections to each other and what they are learning. In selecting a particular approach to learning communities, campuses must recognize that these communities are most effective when the basic structure and characteristics of a particular model are adapted to the organization and to the student and faculty culture of a campus. Choosing an approach first requires an understanding of the basic principles on which learning communities models are based.

Historical Roots

Learning communities take different shapes as they are installed in undergraduate curricula across all institution types. And although programs vary according to the approach to learning communities, location of the program in the undergraduate curriculum, and size of the initiative, they share a rich history with other educational reform movements that emphasizes community, social learning theory, and collaborative learning.

Early Reformers

The early work of John Dewey, Alexander Meiklejohn, and Joseph Tussman had a profound influence on the way learning communities are defined and formed today. Their focus was on liberal teaching, described by Meiklejohn (1932) as "attempts to create and to cultivate insight or knowledge" (p. xix). Their educational plans promoted connected knowledge as opposed to unrelated or unconnected knowledge. These three educators also shared a willingness to challenge the status quo. Creating the kinds of curricular structures that support learning as integrated social experiences required, then and now, challenging traditional notions of teaching and learning.

No discussion of influences on learning communities would be complete without referring to John Dewey. Dewey described education as a purposeful, student-centered social process that required a close relationship between teacher and student. The learning environment should be structured to apply cooperative and collaborative approaches to learning that emphasized learning and not teachers. According to Dewey (1916), education should promote "habits of mind" (p. 57). He saw education as growth. Students should develop ways of understanding situations in which the mind operates. This required forms of skill and habits of judgment and reason. He was committed to learning by doing and saw learning as a lifelong process. Dewey contributed insights into the learning process and a definition of education as a continual process of reorganization, reconstruction, and transformation.

Alexander Meiklejohn's Experimental College at the University of Wisconsin (1927–1932) is considered one of the earliest, organized learning communities initiatives. Like Dewey, Meiklejohn was troubled by fragmentation and specialization in undergraduate education. He recognized the relationship between education and democracy and wanted to promote an education environment that prepared students for their roles as citizens. His Experimental College was a two-year lower-division program built around the study of society: what it is and how it works. In the first year, the learning community explored democracy in fifth-century Athens and in the second year nineteenth- and twentieth-century America. The Athens-America curriculum, as it was known, enrolled students in the program full time. Instruction was discussion based and relied on original texts from the periods to study the civilizations.

In 1928, the second year of the effort, Meiklejohn added another component to the program: regional study. Sophomores were required to conduct an analysis of an American community. The purpose of the task was to help students apply what they learned about Athenian civilization to something more personal and relevant, such as their own home towns.

Meiklejohn (1932) defined the place and function of the Experimental College in "the larger scheme of education" (p. 3). He recognized that students entered Experimental College with twelve prior years of education and that after the sophomore year they would continue with advanced studies.

> In a word, the freshman and sophomore years—which we may call the "lower college"—are not a closed and separate experience. They grow out of experiences which have gone before; they grow into experiences which are coming after. They are an episode within a continuous process of education. They can be understood only when they are seen as making their special contribution to that process as a whole [p. 3].

Meiklejohn built the Experimental College on the principles of connected and integrated learning. He called for a "scheme of reference" running through the instructional plan (p. 3), and he referred to faculty who were teaching in the program as "advisers." In the Experimental College, advisers shared in the teaching of all subject matter.

Meiklejohn's program challenged the popular elective system of education. He struggled against departmentalism and provincialism, a familiar theme in higher education reform. He also had to deal with the separateness of the Experimental College. Fifty years later educational reformers face similar challenges as learning communities programs struggle to shed the "experimental" label that isolates them and prevents them from being a regular part of the curriculum.

Joseph Tussman's Experiment at Berkeley (1965–1969) is another early example of learning communities in undergraduate education. Tussman, like Meiklejohn, was concerned with the need for a quality lower-division education experience for students. He felt the university was struggling with a dual identity: the tension between being a college and a university. He defined universities as highly trained collections of specialists, with departmental interests defining and controlling the upper-division education experience. He saw the lower division as "invaded, neglected, exploited, and misused" (Gabelnick, MacGregor, Matthews, and Smith, 1990, pp. 13–14).

Tussman defined the Experiment as a program, not as a curriculum with a discrete set of courses. Programs were created by teams of faculty representing different disciplines. He saw creating curriculum as a collaborative process. Although the Experiment was short-lived, Tussman's work influenced reform on other campuses, including The Evergreen State College, and Patrick Hill's work at the State University of New York at Stony Brook. These programs are among those recognized for reform and reorganization in Jones and Smith's *Against the Current* (1984), a book that emerged from a national conference on alternative education commemorating the tenth anniversary of The Evergreen State College.

Leaders in the Learning Communities Movement

The creation of The Evergreen State College in Olympia, Washington, in the 1970s is described as "one of the few major experiments in curricular innovation" (Youtz, 1984, p. 93). The college was founded with a curriculum based on interdisciplinary coordinated studies programs. Programs were year long and full time for both faculty and student participants. Programs offered a flexible curriculum design and focused on real-world problems. In the first year, programs included Political Ecology, Contemporary American Minorities, and Environmental Design.

The book seminar, a critical component of both Meiklejohn's and Tussman's work, is at the center of Evergreen's Coordinated Studies Programs. It builds classroom discussion around original sources instead of textbooks. Faculty convene the seminar once or twice a week and serve as facilitators. The seminar is the "social and intellectual nucleus of coordinated studies as it provides students the opportunity to build connections between the texts, lectures and other material presented in the coordinated studies program" (Gabelnick, MacGregor, Matthews, and Smith, 1990, p. 30).

The State University of New York at Stony Brook began its Federated Learning Communities program in 1976, motivated by a desire to sharpen the definition of academic community and challenge existing curricular structures:

> What we are seeking are new structures of association readily intelligible structures of association which engage the intellectual and personal energies of students and faculty in common and shared enterprises, which confirm and work to realize the worthwhile expectations of students and faculty, which effectively challenge the unconstructive and devitalizing practices of students and faculty [Hill, 1984, p. 281].

Stony Brook's Federated Learning Communities reorganized existing courses to focus on contemporary issues in an interdisciplinary context. In addition to the federated (clustered) courses, students enrolled in a program seminar led by a faculty master learner. Federated Learning Communities asked faculty to be a "new kind of teacher" (Hill, 1984, p. 288). Master learners participated in full-time study alongside the students in the learning communities, modeling the benefits of critical thinking, interpreting the expectations faculty and students had for each other, assisting in the development of students' own ideas, and facilitating student learning by identifying opportunities and resources for learning.

Uses of Learning Communities

Historically and today, learning communities programs differ in the ways they involve faculty and the amount of time students spend learning with and from each other. Regardless of the approach, a learning communities classroom is more student centered, with teachers and students sharing responsibility for teaching and learning.

A campus that is considering introducing learning communities is faced with choosing among several different approaches. The administration needs a basic understanding of how campuses use learning communities in terms of general goals and objectives. They also have choices about where learning communities are placed in the organization.

Many campuses build learning communities into existing general education programs or use them as a centerpiece of general education reform. Learning communities can improve general education by bringing students and faculty together in ways that promote greater interaction with each other and deeper integration of the material being studied.

Other campuses place learning communities at the center of first-year-experience initiatives. Learning communities are an ideal setting to introduce students to what it means to be a college student—most important, the differences between high school and college classrooms. Learning communities located within first-year-experience programs often link academic, discipline-based courses to new or existing first-year-experience courses or freshman seminars. These are courses taught by faculty, academic administrators, or student affairs professionals for which students receive academic credit.

Learning communities can also be built into developmental studies programs that provide at-risk students with a support network of faculty, peers, and counselors. Learning communities that pair developmental or skills courses promote student success through an emphasis on basic skills. Communities can emphasize both skill enhancement and academic progress by linking developmental courses with credit-bearing courses in the disciplines.

The STARS learning community at GateWay Community College is a developmental program that focuses on the needs of the student population that is most at risk. The STARS community pairs two developmental courses, English and reading, with a student success seminar. These courses were a natural choice for a learning community because they shared a common student population: students with the lowest skill levels, little familiarity with the expectations of colleges, and the least supportive environments (Maricopa Community College Web site, 1998). STARS aims to improve the retention and achievement of these students by helping them better understand the expectations of college and strengthening the attitudes and skills needed to succeed in college. According to its founders, STARS's "main connection was viewed as the theme of success following from self responsibility" (Rasmussen and Skinner, 1998, p. 3).

An important concept to consider in the planning phase of learning communities work is that a campus does not have to offer learning communities for all students—at least not all at once. In fact, many campuses deliberately start small. There is logic in targeting specific populations for learning communities participation. These programs might build learning communities around a shared academic or career interest such as women in science or premedicine studies. Students enroll in a cluster of courses that typically include a seminar addressing their academic and career goals. In addition, these programs often include tutoring, mentoring, internship, and undergraduate research components. Some programs are collaborations between two or more existing campus programs.

Students participating in the National Science Foundation–sponsored AMP Program (Alliance for Minority Participation in Math, Science, and Engineering) at Temple University enroll in a learning community that links precalculus, the first course in general chemistry, and a freshman seminar. An important objective for this community is to promote minority student academic performance and persistence in degree programs where students of color are typically underrepresented. These students receive tutoring in math and science, undergraduate research experience, and academic and career advising. The community was developed jointly by the coordinators of the Learning Communities and AMP programs.

Learning communities are also an effective way to introduce students to the academic culture of the major. They bring entering students into contact with faculty and peers in the department and facilitate connections with alumni. Introductory courses in the major are easily linked with writing courses to form communities in which students are exposed to the scholarship and language of a discipline. The University of Washington's FIG Program offers students several premajor communities from which to choose. Students in the Business FIG, for example, enroll in an economics, writing, math, and FIG University Resources course that can be applied to the business degree.

Learning communities provide students with an introduction and access to the culture of a profession. The New Engineering Curriculum at Drexel University in Philadelphia brings together faculty from engineering, science, and the humanities to form learning communities. The program emphasizes the interdisciplinary mathematical and science foundations of engineering, the role of technology and the computer, and the importance of experimentation and teamwork in the professional practice of engineering. The first-year humanities course is integrated as an important aspect of the engineer's work (Arms, 1998).

Learning Communities Models

Three of the four approaches to learning communities examined here are adapted from the models originally described by Gabelnick, MacGregor, Matthews, and Smith (1990): paired or clustered courses, cohorts in large courses or FIGs (freshmen interest groups), and team-taught programs. The fourth approach, residence-based learning communities, describes models that intentionally link the classroom-based learning community with a residential life component. Each of the four models is described in terms of the following characteristics:

Curricular structure: How courses and students are organized to form communities

Faculty role: The levels of faculty development and ways faculty collaborate to achieve curricular integration

Cocurricular opportunities: The ways that a learning communities approach integrates students' in-class and out-of-class learning experiences

Opportunities for peer leadership: Leadership roles in learning communities for community members or upper-division students

We pay specific attention to the peer leadership dimension because learning communities provide important opportunities for undergraduates to remain involved with peers and faculty after their enrollment in communities.

There is no one best model or approach to learning communities. On one campus, learning communities might be developed in the spirit of one particular model, while at another they may be built by combining elements from more than one approach. Rasmussen and Skinner (1998) offer this advice:

The best design will depend on institutional environment and the specific disciplines to be integrated as well as the characteristics of the faculty and students who will participate. The goal is to provide a richer range of learning experiences to our students and contribute to a more vibrant and supportive campus environment for students and faculty alike [p. 4].

Paired or Clustered Courses

Curricular Structure. The paired—or clustered—course model links individually taught courses through cohort and often block scheduling. The paired-course model links two courses and is considered the simplest of learning communities models in terms of curricular strategy. A paired-course learning community typically enrolls a group of twenty to thirty students in two courses. Offerings tend to be existing courses that traditionally enroll significant numbers of first-year students.

One of the two courses in the pairing is usually a basic composition or communications course. These courses tend to be more interdisciplinary in nature and promote a classroom environment where students and faculty get to know each other. In paired-course learning communities, classes are often linked based on logical curricular connections and skill areas. For example, a pairing of calculus with general chemistry promotes scientific discovery and quantitative reasoning skills. Other courses commonly used in pairs include college math, introductory social sciences, literature, philosophy, and first-semester courses in science. Exhibit 2.1 shows several examples of paired course learning communities.

A pair might also include a first-year-experience or freshman seminar course, a for-credit offering designed to assist students in the transition to college. Indiana University Purdue University Indianapolis (IUPUI) builds paired-course learning communities linking first-year-experience courses to discipline-based courses. The emphasis in these communities is on skill building, student learning, and connecting undergraduates to the people and resources they need to succeed in college. Each community features a section of either a critical thinking course or a first-year seminar. The success seminar is taught by an instructional team, led by a faculty member, that also includes a peer mentor, librarian, and academic counselor.

This instructional approach to helping entering students make the transition to their new academic experience involves a great deal of cross-campus collaboration. IUPUI's newly formed University College is the administrative home for the IUPUI Learning Communities Program. A faculty committee coordinates faculty participation, the university library assigns librarians, and University College organizes adviser and student mentor involvement. As IUPUI moves toward

EXHIBIT 2.1. EXAMPLES OF LINKED-
COURSE LEARNING COMMUNITIES.

Linked Courses with Stated Themes

Delta College
Learn Economics by Navigating the Internet
   Principles of Economics I + Basic Applications/Internet (5 credits)
Community and Individualism in American Culture
   College Composition I + Introduction to American Government (6 credits)
Chemical Composition
   College Composition II + General and Inorganic Chemistry (7 credits)
The Role of Control
   College Composition I + General Psychology (7 credits)

Linked Courses Without Stated Themes

Temple University
Mass Media and Society + College Composition (6 credits)
General Chemistry I + Precalculus + Learning for the New Century (seminar)
   (9 credits)
American Women's Lives + College Composition (6 credits)
Introduction to Academic Discourse + Learning for the New Century (5 credits)

University of Miami
Elementary Botany + English Composition I (6 credits)
Jewish Civilization: Society, Culture, and Religion + English Composition I (6 credits)
Calculus II + Introduction to Marine Science (7 credits)
Social and Psychological Foundations of Education + English Composition I (6 credits)

mandating learning community participation for all entering University College students, it faces the challenge of identifying resources for the instructional team model. The work of academic advisers and librarians has been redefined to include learning communities assignments, and the undergraduate schools are working with University Studies to identify appropriate rewards to increase faculty leadership and participation in the program (Evenbeck and Williams, 1998).

Even in a simple paired-course model, individual communities can draw energy from interdisciplinary, thematic titles. Themes give students and faculty a head start in building connections between the two courses. For example, students at Delta College can enroll in "The Role of Control," a learning community linking college composition and general psychology.

The cluster approach typically expands the paired-course model by linking three or four individually taught courses around a theme. Clusters are often small and usually enroll cohorts of twenty to thirty students. One course tends to be a writing course, and the cluster usually includes a weekly seminar. The seminar plays an important role in helping students and faculty build curricular connections between the courses. These seminars are often offered for less than full academic credit (one or two credits as opposed to three or four) and become an ideal setting for synthesis and community-building activities because of that flexibility. The University of Texas at Corpus Christi has developed a cluster approach using larger courses. Students enroll in two large lecture sections dedicated to learning communities that are linked to smaller English and seminar sections.

All daytime students in the Liberal Arts and Sciences program at LaGuardia Community College are required to take an introductory cluster in their first semester. Students placed in remedial courses enroll in clusters in their second semester. Clusters include the "Lib 110" (Liberal Arts) hour, a course that meets one hour a week and is usually team-taught by two or three faculty teaching in the cluster. Program directors describe the hour as "a way of making a genuine commitment to the integration of the clusters courses and for students to benefit from this integration" (P. Van Slyck, personal correspondence, Oct. 14, 1998). For example, the faculty coteaching the Lib 110 hour for the Drama, Culture, and Communication cluster help students write a research paper on a theatrical production by using the Lincoln Center for the Performing Arts Library in New York City and lead enrichment field trips to see and critique a Broadway play.

Faculty Role. Because the offerings in paired-course learning communities are individually taught established courses, the faculty role in these communities is often assumed to be minimal. It is a mistake to think that learning communities can be created simply by linking courses through a registration process. A more accurate way to explain the complex role of faculty in paired-course learning communities would be to use a sliding scale of involvement and investment. If faculty invest a minimal amount of time in integrating their curriculum and planning activities for the students coenrolled in their courses, students may gain only the social benefits of taking two courses with a common group of students. When faculty invest the time to integrate their curriculum and design community building activities, students can achieve a deeper understanding of course material and a more meaningful interaction with teachers and peers—the outcomes that learning communities, by design, should offer.

Achieving integrated teaching and learning in linked courses takes a commitment of time and resources. Ideally faculty should plan their courses together, linking syllabi through coordinated readings and assignments. A faculty attitude that there is nothing different about such a course except for the fact that he or she shares students with a faculty member in another department is an obstacle in the linked-course model. Faculty need to understand that the link raises the expectation for collaborative planning and curricular integration between courses.

To achieve integrated teaching and learning in linked-course learning communities, faculty need to coordinate and teach their courses in a campus environment that values and rewards collaborative teaching.

Faculty teaching pairs need to communicate their expectations for students, teaching philosophies, goals for their courses and the community, curricular objectives, and plans for assessing student learning. Under the best circumstances, planning begins prior to the start of the term and continues throughout the semester. At faculty development workshops, time is usually reserved for teachers to discuss their courses and plan their community. More campuses are providing resources for faculty development.

Learning communities in the Freshman Year Initiative (FYI) Program at Queens College in New York City feature three courses, one of them English composition. Courses and faculty come from more than thirty departments, and most faculty in the program are full-time, senior professors. The four to five faculty members who are teaching courses as part of a community meet regularly to exchange course materials, coordinate exams and papers, design community projects, and discuss student progress. Faculty also visit each other's courses.

Faculty commitment in learning community clusters is usually more involved and more time intensive than in paired courses. It is important to note that whether the cluster links two or three courses, faculty commitment in the cluster model varies, with coplanning becoming more difficult to realize when three or more teachers and courses are involved in the learning community. When enrollment in the courses is restricted to learning communities students only, faculty coplanning is easier. Clusters are organized around a theme that is usually faculty generated. Faculty typically coordinate readings and assignments across the cluster and on some campuses share responsibility for teaching the weekly seminar. On other campuses, one faculty member from a discipline-based course assumes teaching responsibility for the seminar. Seminars can also be peer led, providing an opportunity for upper-division students to stay involved in the learning communities while gaining leadership experience.

Faculty at LaGuardia Community College work collaboratively to design clusters and then apply to teach their clusters as part of the college's cluster program. To apply, faculty teams submit a cluster proposal form (see Exhibit 2.2). The description of the cluster must contain answers to the following questions:

- What central questions or themes will this cluster explore?
- How will each course differ from its "stand-alone" version?
- How will specific classroom activities in each discipline contribute to the exploration of the cluster's central themes?
- How do you plan to structure linkages in the research paper?

EXHIBIT 2.2. CLUSTER PROPOSAL FORM, LAGUARDIA COMMUNITY COLLEGE.

This Proposal Form must be fully completed *on both sides* and approved before the cluster will be considered for inclusion in any schedule.

I.   Proposed semester _____ Contact Person _____

II. Name/Title of Cluster
    _____

III. Description to be used in recruitment materials (max. 30 words)
    _____
    _____
    _____

IV. Special room requirements? (labs, filmroom, theater, etc.?)
    _____

V.   Individual Courses which Comprise the Cluster (Attach Grid)
    1. Course number _____ Course name _____
       Instructor _____ Credits ____ Time/Days _____
    2. Course number _____ Course name _____
       Instructor _____ Credits ____ Time/Days _____
    3. Course number _____ Course name _____
       Instructor _____ Credits ____ Time/Days _____
    4. Course number _____ Course name _____
       Instructor _____ Credits ____ Time/Days _____

VI. Faculty cluster meeting time: Please designate the 1 hour time slot when all cluster faculty will be available for meetings. _____ Time/Days (Attach Grid)

VII. Attach student target group data—(contact Harriet Mesulam for data regarding potential student population)

VIII. What specialized recruitment activities are needed?

This form must be received by Harriet Mesulam with all signatures and information complete. Forms missing vital information will be returned to the originating instructor. Additional sheets may be attached. OVER! →

- Is the form complete?
- Have ALL appropriate department chairs signed it?
- If necessary, are completed overload forms attached?
- Is a schedule grid completed?

EXHIBIT 2.2, Continued

Cluster Description

Course Organization—(attach additional page if desired)

1. What central questions or themes will this cluster explore?

2. How will each course differ from its "stand-alone" version?

3. How will specific classroom activities in each discipline contribute to the exploration of the cluster's central themes?

4. How do you plan to structure linkages in the research paper?

5. How do you plan to use the LIB 110 hour?

Approvals: Each course in the cluster must be approved by the chair of the department in which the course belongs.

Department Chair _____ Date _____
Department Chair _____ Date _____
Department Chair _____ Date _____

Source: LaGuardia Community College. Used by permission.

- How do you plan to use the LIB 110 hour [an integrated hour usually team-taught by two or three faculty teaching in the cluster]?

The teaching team must also identify the students that the cluster will target and any specialized recruitment activities needed to enroll students in the cluster.

The first step in the cluster approval process is to gain approval from the department chair for each course in the cluster. The cluster application is then submitted to the Cluster Program Steering Committee, which consists of one member from each of the departments in Liberal Arts. Committee members review and vote on the cluster applications. The program coordinators sit on the steering committee as advisory, nonvoting members.

The process is becoming increasingly competitive, and more and more faculty are interested in developing clusters, which naturally leads to higher-quality clusters. The program coordinators are considering adding student feedback to the cluster selection process in an attempt to build in one more level of quality control.

Cocurricular Opportunities. In the paired-course model, particularly when courses are block scheduled, faculty can take advantage of combined class meetings to plan off-campus field trips or special events, such as film screenings, guest speakers, or pizza parties. Faculty can also plan community-building activities that meet outside class time or on weekends. On campuses with large numbers of commuting students, however, activities scheduled during nonclass time may be poorly attended. In addition, an increasing number of students on all campuses reserve their afternoons and weekends for work. Some learning communities faculty have found that community-building activities tend to be most effective when they take place during class periods or blocks of time reserved for program activities. Bowling Green State University's Chapman Learning Community reserves a block of time on Wednesdays for faculty and student activities.

In the cluster model, the learning community might include an experiential learning or community service component. The weekly seminar, through use of discussion and assigned readings, can help students connect what they are learning in their cluster courses to experiences in the field. For example, students in the University of Maryland's College Park Scholars Program participate in colloquia. The colloquium is a course offering one to three credits in which faculty explore and experiment with interdisciplinary themes. Colloquium curricula often include opportunities for experiential learning. In one case, a faculty member leading an arts cluster assigned his class the novel *Les Misérables* and then arranged for students to attend a performance of the play. The following week members of the cast came to campus and met with students in this colloquium.

Peer Leadership. The paired-course model affords the fewest opportunities to involve upperclassmen in peer leadership roles. When communities are formed by linking only two courses, there are fewer peer teaching roles for undergraduates. Peers, however, can play a valuable role in a community by serving as advisers, tutors, or undergraduate teaching assistants.

In clusters, peers often facilitate or coteach weekly seminars. Peer leadership is an excellent way to connect freshmen with upper-division students. Peer leaders are typically former participants in learning communities who can help communicate to entering students the expectations and objectives for participating in a community. As with the paired-course approach, peers can also serve as peer advisers or tutors.

Campuses recruit and reward peers in different ways. Faculty can nominate students for peer roles. They often nominate former students recognized not only for academic achievement but also for the ability to work well with others. Former learning communities participants are logical candidates for peer roles. When students have a positive learning communities experience, they are more likely to seek out ways to give back to the program. Peer leaders can receive a stipend or weekly paycheck for their involvement. They might also receive academic credit by enrolling in an advanced seminar or leadership course that helps prepare them for their roles as peer educators. A designation on a student development transcript, a service that might be offered by the Division of Student Affairs or Student Activities Office, is another way to acknowledge upper-division student participation in learning communities.

Cohorts in Large Courses

Curricular Structure. These programs are often referred to as FIGs—freshman interest groups. A less commonly used approach is the federated learning community: student cohorts enrolled in larger courses guided by a teacher who serves as a master learner. The federated learning community integrates courses around a theme. The master learner "enrolls" in the courses with the students and facilitates a weekly seminar to help students synthesize what they are learning. The master learner usually has no teaching responsibilities beyond the federated learning community (Gabelnick, MacGregor, Matthews, and Smith, 1990).

FIGs are the simplest model in terms of organization and cost (Gabelnick, MacGregor, Matthews, and Smith, 1990). This approach works well at large universities or at other institutions where freshmen are typically enrolled in at least one or two large lecture courses each semester. In this model, learning communities students represent a subset of the total enrollment. When a large lecture course requires students to enroll in a smaller recitation or discussion session, FIG students are typically enrolled in a designated FIG section.

In addition to one or two large courses, FIGs typically include a smaller writing course and a weekly seminar, with enrollment in these sections usually limited to FIG students. The weekly seminar is often facilitated by an undergraduate.

At the University of Washington, FIGs typically consist of two larger-sized lecture courses; a smaller English, humanities, or arts course; and a one-credit course, "University Resources, Information, and Technology." Each FIG has a theme, typically coordinated around a general area of study such as business, liberal arts, sciences, or engineering. For example, the "Performing Arts: Drama" FIG includes Greek and Roman classics, acting, and survey of music paired with the one-credit seminar.

Faculty Role. Teaching courses that are part of FIGs involve little faculty coordination and virtually no coplanning. Faculty whose course enrollment includes FIG students typically receive general information on the program. They know that FIG students are enrolled in their course but are not usually aware of who these students are.

The weekly FIG seminar plays an important role in achieving curricular integration in FIGS. Seminar leaders, often undergraduates or occasionally graduate students, are encouraged to introduce themselves to the other instructors with courses in the FIG to learn more about the content of these courses. Peer teachers can then help community members process what they are learning in the other courses. The seminar can also function as a student success course, helping to connect community members to resources across campus.

At the University of Washington, a small writing course is usually included in the FIG offerings. Many of these courses are taught by first-year graduate students. FIG program directors attend the teaching assistant orientation to present an overview of the FIG program. These instructors do not receive extra compensation for teaching a course as part of a FIG and are not required to alter their curriculum to reflect the content of the other courses in the pairing.

The extent of curricular integration varies across and within FIG models, but curricular connections are usually minimal. However, at the University of Washington, one department's desire to create deeper connections among FIG courses is leading to greater curricular coherence in a small number of FIGs. Faculty in the comparative literature department approached the FIG program about including more sections of the introductory comparative literature in FIGs. Their intent was to enroll more entering students in these courses and to tailor course content to the curriculum of the other courses in the FIGs.

Cocurricular Opportunities. Because faculty in FIGs typically do not coordinate curricular materials, organizing cocurricular activities is more difficult. In this model, the weekly seminar often becomes the arena for cocurricular planning. Out-of-class activities are encouraged but not required, and events tend to be more social than academic in nature. Students might go out to dinner or attend a cultural or sporting event. Sometimes activities are related to the courses in the FIGs. For example, students in a drama FIG will attend theater performances during the term. Activities are typically scheduled as part of the weekly seminar or during out-of-class meeting time. If the FIG program includes a shared living experience, the residence hall provides the setting for cocurricular activities, which tend to be more social than academic in nature.

Peer Leadership. In FIG programs, peers—usually former FIG participants— typically lead the weekly seminars. Peer leaders can also serve as peer advisers or tutors for the community. Their role is to help orient new students to college life. Sarah Ruhwedel, a FIG peer instructor at the University of Washington, described the role in this manner:

> The role of the peer instructor is a fairly complex one. I like to emphasize to people that we really are two things: a peer and an instructor. The instructor side of the role incorporates teaching students what they need to succeed at the UW [University of Washington]. That is the side that [involves] lectures during class and [bringing] in guest speakers. The flip side of the role is that of peer. The role of the peer is to be an older college student that is willing to take the time to help a new freshman to adjust. This goes beyond preparing a 50 minute class agenda, and touches on the more personal lives of the students [S. Ruhwedel, personal communication, Nov. 4, 1998].

In the University of Washington FIG program, peers teach the one-credit "University Resources, Information, and Technology" course. They develop the syllabus, facilitate discussions, arrange for faculty and other guest lecturers to visit the class, help students with academic advising, and organize field trips around the greater Seattle area.

The learning communities in the Connections Program at Illinois State University feature sections of the Connections Seminar. The seminar is a noncredit course led by University College academic staff members or faculty, student affairs professionals, or graduate students paired with a peer adviser. These peers meet weekly with their coteachers to develop the seminar outline and plan activities. They address important personal and social issues from a student perspective.

FIG students often connect with student organizations and upper-division students to become more actively involved in their majors. The University of Missouri-Columbia has learning communities for students in engineering and other academic majors and interests. Students in the Women in Engineering and Men in Engineering communities coenroll in courses and live in dedicated residence space. A significant portion of the membership of the Society of Women Engineers are FIG students. The society and the learning communities students cosponsored a career fair held in the residence hall space. The groups also participated in Engineering Week activities, including hosting prospective students for overnight visits.

Team-Taught Programs

Curricular Structure. Team-taught programs, sometimes called coordinated studies programs, enroll varying numbers of students in two or more courses organized around an interdisciplinary theme. These programs are the most complex in terms of curricular integration and faculty role. Some require full-time faculty and student involvement. Participation can also be part-time, involving two, three, four, or even five courses. In most instances, the learning community constitutes students' entire schedules for at least a semester and sometimes an entire academic year.

Themes are faculty generated and interdisciplinary; they can be broad and liberal arts based, or emphasize skill development in related disciplines, such as math and science. Small-group discussion sections, sometimes called book seminars, are an important part of the community. Students and a faculty member break off into smaller groups to discuss an assigned text and build on what they are learning in the other courses in the community.

Total community enrollment varies, but can range from forty to seventy-five students. In larger team-taught programs, the cohort is often subdivided into smaller seminar groups to achieve a faculty-to-student ratio of one faculty member to twenty or twenty-four students (Gabelnick, MacGregor, Matthews, and Smith, 1990). Due to increasing fiscal pressures, typical enrollment in these programs is now more likely to be closer to seventy-five students and three teachers, with a teacher-to-student ratio of twenty-five to one.

William Rainey Harper College offers semester-long coordinated studies programs. A team of faculty from a variety of disciplines determine the theme and schedule coordinated studies offerings. Offerings involve two to five courses and can enroll as many as seventy-five to one hundred students. For example, "As the Hem Falls: Women in Creative Careers" was a two-course coordinated studies community pairing humanities and fashion history. "Life Choice: People, Power, and Paychecks in a Changing World" involved business management, philosophy, political science, and two psychology courses.

Seattle Central Community College offers students ten-, thirteen-, fifteen-, or eighteen-credit integrated links or coordinated studies programs each quarter. These programs are team-taught and interdisciplinary, and draw in courses from all disciplines. For many program activities (lectures, presentations, films, field trips) students and teachers meet together in a large room. At other times, students and teachers meet in smaller book seminars. Students are organized into groups of twenty to twenty-five and meet with one teacher to discuss selected books. Selection of the books is critical since readings are closely related to the theme and content of the coordinated studies program. In the "Joy of Math and English" program students use writing skills to understand and master mathematical concepts. In the book seminar they discuss stories of plays such as August Wilson's *The Piano Lesson* that includes mathematical concepts (Bystrom, 1999).

At Seattle Central, faculty may propose a ten-credit integrated link consisting of two courses, larger fully integrated links (thirteen to fifteen credits), or a coordinated studies program that accounts for students' full course loads and faculty members' teaching loads. A unique feature of the Seattle Central program is that at midquarter, students select how they want the credits allocated in terms of transcript credit. For example, in the ten-credit "Dynamic Cities: Spaces and Peoples" integrated link, students can select ten credits from the following: Composition (English 101 or 102, five credits), Introduction to Human Geography (Geography 200, five credits), or Geography of Cities (Geography 277, five credits). Faculty grade as a team, although students receive individual course credit. Students can receive partial credit for the program if they do not successfully complete a component.

The first-year program in George Mason University's New Century College is an interdisciplinary, team-taught program consisting of four courses. Each course is six or seven weeks long, constitutes students' entire schedules, and meets for full days, Monday through Thursday. The first course, "Community of Learners," explores interdisciplinary issues in education, philosophy, and intellectual development, with an emphasis on writing and computer skills. The second course, "The Natural World," draws on interdisciplinary themes in math, science, and communications. The third course is offered in the first half of the second semester. "The Socially Constructed World" explores interdisciplinary issues in the humanities, social sciences (psychology and sociology), and fine arts. The fourth and final course in the first-year program, "Self as Citizen," studies the relationship between the individual and society from the perspectives of the social sciences (government), philosophy, and literature.

Each course involves eight faculty members and two hundred students, with students divided into small groups for writing workshops. The instructional emphasis is on small-group discussions, collaborative assignments, and self-paced learning. Students are brought together for "spotlight lectures" based on course themes.

Faculty Role. Team-taught programs are one of the most intensive models in terms of faculty involvement and faculty development. The community assignment typically constitutes a teacher's course load for the term or academic year. In these programs, two to four faculty members form a teaching team. Faculty are involved in all aspects of the program, from the development of the community theme to curriculum planning to the teaching of the courses. Courses vary from highly interdisciplinary to team-taught courses in which the individual faculty "own their own expertise" (J. MacGregor, personal communication, Dec. 21, 1998).

For faculty teaching in the First-Year Program at George Mason University, New Century College is their primary assignment. New Century faculty can be grouped into one of four categories:

- Tenure-track faculty in New Century College
- Tenured faculty who move their FTE to New Century College
- Faculty with shared appointments between New Century College and another academic unit at George Mason University
- Faculty on loan to New Century College, with their departments receiving a payback

The teaching team engages in presemester planning during the summer and on Fridays during the academic year. In addition, the faculty often eat lunch together and informally gather in their seminar or unit room to discuss the course and student progress.

Cocurricular Opportunities. Because students and faculty in team-taught learning communities participate full time in the learning community, class time scheduling is flexible. There are many opportunities to incorporate cocurricular learning experiences, such as field trips or lecture series. The seminar is often the center of community-building activities. Depending on how courses in the community are scheduled, there might be time for students and faculty to gather over lunch or a cup of coffee or work together on service projects either on or off campus.

New Century College offers a variety of out-of-class learning opportunities for students. Prior to the start of the academic year, New Century College students, along with the faculty team for the first course, participate in the Student Transition Expedition Program (STEP), a four-day camping excursion that provides faculty and students the opportunity to engage in team-building activities in small groups of about twelve students. Students are also required to complete a summer reading assignment. At the start of the first semester, faculty and area business leaders cofacilitate small-group discussions based on the assigned reading.

Peer Leadership. Peer leadership is embedded in this approach. Team-taught programs often include a synthesis seminar, book seminar, or weekly discussion group that can be peer facilitated. Another innovative use of peers is to involve current and former learning communities participants in councils or committees that work with faculty and program leadership to plan the direction of the effort. The Student Leadership Group in New Century College includes students in all four years of the college. Students in the First-Year Program work alongside upper-division students and faculty to plan for the college.

Residence-Based Programs

Residence-based programs adapt a particular curricular model to include a residential component. Many of these programs draw from principles of the residential college model. Residential college programs share a common core of characteristics with learning communities models: faculty commitment, students' learning from each other, and the intentional linkages between the academic and social components of the undergraduate experience.

A primary goal of residence-based education is the integration of students' living and academic environments. Educational programming in residence halls centers around the belief that not all learning occurs in the classroom. Rather, a significant amount of what students learn during college comes from their experiences of daily living, and there is natural overlap between students' academic and social learning activities.

Smith (1993) offered the following differentiation between the classical residential college model and a living learning center: "A classical residential college is characterized by one factor: faculty reside among their students" (p. 5). A living-learning center, on the other hand, is typically defined as student living space with intentional academic programming and services, such as in-hall tutoring, ongoing lecture series, and academic advising. It is also common for living and learning programs to feature academic courses taught in the residential facility.

According to Schroeder (1994) "Learning communities are fostered by commonality and consistency of purpose, shared values, and transcendent themes" (p. 171). In residence-based learning communities, the role of residence life is to create conditions that promote these values. Residence-based learning communities involve more than assigning students with similar majors to the same floor of a residence hall. In these learning communities, intentionally organized student cohorts enroll in specified curricular offerings and reside in dedicated living space.

Residence-based learning communities are designed to integrate diverse curricular and cocurricular experiences. For this reason, they may be the most radical of the four learning communities approaches described in this chapter because they challenge and require change within multiple university systems: curriculum, teaching, and housing.

When the University of Michigan launched its Pilot Program in 1962, a project described as an "experiment in community learning" (Center for Research on Teaching and Learning, 1972), program leaders recognized they were embarking on a bold initiative: "Few administrators in large universities tolerate wide-ranging innovative experiments designed to foster student development and academic progress at the risk of complicating already complex management procedures" (p. 1).

The program functioned within the College of Literature, Science, and the Arts and the Office of University Housing and was developed in response to a small group of faculty and housing staff who had become increasingly concerned with the anonymity experienced by undergraduates, particularly freshmen. The purpose of the pilot program was described as "an experimental program for freshmen predominantly that combines residential-academic experiences and that seeks to provide a structure that will enable freshmen to make a better and more productive adjustment to university life" (p. 7). The hope was that by enrolling students from a particular residence in common courses, the students would continue to develop and discuss in the residence halls ideas generated in class. This Michigan program is an example of residence-based attempts to reorganize the out-of-class living and learning environment of its students. Residence hall–based learning communities programs seek to provide similar learning experiences for students.

Curricular Structure. The curricular component of residence-based programs typically resembles one of the other three learning communities approaches: clusters, FIGs, or team-taught programs. Residence-based programs include a deliberate link to residential life that goes beyond students living in shared space. Academic and cocurricular community activities are scheduled in residence, and in many instances classes meet in classrooms located in the residence halls.

These programs seek to arrange students' curricular and living experiences in new ways. Residence-based learning communities challenge traditional curricular structures, as well as residence hall systems and organization. This approach requires levels of collaboration and cooperation that may feel new and different to all involved—residence life staff, faculty, and students—and also places more responsibility on students for shaping their living and learning experiences.

Faculty Role. The faculty role varies in residence-based learning communities. Minimal involvement might be to ask faculty to attend occasional programs in the residence hall or join students for a meal in the dining center. In other programs, faculty have offices in the residence halls. The most extensive faculty commitment, the residential college model, asks faculty to be in residence.

A residence-based learning community program provides opportunities for faculty to visit and meet with students in their learning environments. Lecture series and small-group discussions provide excellent opportunities for faculty to pursue multidisciplinary issues with students outside the classroom.

Residence life and student affairs personnel also benefit from participation in residential hall–based learning communities. Participation in the planning, implementation, and assessment phases of learning communities effectively connects residence life to the educational mission of the institution. This work is time-consuming and constant and must be inclusive, involving faculty, residence life, and students in all aspects of the planning process.

FIGs at the University of Missouri-Columbia evolved out of the collaborative efforts of academic and student affairs. Missouri's FIGs are residential learning communities, involving courses from across the freshmen curricula, that are located in more than three-quarters of the university's residence halls. Small cohorts of fifteen to twenty freshmen enroll in three sections of the same general education courses, share living space, and complete a one-credit seminar designed to integrate material from the general education courses and introduce students to university resources. The collaborative relationship between residence life and academic affairs has created opportunities for more partnerships, including the development of residential colleges (Schroeder, Minor, and Tarkow, 1999).

Cocurricular Opportunities. The residential component of residence-based learning communities provides ample opportunities for cocurricular activities. Community members can participate in a semester-long service project or in a series of activities related to their course objectives. Activities can also be designed to build community and assist students in their transition to college life. In residence-based programs, community members often assume responsibility for planning this aspect of their learning communities experience. Student governance is common in residence halls and provides a valuable leadership experience for learning communities students.

The Residential College at Mary Faust Hall at the University of North Carolina Greensboro (UNCG) is a two-year program involving approximately 120 students. Each semester, students are required to enroll in an interdisciplinary core course on the American experience along with one or two other residential college offerings—often seminar versions of courses available to the greater university community. Academic offerings also include opportunities for community service and independent study.

A full-time counselor is in residence, and faculty have offices in the hall. Members of the residential college participate in committees and pay student program dues. The committees sponsor extracurricular activities such as student-faculty mountain retreats, theater productions, parties, coffeehouse sessions, and dinners. Former residential college students visit for reunions. A newsletter, *Residential Collage (sic)*, keeps students, faculty, former participants, and the UNCG community connected to the program.

Peer Leadership. In residence-based programs, students typically exercise more authority and decision-making responsibility for their living environment and cocurricular programming than do students in residence halls without a connection to the formal curriculum. Students participate on learning communities councils or committees and work with residence hall staff to govern the living space and plan events for the community.

The residential component also means more opportunities for upper-division students, second- and third-generation learning communities participants, to be involved with new cohorts of learning communities students. Resident assistants (RAs) are often assigned to a community and in some instances peer-teach the weekly seminar. Another role for upperclassmen is as tutors in residence.

Special Characteristics of Learning Communities Models

Many campuses find that the flexible nature of learning communities models allows them to customize or upgrade their approaches to meet their broader goals for undergraduate education, as well as achieve specific educational outcomes. *Customizable* and *upgradable* are becoming two phrases closely associated with learning communities models.

Customizability

In making decisions about learning communities models, many campuses face the task of choosing between the benefits offered by one approach and the feasibility of another given the institution's organization and faculty culture. The

FIG approach may work best at large universities given course sizes and the large numbers of entering freshmen. FIGs require the least amount of change to the culture of a large university, which typically values research over teaching and is characterized by departmentalization and specialization as opposed to collaborative teaching and cross-discipline partnerships. On the other hand, the multidisciplinary nature of coordinated studies programs offers the deeper involvement between students and faculty that is at best difficult, if not impossible, to achieve on large campuses, particularly those with significant populations of commuting students. Developing a learning communities program involves compromises but can also lead to new opportunities for experimentation with alternative approaches and models.

That each campus brings a unique set of opportunities, goals, and resources to learning communities work leads to rich and diverse examples of learning communities. Although we certainly advocate campuses' learning from the experiences of others, we do not recommend that campuses replicate another campus's learning communities work by simply plugging in another's model on their own campus. Customizing learning communities to fit the culture of a campus means dedicating time and resources to build learning communities that are the right fit for the institution (W. Zeller, personal communication, Dec. 1998).

Many campuses select a particular approach and then customize their model as they learn more about student and faculty needs in learning communities. The practice of tailoring or customizing learning communities programs to meet the needs of unique student populations is becoming a common practice across learning communities programs. A customized approach can be highly effective when there is strong faculty or student interest in a more structured learning communities experience or narrowly defined outcome, such as improving retention of female students in engineering programs.

The use of multiple learning communities models on a single campus is becoming more common. It is an attractive approach because learning communities by design are flexible. Relying on different approaches affords campuses to spread resources across programs and support the diverse needs of different student populations. As campus interest in learning communities increases, collaboration among different academic departments and units within an institution, such as academic affairs and residence life, becomes more possible.

Priorities and resources shift, and campuses can use the multiple-models approach to offer students different ways of becoming more involved in their undergraduate experience. A residence-based, linked-course program will not work for a student who needs to commute to campus, but it can offer a residential student a more integrated living and learning experience. A student unsure of his or her major can benefit from the increased faculty and peer support that comes from completing general education requirements as part of a FIG program, and a premed student can benefit from enrolling in a faculty-led cluster of math and science courses.

The learning community initiative at William Rainey Harper College uses three models: linked courses, coordinated studies, and clusters. This multimodel approach evolves from the belief that the learning communities framework—students and faculty experiencing courses or disciplines through a complementary and connected curriculum—can be structured in different ways (*William Rainey Harper Faculty Handbook,* 1998, p. 4). Programs are differentiated by the amount of coordination among disciplines. In links, faculty coordinate assignments and syllabi but do not teach together. Coordinated studies involves a cohort of students enrolled in two to five courses taught by a team of faculty from different disciplines. Clusters are a group of courses organized around a common theme. Faculty serve as discipline-specific advisers and participate in interdisciplinary cluster activities.

Customizing learning communities might also involve modifying a particular approach to meet the needs of a specific student population. Delta College in Michigan offers students linked-course learning communities—pairing courses taught by at least two instructors from two different disciplines. For example, the learning community Learn Economics by Navigating the Internet pairs an economics with a computer science course. To address the achievement and persistence problems facing many nontraditional male students of color, teachers and administrators at Delta College's Ricker Center developed a unique learning community, Which Way Is Up? This learning community contains three academic courses (psychology, English, and sociology) and a two-hour community forum that meets on Saturdays. The community is described as

> a collaborative learning community with a non-traditional approach to social science, and an orientation to ethnic minorities. This community will use the principles of psychology and sociology to discover and understand patterns of individual and group behavior from the perspective of African-American and Hispanic males. Particular emphasis will be given to initiating the expression, both written and oral, of self-discovery, dialogue and community among men of color [Jones, Thompson, and Ketchum, 1998].

The community is based on a core of values that includes shared aspirations, interactive learning, individual growth, caring behavior, group collaboration, open communication, and diversity.

Upgradability

During the process of developing and implementing learning communities, a campus may discover other areas of need within the program itself or in related areas of the undergraduate experience. For example, it is not uncommon for the implementation of learning communities to lead to changes in residence hall or new student orientation programming. In other instances, bringing faculty together to talk about teaching and learning can lead to productive dialogue on how to support student achievement better. This in turn may lead to the linking of freshman-year experience-type courses or tutoring programs to learning communities models. By design, learning communities are flexible, student-centered approaches to teaching and learning, making add-ons not only possible but desirable.

Upgrades can also be achieved by linking learning communities to other initiatives that share similar characteristics, such as residential colleges. For example, at the University of Missouri-Columbia, some FIGs are nested in residential colleges that are supportive or reflective of the general theme of the FIGs. The FIGs with arts and theater, and music and creative writing themes are housed (nested) in the Fine Arts Residential College. The freshmen participating in these FIGs are surrounded by upper-division students who may have participated in an arts-related FIG themselves and chose to renew their ties to the community and its goals by joining a residential college (L. C. Eimers, personal communication, Jan. 26, 1999).

Conclusion

The philosophy and theory behind the learning communities approach to curricular reform is not new. Past attempts and initiatives now under way share an intentional reorganization of curriculum and the creation of new roles for students, faculty, administration, and staff in efforts to develop transformed learning environments. Regardless of the learning communities model—paired courses, cohorts in large classes (FIGs), or team-taught program—building communities requires change.

CHAPTER THREE

CREATING A CAMPUS CULTURE FOR LEARNING COMMUNITIES

At their best, learning communities generate their own synergy, creating a campus culture where the whole is greater than the sum of the parts. Learning communities create opportunities for greater faculty-student interaction, build on the strengths of interdisciplinary curricula, foster collaboration between academic affairs and student affairs, and generally provide creative space for thoughtful members of the college community to work together. They do this by bringing together different units of the campus that have separate and distinct missions.

This chapter offers a process model for introducing learning communities on a campus, based primarily on a case study of College Park Scholars at the University of Maryland, College Park. Although we draw specific examples from the Maryland program and others, our broader goal is to offer a template for assessing campus culture and anticipating opportunities and resistance.

In *The Fifth Discipline* (1990) Senge describes a key concept of his theory about creating a learning organization: "Real learning gets to the heart of what it means to be human. Through learning we re-create ourselves. Through learning we become able to do something we never were able to do. Through learning we perceive the world and our relationship to it. Through learning we extend our capacity to create, to be part of the generative process of life. There is within each of us a deep hunger for this type of learning" (p. 14). His is a particularly appropriate message for institutions of higher education, which are learning organizations in multiple senses of the word. In mission and motive, universities and colleges should validate what it means to become learning organizations. These institutions are being accused of moving away from their primary mission and developing identities closer to those of corporations and industries, and as such, are challenged by competition from other "learning organizations" that are forcing those at colleges and universities to rethink their definitions. The learning community model may be one that can bring renewed awareness and energy to our primary mission.

Colleges and universities have sometimes been seen as more conservative than market-driven industries, although that is changing. Society depends on universities and colleges to preserve cultural and societal norms, so it is not surprising that resistance to change runs deep in higher education. Nevertheless, changes in demographics, access, student preparation, faculty roles, and costly technology innovations are forcing new initiatives at a new pace.

Universities serve society best when they bring their considerable creative and analytical talents to bear on the problems society deems most critical. Today one could make the case that their most serious challenge is educating a generation of responsible citizens who will be ready and willing to accept leadership roles and participate as citizens. Learning communities are particularly good at fostering that kind of coherent, purposeful education.

Like any other broad-based campus innovation, learning communities are most successful when they are fully integrated into the college or university structure. Those who wish to introduce learning communities on their campus need to be sensitive to their institutional culture and find ways to meet the resistance to change that lurks on every campus. Yet every campus has a number of different institutional structures that could become vehicles for starting a learning community. In some ways, how the learning communities are organized, where they plant their roots, and how they eventually evolve depend in large part on what motivated them and where the initial inquiry and idea began.

Identifying Change Levers

Although there is no model of institutional change applicable to all campuses, there are some common change levers advocates of learning communities can use to move the agenda forward. Students of higher education have spent considerable time analyzing and describing the barriers to change at a university. When we refer to a fully integrated program, we mean one that has been embraced by all the units at a university, from the facilities maintenance people, who take pride in the physical appearance and functioning of the physical sites, to the faculty on general education committees, to the registrars' offices where linking courses and blocking schedules are part of their regular service to the campus rather than a special one-time favor.

Making the Big Store Small

Large research universities are frequently struggling to bring their institutions down to a human scale. The editors of *Metropolitan Universities,* a publication of the Coalition of Urban and Metropolitan Universities, devoted its June 1998 issue to the topic of learning communities, targeting large, land grant institutions. It is not by accident that learning communities are emerging more frequently at larger universities where there is an increased sense of urgency to create a personal scale for students and teachers.

Frequently the first step toward creating learning communities at a college or university comes with the recognition that something needs to be fixed—usually the perception that the university is unfriendly to undergraduates. Some campuses are driven by a desire to attract more and better-quality students and are drawn to learning communities as a way to change their image. Others want to do a better job of educating and retaining all students. Linking learning communities to undergraduate recruitment and retention—the bread and butter of any institution of higher education—creates a real motive for change.

A professor and former dean of undergraduate studies at the University of Maryland described how the idea for College Park Scholars originated out of a desire to improve enrollment and the overall quality of students.

> CPS [College Park Scholars] originated in the general crisis of enrollment and my own belief that we could not get better as a university unless our students got better. For the most part, we are an open enrollment university. Hardly anyone came to the University as a student in the humanities and social sciences. There was also the general impression that the university was large, formless, bureaucratic and uncaring—we needed something to attract better students [Ira Berlin, personal communication, Sept. 1997].

When change is initiated from the top, it is usually linked to some broad campus needs. In the Kellogg Commission Report, *Returning to Our Roots* (1997), the committee catalogued the challenges to public higher education, including "the emerging enrollment boom, new competitors on the horizon, constrained public funding and growing resistance to price hikes, eroding public trust, and limited institutional flexibility." It then proposed learning communities as a response to these institutional challenges (p. v).

Learning communities are now more widely viewed as a promising model for restructuring undergraduate education. Frequently faculty committees charged with reviewing undergraduate curriculum and general education outcomes look to learning communities as a way of thinking outside the box of traditional majors and minors. When issues of recruitment, retention, student learning outcomes, and student satisfaction capture the attention of the university as a whole, a campus is ripe for the introduction of learning communities.

Change Levers

Five change levers in higher education—institutional mission statements, strategic planning processes, periodic campus reviews of departments and colleges, collaboration between departments and colleges, and external reviews—represent change as a process and involve large parts of the campus in sustained debate and discussion.

Institutional Mission Statements. When a campus is reallocating resources, the committees charged with making recommendations periodically turn to the institution's mission statement for direction. Learning communities can become an ideal vehicle for realizing a stated mission, especially if the mission already makes a strong commitment to the importance of undergraduate education and the concepts inherent in a student-centered college. Mission statements might include phrases or statements that embrace some or all of the characteristics of learning communities—for example:

- Movement toward restoring the role of general and liberal education in the curriculum
- References to increasing interdisciplinary curricular options
- Statements valuing pedagogy and the teaching-learning continuum
- Commitment to promoting educational goals outside the classroom as well as inside the classroom

When a campus is on the verge of committing resources to a new venture, the mission statement can serve as a beacon to help focus on a common goal. Mission statements generally include an emphasis in the areas of leadership, citizenship, diversity, and internationalization—all areas that can be supported by learning communities. They allow for the development of mutually beneficial partnerships and are a setting where common ground can be found among academic disciplines and between academic affairs and student affairs. It is important to formulate a clear position on learning communities that is communicated throughout the campus. By linking the introduction of learning communities to the mission statement of the institution, the campus sends a consistent message to its constituents and publics.

Strategic Planning Processes and Documents. It is much easier to get a favorable hearing for learning communities from campuswide administrators and faculty if there is already a change process in place on a campus. A campus that is engaged in strategic planning or Total Quality Improvement is in the position to explore the option of starting learning communities in pursuit of newly defined goals. When the University of Maryland initiated a strategic planning exercise in the mid-1990s, someone at every college forum advocated the introduction of learning communities as a way to achieve strategic goals. By the time the provost had visited all the colleges and engaged the faculty in hours of dialogue, it became clear that learning communities were the intervention of choice, placed near the top of the strategic plan. A campus strategic planning process leads directly to a set of budget priorities, and change happens most readily when funding priorities are identified and supported.

When a campus undergoes a serious strategic planning process, the stakes are high. Depending on the primary mission of the institution, undergraduate education can come out as one of the winners if proponents of learning communities give a clear, consistent message each time they are called on to describe their contribution to the overall good of the institution.

Periodic Reviews of Departments, Colleges, and Campuses. Like strategic planning, a periodic review presumes a public and predictable process. It is easier to inject the concept of learning communities into a process of inquiry than it is to try to sell the idea around campus. Taking an opportunity to be proactive with respect to external and internal reviews can sometimes facilitate discussion of new campuswide commitments and strategies.

For deans and department chairs who are working to increase enrollment in their units or need to respond to an external review, the learning community model offers a concrete way of addressing felt needs. University of Maryland deans were anxious to participate in the learning communities program because they hoped to generate early interest in their departmental majors. The learning community philosophy opens opportunities for creativity in course development and interdisciplinary studies that enliven a major or a college, and maximize faculty resources.

Collaboration Between Departments and Colleges. The best way to incorporate the idea of learning communities into a college is to involve every segment as owners of the project. Learning communities are an innovation that allow campuses to shape a completely new response to a local problem.

When the University of Maryland initiated College Park Scholars in 1994, the impulse and the funding came from the division of academic affairs. In the first round, the requirements were minimal. College Park Scholars considers each learning community a program. Each thematic program had to be interdisciplinary, be sponsored by an academic college, have a tenured professor as a director, and convene a cross-disciplinary advisory board of faculty from different departments and colleges. The necessary collaborations that grew out of the discussion of curriculum and course offerings created new alliances on campus among faculty in different departments and different disciplines. For example, the Science, Technology, and Society program had an advisory board that included faculty from engineering, history, and philosophy. These cross-departmental collaborations expanded the pool of potential majors by tapping undeclared students who had an interest in this area. They also allowed faculty to explore innovative courses since they had dedicated resources—time, graduate assistants, supplemental money for curriculum enhancements—with which to experiment.

External Reviews. Bringing an external review committee to campus to make recommendations for strengthening the undergraduate experience is another way of introducing new ideas. An external team is not constrained by any internal hierarchy or boundaries and is free to make innovative recommendations.

In the fall of 1997 the Iowa State campus was about to invest in significant renovation of the residence halls. The department of residence assembled an external review team to analyze and assess how the department could best support the academic mission of the institution. The department asked this team to help them set priorities and provide advice on allocating resources. The selection of the external review team and the charge to that team generated a set of recommendations specific to that campus.

In anticipation of a major renovation of the residential facilities, Iowa State asked the consulting group to help the department of residence assess the needs and potential for creating learning communities and other ways to support student learning. The most important recommendation the consultants offered was that the committee designated with the planning authority be sanctioned by *both* the vice president for academic affairs and the vice president for student affairs. Collaboration at that level established new, powerful alliances for change on the campus.

Creating Structures to Accommodate Learning Communities

Creating learning communities requires working simultaneously within and outside existing structures. The recommendations that follow have been sifted from interviews and conversations with many different participants in learning communities and suggest a model for change that is broadly applicable.

What happens, for example, if the idea for learning communities comes not from an administrative mandate but rather from faculty who have, through workshops or professional development experiences in their disciplines, come together to explore new curricular structures? These committee-generated initiatives might be the brainstorm of an individual faculty member or evolve as a response to some more general considerations of a curriculum committee. Assistant deans and advisers might want to initiate new advising structures; faculty on core general education committees might want to experiment with interdisciplinary courses; residence life staff might want to bring more learning activities into the residence halls. Any one of these scenarios sets a slightly different course in motion and requires slightly different approaches to change.

Whether the impetus for learning communities comes from faculty or administration, from academic affairs or student affairs, the same principles are at work. Campuses work through committees and consultation, and the first question that must be addressed is, Who should be at the table? A general rule of thumb is to be as inclusive as possible, as early as possible.

Identifying Roles for Stakeholders

Collaborative relationships develop through personal contacts, so it makes sense that early planning for learning communities should bring the key players together in frequent, informal discussions. Who convenes the group is as important as who is invited to participate in the initial discussions; a wise administrator knows how to balance inclusivity with exclusivity to give the matter appropriate weight.

Putting together a task force or planning committee for a learning community is as politically sensitive as putting together the right search committee for a campuswide administrative position. A department chair or a dean can have faculty begin exploring the possibilities, but the most compelling invitation comes from the provost's office. To be appointed by a college dean, at the request of the vice president for academic affairs or chief academic officer, sends an important message to the campus, particularly to faculty, that outcomes will receive serious consideration, especially when budgets are determined. Once the campuswide committee is formed, the participants share ideas, explore assumptions, and develop trusting relationships. Learning communities are built on the friendships and relationships forged early in the planning process, and planning committees are crucial to the success of the project. If students can be part of the planning, the outcome will be that much stronger. Students often stimulate some of the best, most creative thinking in such planning committees.

Identifying and naming a campus committee is not trivial, as can be witnessed by this e-mail exchange among faculty and administrators subscribed to a learning communities listserv:

> [The first posting:] Last night, a group of us who teach in learning communities on our campus decided to form a committee, in part, to help market our courses. We need a name for ourselves, but are avoiding "The Learning Communities Committee." We'd like something with a little more panache, maybe like Illinois State U.'s "Connections." Ideas Council for Learning Communities

> [The reply:] Thanks for the kudos to the Illinois State University "CONNECTIONS" program name:) As for your query about the "committee's" name, we refer to our committee as the Learning Community Council. Also, the committee is made up of representatives from academic departments, student affairs professionals, and campus staff that all are "stakeholders" and/or work with learning community students. You could call your committee an action team or implementation team and find a catchy name to relate to this. Good luck with recruitment and implementation! [Timothy Gordon, personal communication, Jan. 28, 1999].

Identifying Priorities

The project goals should be based on the participants' needs, concerns, ideas, and strengths. At the University of Maryland, when the first conversations began to surface, the dean of undergraduate studies brought together the director of admissions, director of resident life, and several deans to explore what a learning community model might look like and how it could serve different purposes for different constituencies. Later that group became the advisory group to the pilot project, meeting weekly to discuss the issues of the day: How should we decide how many students to invite? Should we do telephone interviews with students to anticipate their response to the ideas? Who will be responsible for that process? If we want to renovate the residence halls to meet the needs of faculty, how do we get them on board in the planning stages? Who should pay for the conversion of residence rooms into faculty offices? All these conversations took place in a positive atmosphere because the initial committee was broad-based and representative. Exhibit 3.1 provides an overview of the stakeholders who participated in the development of College Park Scholars at the University of Maryland.

The notion of stakeholders is important. When the project gets going, the stakeholder group gets larger. Whether the idea of a learning community is generated from the top down or from the bottom up, broad-based participation is critical to the success of the project.

Creating Opportunities for Shared Learning: A Case Study

When the University of Maryland seriously began to explore creating learning communities on campus, faculty directors and student life staff were brought together almost a year before the first students were invited in order to discuss life in residence halls. Faculty had memories of their own undergraduate residential experiences, but they bore little resemblance to the reality described by the residence life professionals.

The first time the University of Maryland attempted to create a jointly sponsored living learning center for honors students in 1992, Jane Lawrence, then the director of the university honors program, described a critical impasse:

> The most problematic aspect of developing our Honors House at UMCP was the tension that arose between the student affairs culture and the academic culture. . . . Student Affairs [had an] emphasis upon basic services, student development, and facilitating students' psycho-social development. Although all of these are important goals, when creating special thematic living learning centers, especially ones of an academic nature, they [came into] conflict with faculty members' interest in having academics be the priority of the new facility. In my opinion, there was little understanding initially among some Student Affairs/Resident Life staff that these new facilities—with their distinct missions and faculty constituencies—needed to be operated differently from other residence halls. There was a tendency to value uniformity over creativity and flexibility, and control over empowerment or collaboration. In addition, there was a sense that all existing processes and procedures must be followed regardless of changing circumstances ["Lessons Learned . . . ," 1995, p. 21].

Determined not to make the same mistakes with College Park Scholars in 1994 and energized by the recently published *Student Learning Imperative* (American College Personnel Association, 1994), which redefined the role of student affairs in the academic mission of the institution, the University of Maryland residence

EXHIBIT 3.1. PARTICIPANTS' NEEDS AND CONCERNS, UNIVERSITY OF MARYLAND COLLEGE PARK SCHOLARS.

Players	Issues	Goals	Constraints	Resource Demands
Admissions	How can we recruit better students and achieve a higher yield of talented students? Is there a way to hold on to the talented students (B+ range) who could not be accommodated in honors programs?	Improve overall SAT of entering freshman class. Improve retention between first and second year. Create a "new product" to promote.	Technical computer programming did not exist to track admitted students into different programs. Students did not always get their first choice of program. Who decides who gets into what program?	High cost of publicity brochure. Need for infrastructure in College Park Scholars (CPS) (admissions, phone receptionist, tours of facilities). New computer programs, and much more.
Resident life/ residential facilities	What can we do to enhance residential experience for our students and create links to academic activities and programs?	Fill empty residence halls. Enhance programming in residence halls, linking to academic experiences.	Should students be required to live in residence halls linked to academic programs? How to ensure safety and security of residence halls that are being used as academic centers (easy access versus security). Who controls spaces in residence halls that are used by program faculty?	$2 million renovation of first residence hall, computer jacks for all rooms, additional residence life staff for floors, new security system for building, unanticipated rapid growth required program to expand to second building in less than a year.
Colleges	How can we reaffirm our commitment to under-graduate students and also recruit more talented students into colleges?	Recruit more majors. Give undergraduates a more interdisciplinary connection. Take advantage of strong teaching faculty. Develop links to other units on campus.	If we limit programs to majors, we lose inter-disciplinary breadth. Faculty need to incorporate courses from across campus into their programs. Our best teachers become tied up with administrative details of admissions and behavioral issues of a small group of students who are not majors.	Campus funding for 1/2 line and add two additional teaching assistants to each college that sponsors a CPS program (4). Colleges count CPS courses toward campus obligation for general education. Some receive extra funds from campus to offer additional sections of popular courses oversubscribed because of CPS requirements.

Players	Issues	Goals	Constraints	Resource Demands
Department	Can we attract more undergraduates into our honors programs in departments? How can we create rewarding experiences for our top faculty to work with undergraduates?	Recruit more majors. Create new opportunities to recognize and reward outstanding teaching faculty. Create new interdisciplinary programs, courses, and majors or minors.	No department wants to sign away its best teaching faculty to a nondepartmental program half-time. Departments felt a burden to create new sections of popular courses.	Resources from campus to colleges filter down to departments. College in-kind contributions are recognized as supporting overall mission.
Faculty	Will I ever be rewarded for quality teaching? Can I be rewarded for working with under-graduates? Is there an opportunity on campus for innovative interdisciplinary programming and profes-sional development? What kind of support will I get?	Richer experiences teaching undergraduates. Opportunities to collaborate with faculty from different fields. Professional advancement, higher salary, improved status in department and college, professional satisfaction.	No clear way of crediting faculty for contribution (teaching? service?). Faculty rarely have appro-priate level of administrative experience, and there are numerous details to making a learning community work. Burnout potential because of heavy time demands.	President's reception for learning community faculty. $5,000–$10,000 in pro-gram money, plus 10 percent summer salary for faculty directors. Student affairs provided assistance to faculty for programming. Departmental teaching assistants for programs. Additional office and com-puter for program offices in residence halls. Intangible of new faculty developing and supporting each other.

EXHIBIT 3.1, Continued

Players	Issues	Goals	Constraints	Resource Demands
Students	The University of Maryland is too big; undergraduates get lost. How can we give undergraduates more value for their tuition dollars? The first two years are dominated by teaching assistants, not professors.	A small college experience, faculty mentors, connections with students from diverse backgrounds. A sense of community and connection to the intellectual, cultural, and career opportunities on the campus. Opportunities to interact with students who share their interests. Career internships and travel experiences.	Brand-new program, no one knows what to expect, no ground rules early in the process. Need clearer communication about the extra work involved. Required activities compete with Greek rush, athletic practice, band practice. Facilities designated for each program must be equally attractive. Other students on campus view CPS as elitist.	Students get extra attention from faculty, program office staff (for example, "one-stop shopping" at program office for registration). Field trips, speakers, computer labs, and classrooms in residence halls, classes in residence halls.
Institutional advancement	How can we raise our profile with respect to nationally recognized rankings? How can we advance our objectives of positive publicity and increase fundraising opportunities. Can we generate greater appeal to alumni, parents of students, state legislature, business community of Maryland?	Attract more attention—national publicity. Attract corporate donations and large gifts. Increase alumni connections over the long term. Rise in national rankings. Excellent opportunity to seek grants from both public and private funding agencies.	No track record. Must be cautious about treading on college fundraising turf. Time-consuming for directors to reach out—when program demands constant attention. New development infrastructure needs to be created.	Institutional advancement designated staff to support the new program needs. CPS became a president's priority. Advancement was able to take advantage of previously untapped faculty contacts. Parents became active from the beginning. In time, the program worked to create alumni network.

life staff came to the project with some specific expectations of faculty roles in the residence halls. Faculty, for their part, were determined not to be seen as glorified residence counselors, yet they were intrigued by the thought of being able to participate in decisions that would shape the living environments of students. Residence life staff took time to orient faculty to their mission, providing documents such as the *Student Learning Imperative* as part of the background reading for faculty, and the faculty included resident life staff in the meetings where they discussed curriculum and planned related cocurricular programs.

A somewhat unusual example demonstrates the connections forged between faculty and residence life staff. We call this example "The Fish Tank." Students in College Park Scholars' newly formed Life Science cluster were housed together on one floor of a residence hall and registered for several common classes. The faculty director was given a first-floor office in the residence hall and was expected to hold some of his office hours there. The faculty director was an entomologist by training, and his office housed terrariums and aquariums full of spiders and millipedes. This situation made for one of our first encounters with the housekeeping staff.

Who would clean the office with the bugs? Technically it existed in the residence hall, but it was used as academic affairs space, and the housekeeping staff was none too pleased to have to work around the insects. The faculty member, however, was not ready to abandon the environment he had created. Eventually a compromise was worked out, but just as the fumigation and cleaning issues were resolved, another issue cropped up.

The faculty director was awarded a grant from his department to do something special for his College Park Scholars students, and he suggested building an aquarium in the residence hall lobby. A committee was established to explore the issue. How much would it cost? Who would take care of it? What did it need to become a reality? Could we afford it? Faculty, students, and residence life building representatives reviewed the plan. They discussed pros and cons, feasibility, and cost and ultimately decided to proceed, with several stipulated understandings:

The faculty member would pay for the tank and the fish and be responsible for the upkeep of the tank (even during university holidays) and the replacement of dead fish.

Students would help keep the fish fed and clean the tank.

Housekeeping would clean any water leaks and regularly check that the pump was working.

Residential facilities would install a built-in wall unit for the tank with a locking storage case and secure Plexiglas sides to protect it from pranks and vandals.

When the tank was finally in place in the main lobby of the residence hall, the reality of the brilliant tropical fish and rainbow coral was breathtaking. Students, faculty, guests, and facilities staff regularly congregate on the benches to gaze through this watery window on another world. In this way, the fish tank contributes to creating community and the community sustains the fish tank.

Developing a Planning Calendar

A planning group that has the benefit of staff support to keep its calendar and retain records of the meetings brings a sense of seriousness of purpose to the enterprise. We recommend assigning a coordinator or graduate assistant to help the group maintain a focus based on regular meetings and reports or minutes to help ensure the project moves forward. Regular meetings help keep everyone informed of progress.

As with most other large projects, it helps to develop a planning calendar consistent with regularly scheduled events, procedures, and deadlines for the campus planning process. A start-up calendar may run as follows:

September–December	Schedule a series of initial planning meetings, and establish decision deadlines.
January	Send letters to newly admitted students informing them of the program and inviting them to participate.
January–May	Recruit students. Schedule faculty meetings for curricular planning and program development.
June–August	Faculty, new students, and program staff participate in orientation. Students register for communities. Faculty planning continues. Schedule faculty development workshops. Schedule any necessary facilities renovations.
September	Learning communities begin.

This calendar suggests a planning cycle that begins a full academic year before students and faculty meet in the classroom.

William Rainey Harper College includes a learning communities calendar in its faculty handbook (see Exhibit 3.2). The calendar provides important in-

EXHIBIT 3.2. LEARNING COMMUNITIES CALENDAR, WILLIAM RAINEY HARPER COLLEGE.

July and August
New student orientations
- Informal flyers and posters developed and posted
- Special interest mailings

August
- Open registration—new student orientations
- Faculty orientation information meetings and/or receptions to promote learning communities
- SUBMIT LEARNING COMMUNITIES APPLICATIONS BY SEPTEMBER 1

September
- Schedule and room requirements for spring programs submitted to divisional administrative assistants
- Course schedule newspaper deadline for spring programs is September 15
- Administer pretests to all students in learning communities

October
- Textbook orders for spring programs due

November and December
- Administer posttests to all students and complete surveys and submit to Jacque Mott
- Continue publicity efforts for spring programs
- Mailing to and meeting with counselors regarding spring offerings

January
- Application deadline for new learning communities programs—January 31
- Advertise and recruit for spring programs
- Attend orientations

February
- Review and approval of new applications by Learning Communities Committee
- Schedule and room requirements for fall programs submitted to divisional administrative assistant
- Submit program information for fall publications to develop promotional materials.

March
- Textbook order for fall due by April 1
- Course schedule (newspaper) information due March 1

April
- Letters to high school counselors recruiting for fall
- Meetings with counselors concerning upcoming programs
- Visit classrooms to promote learning communities

May
- Evaluation meeting—academic year teams are asked to discuss and evaluate their programs
- Set goals for the following year

Source: William Rainey Harper College. Used by permission.

formation for faculty: recruitment events, scheduling deadlines, and assessment information.

Reaching Out to the Campus and Local Community

Having a broad representation on the committee that is charged with offering a model for change is vital—but not enough. Campuses are slow to change, and committee members need to have a direct link to their deans and departments:

> Consider asking department chairs to list "updates on learning communities" on agendas for regularly scheduled department meetings or scheduling regular briefings for faculty senate and curriculum committees.
>
> See that the program is represented on various campus committees, including those charged with reviewing academic advising or admissions policies.
>
> Keep the campus community informed of the learning communities committee work to create shared ownership. Consider giving interviews to the student and faculty newspapers. Invite others on campus not involved with the program to visit classes and talk to learning communities faculty and students.

Meeting Sources of Resistance

In 1972 Robert Halfman and colleagues at the MIT Education Research Center published *Tactics for Change: Checklists for the Academic Innovator.* Numerous items on the lists they produced still resonate in today's academic climate and provide a useful starting point for campus faculty and administrators looking to institutionalize learning communities on their campuses.

Make Sure the Idea Is Not Seen as Being Owned by One Individual

Halfman called this the "entrepreneur effect" and suggested that any innovation that is too closely linked with a single person will survive only as long as the person who initiated it keeps it alive. In this book we have emphasized the importance of working through committees in part to address this potentially damaging scenario. A related danger is the "isolation of infection" effect. Any program thought to be the exclusive purview of one administrator or faculty member gets quarantined and effectively isolated.

Be an Advice Seeker, Not a Permission Seeker

For both faculty and administrators who want to begin discussions of learning communities on their campuses, the best advice is always to invite campus participants to consult on the project. This strategy accomplishes two goals: first, the more people who contribute to an idea, the more they feel ownership of it; second, the more people involved in defining the idea, the fewer surprises when the group begins asking for resources.

Protect the Program from Too Many Levels of Approval

If the proposal for the learning community has to pass through an exhaustive committee process before it is piloted, the faculty and administrator sponsors of the learning community could easily lose their enthusiasm before they begin the real work of creating the new model. The decision makers who have the authority to approve (or not approve) must come to the table from the beginning or as soon as possible.

Use Shared Governance to Your Advantage

Institutions of higher education are sometimes faulted for the cumbersome structural organization of shared governance, which some on the outside think ties the hands of visionary administrators and slows change to a glacial pace. Yet the advantage of shared governance is that a structure is already in place to integrate a new idea into the very fabric of the institution. It is precisely because of the concept of shared governance that we can talk in terms of changing the campus culture, which can happen only through this transformative process.

Be Realistic About Costs

Burgess (1994) recognized a number of institutional features that affect teamwork at a university, among them faculty autonomy, discipline boundaries and biases, administrative obstacles, and dysfunctional reward systems. These are formidable obstacles to any collaborative enterprise at a university and can become significant barriers to an initiative as integrated as learning communities.

Any effort to get learning communities started on campus must be realistic about the costs to departments and colleges in faculty time and work with units to reach compromises on sharing resources and costs. Frequently change within a department looks more viable than collaboration between departments and colleges. Departments are leery of sacrificing their autonomy, yet central administration can leverage cross-departmental collaboration by offering small carrots.

Because cross-disciplinary learning communities are more interesting and more viable in the long run than individual courses taken in a predetermined sequence, it is worth the extra effort and time it takes to work out the details between departments.

Maryland's College Park Scholars Science, Technology, and Society Program was created collaboratively between the College of Engineering and the College of Arts and Humanities. Operationally the provost's money went into the engineering college budget to buy out the faculty director's time and the extra funds for the graduate assistant and staff support. However, since the whole concept of Science, Technology, and Society required a partner from the humanities (history or philosophy of science, or social sciences), the director of the Science, Technology, and Society Program redirected resources to provide course release to a historian, who became a codirector for the program. Eventually they added an instructor from the history department who helped shape the colloquium and worked with the writing instructors to suggest composition assignments based on the Science, Technology, and Society curriculum. Thus, learning communities money went through the engineering college to the history department, ultimately strengthening the program.

Identifying Resources

Identifying resources for major projects on campus involves more than merely finding funding sources. Elliot and Decker (1999) find that campuswide support for learning communities comes from four sources:

- People (faculty administrators, academic support staff, and student affairs professionals)
- Organizational culture (the administrative placement within an institution and connections that placement entails)
- Context (the role and purpose of the learning community on a campus)
- Financial support (redirected funding and new money)

Here we address specifically the question of money.

Budget Structure and Funding Expectations

Different learning communities models require different structures and commitments. Jean MacGregor, the director of the National Learning Communities Dissemination Project, which is supported by Funds for the Improvement of Post Secondary Education, has researched this question and writes:

The funding and costs for learning communities on various campuses reveal apples and oranges and chili peppers—all over the place in terms of whether the learning community is a rearrangement of curriculum and course-loading, or is embedded in the existing curriculum (staff time to work this out), or whether it is driven primarily by student affairs professionals or residence life (again, rearrangement of and possible additions to professional or student staff). Some institutions have created these programs entirely on internal money, with redeployment of existing resources, while others have made major new investments with grant money or special state funds [J. MacGregor, personal communication, Dec. 6, 1998].

Some basic principles do apply across the board. The earliest discussions of learning communities should address the needs of the campus, the purpose of instituting the learning community, and ways to build a coalition across campus to support the learning community. Budget discussions should be raised in the context of the planning discussion but should not drive the early discussions.

Under the best circumstances, a learning community budget begins within a total campus context rather than in one department or division, where all of the major players can imagine the benefits of supporting a learning community model on the campus. Thinking about learning communities from this perspective requires some serious internal public relations efforts around campus and leadership on the part of high-level administrators. Campus leaders are conveners of broad-based task forces or committees charged with looking at reorganizing campus resources, prioritizing campus goals, and agreeing to cooperative participation.

During the strategic planning process at the University of Maryland in 1995, the campus rallied around undergraduate education as among the highest priorities. That consensus created a framework for each division to submit a request for supplemental funding to support those priorities. Learning communities became the vehicle of choice to support undergraduate education initiatives, and the resources flowed to areas that proposed making a contribution to the establishment and sustainability of learning communities on campus. The registrar's office supported creating linked or blocked courses, the academic departments assigned special sections from their course listings to learning communities, and residence life designated space in residence halls to learning communities. These decisions resulted in internal reallocations of resources and in many cases justified requests for supplemental funding to fulfill these expectations.

On some campuses, university structures are such that the colleges themselves are the strongest home for learning communities. Funding that is then added to the base budget of a college expressly for support of a learning community or finds its way into a college budget sends the strongest institutional message: if this program is important to the campus, we will fund it in accordance with our priorities. This strong message paves the way for an enthusiastic reception from the college deans and their administrative officers. When deans see the direct advantages of learning communities for their colleges, they invariably become among the strongest and most influential advocates on campus for the program. Once college deans and the campus administrators negotiate the money and the responsibility for supporting learning communities, it is in everyone's best interest to identify the strongest faculty to make the learning community work. It would be counterproductive to invest in a learning community that had second-rate teaching. Typically these types of programs have high visibility; cutting corners by assigning second-best teachers inevitably backfires.

On a continuum of complexity, residential models require a higher budget, and linked courses require a lower budget; large universities have more expenses than small colleges, and faculty-driven programs cost more than auxiliary support programs. The richer the resources and the less that learning communities are seen as adding on to everyone's workload, the more easily change is accepted by the campus.

Financial resources are not sufficient to transform a campus culture. Resources are only one motivation or obstacle to change. Certainly ample funding helps, but faculty may resist change on intellectual principles even in the face of adequate funding. This is especially the case if faculty perceive that this is a pet project of administrators and will ultimately take money away from their colleges and departments and their own pet projects. In the best case, funding supports something that the faculty find to be an important priority for the campus, and they collaborate with campus administration to make it successful. In some cases, small campus-funded pilot projects might be a way to involve faculty before engaging in wholesale restructuring.

Can Learning Communities Pay for Themselves?

It is easy to fall into the trap of assuming that anything done to improve undergraduate education will necessarily cost a campus money, but many associated with learning communities across the country would contend that under carefully constructed circumstances, some learning communities can pay for themselves, and even become revenue generators for a campus. Entrepreneurial administrators can use partnerships to promote participation in institutional alumni and capital campaign activities. Partners can seek external grants and corporate sponsorship. Existing budget structures need to be evaluated and challenged to encourage the campus to take advantage of resource blending (that is, auxiliary housing funds, schools and colleges and central administration). In some cases, state institutions may be able to leverage base budget increases from the state legislature to support this undergraduate initiative.

Some programs, including those at Temple University, are initiated through a grant. The FIGs at Indiana University, in their first year of student enrollment, were also grant funded (S. B. Westfall, personal communication, Dec. 7, 1998). Grant funding typically requires campuses to provide matching funds, but still eases the cost of start-up for an institution. One word of caution: moving from grant to institutional funds requires careful budget analysis and planning.

Ferren and Slavings (1999) have been engaged in institutional research at Radford University and have developed tools for analyzing the cost-effectiveness of the curriculum. Their data strongly support the value of program innovations, which can be proved to reduce freshman attrition. If a campus can develop programs that improve student retention, Ferren and Slavings maintain, "An analysis designed to compare retention rates before and after implementing special retention efforts shows significant increases in revenue streams due to increased retention. An institution that averages 1600 new freshmen per year might increase retention as a result of the new program by as much as seven percent in a two year period, increasing tuition revenue by as much as $1.9 million per year." Allowing for some costs associated with the program, they suggest that most campuses would still realize significantly increased revenue.

Retention savings obviously are not realized until a program is up and running. In order to fund a new program, some campuses have developed supplemental fee structures. At Bowling Green State University, students in the program are charged an extra fee (approximately $250 to $300 per semester in the first year of the program). The program uses some of the money for community activities and events, and the bulk of the fee goes to the university toward the costs of smaller classes, more faculty involvement, and additional faculty offices. Yet there are still questions of how such fees should be set, what constitute the extra costs, how to apportion the revenue, and how to put a dollar figure on the value added for the students (B. Midden, personal communication, Dec. 3, 1998).

The University of Missouri-Columbia has invested heavily in residence-based FIG communities. The program is currently funded by contributions from the chancellor, provost, vice chancellor for student affairs, and some academic departments. In 1999 they projected having 65 percent of their fifty-three hundred students participating in some form of living and learning experience. When close to two-thirds of the student body participate in some form of learning community, a different kind of question needs to be asked: should the university charge only participating students for the extra services or distribute the costs to all residential students, in the same way they do cable television, ethernet access, and voice mail (F. Minor, personal communication, Dec. 2, 1998)? These considerations reflect the uncharted nature of the learning communities movement across higher education. Different institutions are creating different home-grown models for funding and implementation.

Categories of Costs

A campus that is beginning to project the cost of learning communities needs some outline of the predictable expenses. It might be useful to think of three categories of costs for learning communities: start-up, one-time costs that have a good chance of receiving outside grant support; logistical and operating expense support that allows the learning community to become part of the sustainable infrastructure of the institution; and faculty development and reward structure costs that should be considered long-term investments in teaching and learning.

Start-Up Costs. When a campus convenes a committee or task force to study and prepare for learning communities, the initial investment in faculty and administrative time may offer an attractive opportunity for grant funding. Even if external funding is not immediately available, campuses usually have some resources to apply to improving teaching and learning on campus, and these can be tapped for exploring or piloting learning communities. Negotiating for sample sections of popular courses, offering faculty summer stipends to prepare coordinated curricula and syllabi, and preparing preliminary publicity around the pilots represent legitimate expenses for which minimal supplemental funding can be requested.

Some costs, like registration, advising, and special sections of common courses, can be absorbed and reallocated within the existing budget structure. Other costs, such as faculty retreats or workshops, might be externally supported through grants until the project is well under way. Still other expenses, such as the development and distribution of marketing and recruitment materials, must be understood as part of the reorganization of the campus around a new set of priorities.

Logistical and Operating Expenses. Administrators cannot expect to establish a learning community without the realistic understanding that it will cost something. Although it may be possible to reorganize and reallocate funding if and when the project is fully implemented, there needs to be a realistic projection of operating expenses early in the budget planning process. Such expenses might include everything from salaries for a part-time or full-time director and some secretarial support, to telephones, computers, and office furniture. There might be other categories of operating costs too:

- Publicity (outreach) to prospective students and parents
- Recruiting
- Student activities (for example, trips to museums, special receptions for speakers, newsletters, and student publications)
- Evaluation
- Printing and publishing costs for special course descriptions or new programs
- Facilities (setting up spaces conducive to learning communities)
- Audiovisual, technical, and computer support

No two campuses will fund the learning communities in the same way, and expenses will vary by program. New programs have different needs from mature programs. And campuswide programs have different needs from select, targeted programs.

Faculty Development and Program Support

Throughout this book we return to the centrality of faculty for the success of a learning community. How an institution estimates the budgetary implications of faculty involvement is a complex issue. Elliot and Decker (1999) suggest that for the long-term sustainability of learning communities, the conversation must be refocused to include student learning outcomes as part of the added value of learning communities. Typically a campus is more inclined to frame the discussion in terms of retention, or in terms of cost-effective staffing analysis. Yet Elliot and Decker make a case for a redefinition of funding criteria:

> [A] faculty member whose stand-alone class becomes part of a learning community learns to approach the material in that class from an interdisciplinary perspective, using a broader range of pedagogical strategies. In subsequent semesters, the faculty member will be able to teach the stand-alone course from an altered perspective to the benefit of all students enrolled. So, while these students have not been part of the original learning community, their learning has been shaped by it [p. 24].

To change the nature of undergraduate education on a campus, there must be an investment in faculty development. At the same time, the reward structure must be rethought to include recognizing and valuing teaching. Learning communities are among the most cost-effective ways to involve faculty in sustained professional development activities around teaching and pedagogy. Faculty in learning communities are constantly reporting that the experience has changed the way they teach all their classes, not just their learning community sections.

Costs associated with faculty release time to work collaboratively with others in different departments, summer stipends, incentive grants, and travel support are investments in improving undergraduate education. These costs can sometimes be included under the umbrella of funding already targeted for faculty development.

Budgeting Priorities

Learning community funding is a matter of priorities. Different campuses with different missions, resources, and expectations for learning communities will allocate more or less money to support the program.

Sooner or later, if learning communities catch on, there will be a need to provide staff support to faculty in their expanded roles. Some campuses have identified a faculty member and offered release time to help manage the program. Some have hired graduate student assistants to support the extracurricular elements or extra sections of current courses. Others have created new line staff positions as their programs have grown and expanded beyond departmental bounds. Exhibits 3.3, 3.4, and 3.5 are examples of job descriptions for learning communities staff support. These examples, from mature programs, suggest how the multiple activities and roles come together in an integrated learning community.

Conclusion

The ultimate success of the campus culture transformation depends on how change is managed on a campus, who authors it, who supports it, and who benefits. It is also true that the campus structures put in place to begin developing learning communities (collaborative committees, faculty liaisons between colleges, and policy committees) may not be the structures that emerge once the learning communities begin operating. We urge, whenever possible, bringing together all of the partners in the enterprise to participate in an ongoing review of the opportunities, challenges, and resources that affect learning communities work.

EXHIBIT 3.3. POSITION DESCRIPTION FOR COORDINATOR OF STUDENT SERVICES, COLLEGE PARK SCHOLARS PROGRAM, UNIVERSITY OF MARYLAND.

Purpose: Coordinate the student services with the academic components of the College Park Scholars Program. This position reports to the Executive Director, College Park Scholars.

Responsibilities

- Serve as ombudsperson for students in the College Park Scholars Program.
- Serve as the liaison to the faculty directors of College Park Scholars and the resident life staff on programming in the residence halls and in the faculty-led colloquia. This may include providing support on program administration.
- Coordinate special programs, such as orientation, parents' receptions, sophomore send-off, citation ceremonies, study breaks, ice cream socials.
- Coordinate the CPS programming calendar.
- Assist in developing, producing, and disseminating information on courses and student advising to students and the advising community.
- Coordinate with resident life in providing academic support for students, such as tutoring, developing a writing center, arranging special sessions for students in academic difficulty.
- Prepare semester and year-end program evaluations.
- Supervise students who work in the central office of CPS.
- Serve as a liaison with Residential Facilities Office in troubleshooting and communicating facilities issues.

Requirements

- Bachelor's degree requiried; master's degree preferred.
- Ability to work with staff involved in various activities.
- Ability to analyze situations and facts from a variety of sources and to exercise creativity and independent sound judgment in suggesting solutions and resolving conflicts.
- Ability to use tact and discretion in interactions with a broad segment of the campus community from students through vice-presidents.
- Ability to deal with the pressures of multiple activities and deadlines.
- Ability to compile, organize, and analyze data and prepare and present recommendations, charts, and reports.
- Ability to present ideas effectively, both orally and in writing.
- Experience with word processing, spread sheets, computer graphics.

Source: College Park Scholars Program, University of Maryland. Used by permission.

EXHIBIT 3.4. POSITION DESCRIPTION FOR ASSISTANT DIRECTOR, COLLEGE PARK SCHOLARS, UNIVERSITY OF MARYLAND.

Purpose

Primary function is to assist the Executive Director with managing the CPS program, principally in terms of the admissions process, as well as data maintenance, analysis, and presentation. Also coordinate freshmen orientation program, assist with special events, and assist with general office maintenance.

Responsibilities

1. Coordinate CPS admissions and recruiting activities. Represent program at admissions and recruiting functions. Answer public inquiries regarding admissions/new student issues. Liaison to University Undergraduate Admissions Office. Coordinate the CPS Student Ambassadors program.
2. Data, Maintenance, Analysis, and Presentation. Maintain database for 1,000+ students. Prepare enrollment reports for CPS Annual Report. Prepare GPA and retention reports for program evaluation. Assist with audits for CPS citation awards.
3. Liaison with CPS Faculty Directors. Prepare admissions reports for executive and faculty directors. Maintain enrollment database for faculty directors. Provide GPA and retention reports for faculty directors. Provide student academic data to directors for advising and citation awards.
4. Liaison with Department of Resident Life Assignments Office concerning enrollment.
5. Coordinate Orientation Program for first-year students.
6. Assist with planning and orchestration of special events.
7. Handle public inquiries and promotion concerning CPS program. Publish *Sunspot* newsletter. Write articles for various campus newsletters regarding CPS.
8. Represent CPS for various Division of Undergraduate Studies committees and initiatives.
9. Assist with office maintenance and personnel training.

Source: College Park Scholars Program, University of Maryland. Used by permission.

EXHIBIT 3.5. POSITION DESCRIPTION FOR CAMPUSWIDE LEARNING COMMUNITIES SUPPORT COORDINATOR, IOWA STATE UNIVERSITY.

Desired Qualifications

1. Ph.D. in a relevant discipline
2. National reputation as a researcher and author in higher education or a related field
3. Senior-level administrative experience at the undergraduate level
4. College and university teaching experience
5. Knowledge and understanding of both academic affairs and student affairs

6. Knowledgeable and experienced in undergraduate educational innovation
7. Knowledgeable and experienced in faculty and staff professional development
8. Knowledgeable and experienced in student and program assessment and evaluation
9. Knowledgeable about curriculum, teaching, educational learning communities and collaborative learning and outside the classroom
10. Credentials that qualify the person for faculty rank at the associate professor or professor level in the Professional Studies in Education Department
11. Excellent interpersonal and communication skills
12. Intellectually stimulating and can relate effectively with university faculty, staff and students at both the undergraduate and graduate levels

Responsibilities

1. Stimulate the formation of, oversee, and monitor implementation of effective learning communities campuswide.
2. Convene and chair the meetings of the learning communities support steering committee and advisory committees.
3. Assist the faculty and staff in selecting student and faculty outcome variables and related indicators/measures for their autonomous learning community projects.
4. Provide useful orientation and training seminars, workshops, and consultation to the ISU faculty and staff volunteering for participation in the learning community projects.
5. Design and oversee creation, implementation, and operation of a tracking system for the learning communities.
6. Coordinate and be involved in support for in-depth assessment, evaluation, research, data interpretation, and research findings dissemination endeavors related to ISU learning communities and their effects.
7. Stimulate campuswide comprehensive planning for the following year's learning communities and their activities based on the pattern of results from the preceding year.
8. Devise—and promote implementation of—strategies for optimizing the effectiveness, efficiency, and positive impacts of learning communities.
9. Promote active involvement in the learning community projects by ISU faculty, staff, and students.
10. Serve on thesis and dissertation committees and act as a mentor to graduate students conducting research on university learning communities.
11. Teach graduate courses within the professional studies division.
12. Promote and assist the expansion and institutionalization of learning communities across the ISU campus.
13. Assist departmental faculty to develop presentations and articles on their ISU learning community and its effects for disciplinary conferences and journals; and make presentations about the learning communities program and its findings at selected higher education conferences and initiate articles for the popular press as well as for higher education journals.
14. Supervise learning communities support staff.
15. Report to, and conduct additional activities as directed by, the Director of the ISU Center for Teaching Excellence and the Chair of the Professional Studies in Education department.

Source: Lenning, O. T., and Ebbers, L. H. *Developing Optimum Learning Communities and Documenting Their Effectiveness.* Unpublished manuscript. Used by permission.

CHAPTER FOUR

DEVELOPING THE CURRICULA

Historians of higher education will look back on the 1980s and 1990s as a time of great transition for American colleges and universities. A 1999 study by the National Center for Educational Statistics revealed that the educational aspirations of high school seniors soared between 1982 and 1992. In 1982 only 39 percent of students graduating from high school indicated that they had plans to pursue postsecondary education; by 1992 that number had risen to 69 percent. And now it is even higher (Forgione, 1999). In order to respond to the challenge of an increasingly diversified undergraduate population, colleges and universities are reexamining the goals of their general education curriculum and redefining the student learning outcomes for the baccalaureate degree. The American Council on Education reported that between 80 and 90 percent of its member institutions reexamined their undergraduate curricula during the 1980s (Gaff, 1999). Institutions of higher education are turning to new curricular structures and innovative programs, including first-year seminars and learning communities, to meet this challenge.

A flood of studies and commission reports, charges and mission statements, debates and national agendas is targeted at renewing the energy and focus of higher education toward general education. In 1999 the Association of American Colleges and Universities commissioned a new series of study papers on the theme of the academy in transition. The studies we cited in Chapter One, such as those released by the Kellogg Commission (1997) and the Carnegie Foundation for the Advancement of Teaching (Boyer Commission on Educating Undergraduates in the Research University, 1998), all converge on the same question: What has happened to the college experience of integrated coursework, critical questioning, and the engagement of faculty and students together in making meaning? How can we reinvent undergraduate education to serve a broadly expanded student population?

In 1987 the influential Boyer report, *College: The Undergraduate Experience in America,* challenged all colleges and universities to rethink their missions: "The nation's colleges and universities must ask hard questions about the quality of their own work. . . . The vitality of undergraduate education affects, we believe, all the others" (pp. xi-xii). The report was among the first to redefine the general education mission. In examining the overriding goals of an undergraduate education, Boyer found that the college experience had drifted away from its mission to educate students to their potential and had created a limiting, confining curriculum: "Separations and divisions, not unity, mark the undergraduate program. Narrow departmentalization divides the campus. . . . The danger is that in a bid for survival colleges will offer narrow skills training with a cafeteria of courses devoid of deeper meaning" (p. 66).

Boyer stated that the traditions of individuality and community lie at the heart of the undergraduate experience, and he challenged higher education to respond by redefining the undergraduate experience with those goals in mind:

> Colleges exacerbate [the] tendency toward self-preoccupation and social isolation. We found during our study that general education is the neglected stepchild of the undergraduate experience. . . . Too many campuses, we found, are divided by narrow departmental interests that become obstacles to learning in the richer sense. Students and faculty, like passengers on an airplane, are members of a community of convenience. They are caught up in a journey with a procedural rather than a substantive agenda [pp. 83–84].

Boyer's report set the stage for a variety of student-centered curricular innovations: collaborative learning, experiential learning, cooperative learning, mentored learning, internships and experimental interdisciplinary courses, and team teaching, among others. He also anticipated and triggered renewed attention to the extracurricular aspects of student life, among them athletics, health education, food service, and residence life experiences. Learning communities evolved in part in response to this challenge.

Boyer generated widespread debate and rethinking of the undergraduate general education curriculum, and over the past decade, creative curricular models and revisions have taken hold on many campuses. It is in this context that we find the roots of the current learning community model.

Well-crafted learning communities are much more than merely communities of convenience. They are by definition and design intentional and purposeful communities that generate synergy by linking courses, extracurricular activities, and multiple pedagogical strategies. A campus that embraces a learning community model gives a clear signal to prospective students and parents that it treats undergraduate education as a high priority and is committed to investing in the general education of undergraduates. In today's higher education market, with parents and students asking for more clearly defined learning outcomes from the college experience, that is an important message.

At its best, a strong general education curriculum supports students in formulating their own coherent view of knowledge as they participate in shared classes and learning activities. The shift from a teaching model to a learning model in higher education opens opportunities for faculty to rethink their roles and the inherent limitations on their own disciplinary specialties. Not all faculty will embrace these goals simultaneously. Yet every campus has faculty who are ready to rise to the challenge, and learning communities create opportunities to bring these educational innovators together across disciplines.

This chapter looks at five curricular elements that are embedded in many learning communities: general education, interdisciplinary courses, writing courses, freshman seminars, and experiential learning. Although the list is not exhaustive, it suggests the potential for learning communities to transform aspects of undergraduate education on a campus that is ready for change.

General Education

Gaff (1999) has described a number of contemporary trends in general education reform. Prominent among those trends is "the recognition that the freshman year amounts to a critical transition, and the creation of special courses and new support systems . . . promote greater academic successes" (p. 2). For many colleges and universities, learning communities act as a lens for students to help focus their choices among the dozens or sometimes hundreds of courses that could fulfill general education fundamental studies and distribution requirements. The larger and more diverse the campus is, the more choices a student is likely to have.

Most campuses over the 1990s have designated faculty committees to reexamine the requirements for liberal or general education for all students, regardless of major. Common general education requirements typically include a broad distribution of courses in humanities, sciences, social sciences, written and oral communication, mathematics, foreign language, diversity, and technology. University of Maryland students, for example, are required to take three fundamental studies courses (including two writing courses and one mathematics course) as part of their general education requirement; three courses in humanities, selected from approximately 170 courses; three courses in mathematics and science, out of approximately 100; three courses in social science and history, out of approximately 200; and two upper-level advanced studies courses outside their major. In addition, one of these distributive courses must fulfill a human cultural diversity requirement.

As student choices expand, universities are challenged by parents and prospective employers to give undergraduates quality undergraduate advising. Learning communities provide one possible solution to this dilemma—not limiting choices but organizing them and offering a sophisticated support system for students to make the most of their undergraduate experience.

Proponents of a broad liberal education model moved to an accumulation of individual courses as a way of ensuring that many students in many different situations would be exposed to a diversity of disciplines and ways of knowing. In reality, no one was ever really satisfied with a general education program that merely counts credits. Rather, we are looking for a high level of multiple literacies, technological comfort levels, and depth of knowledge that will guarantee that graduates have the competencies to live successful and fulfilled lives.

In the current climate of public school reform, we are witnessing a reexamination of the traditional Carnegie unit credit counting in K–12 education. Grade inflation, low test scores, and extensive remediation at the college level are challenging K–12 educators to rethink traditional curricular models and objectives. A parallel challenge is now facing higher education: to take a critical look at the value and nature of the traditional model of general education defined by credit accumulation, compared to performance assessment (Schneider, 1999). Too many students are coming through the higher education system without an adequate grasp of general education competencies.

One of the most dramatic demonstrations of the failure of the current general education programs was illustrated in July 1998 when Massachusetts revealed that close to 60 percent of the teacher candidates graduating from college failed the general knowledge exam for teacher certification (Bombardieri, 1998). The resulting firestorm of publicity focused attention on the failure of higher education to guarantee undergraduate educational outcomes across the board. The real goal has always been to build students' capacities to learn. The world is changing at such a rapid pace that it is folly to try to equip students with the "answers." Rather, the goal is that when they graduate, they understand how to ask the right questions, organize an approach to problem solving, and apply that understanding to real-world situations.

Learning communities offer different models for delivering general education to undergraduates. Three programs can serve as examples: Portland State University, which delivers general education to all students through interdisciplinary learning communities; New Century College, at George Mason University, designed around learning competencies; and Temple University, which offers an alternative approach to organizing clusters of courses for general education.

Portland State University. In 1994 Portland State University introduced the University Studies program aimed at offering all students a coherent, integrated program that would lead to "the development of the skills and attitudes needed to pursue lifelong learning" (*Portland State Advisor's Guide to University Studies*, 1997). All students at Portland State are assigned to an interdisciplinary learning community and are required to complete the year-long freshman inquiry program. Teams of interdisciplinary faculty design the thematically coherent curricula ("Einstein's Universe," "City Life," "Communities and Conflict"), and those courses explicitly emphasize faculty-student and student-student interaction (White, 1998). This program offers all students an opportunity to participate in theme-based, team-taught, interdisciplinary courses in the freshman year, followed by upper-division cluster coursework.

The University Studies program is designed around specific learning outcomes in the areas of communication skills, inquiry and critical thinking, research methods, computer literacy, diversity and multiculturalism, ethical issues and social responsibility, community building, and group process skills. Students progress through a scaffold of interdisciplinary freshman inquiry seminars, to sophomore inquiry courses, which serve as a gateway to upper division clusters and a senior capstone. According to Charles White, faculty chair of the committee that redesigned Portland State general education in 1993,

> The defining feature is that the courses emphasize academic foundations (writing, oral communication, basic statistics, technology literacy, visual and graphics communication) in an integrated manner. A single project may ask students to analyze data, report and display the results, and present their findings in written and oral form. The constant sharing of work with peers and the functioning of faculty as motivators, guides, and instructors results in the creation of strong classroom communities [White, 1998, pp. 60–61].

New Century College, George Mason University. New Century College is a college within a college offering a B.A. or B.S. in integrative studies. The degree program constructs its general education requirements around competencies rather than disciplines. The Integrative Studies Program offers an alternative curriculum, including a first-year program where students enroll in learning communities and take common courses. The curriculum focuses on eight competency areas: communication, critical thinking and analysis, problem solving, social interaction, effective citizenship, global perspective, aesthetic response, and valuing. Descriptions of the competencies are posted on the New Century College Web site (http://www.ncc.gmu.edu/competency.htm).

Temple University. Temple University implemented a new general education program, the Core Curriculum, in the 1980s. Concerns that the new courses had accomplished little to improve teaching or student learning led to the creation of the Learning Communities Program. Most of Temple's learning communities link general education courses with first-year writing courses, or other courses in the core, to create opportunities for students to study together and collaborate on joint projects. The goal is to help students realize the rich curricular connections that can be built between courses from different disciplines. For example, students in a learning community pairing a college math and introductory psychology course use psychology journals as their textbook to study statistics in their math course. The math teacher loves teaching his course as part of this community because his students learn that they can use math outside the math classroom.

Interdisciplinary Courses

Two curricular elements related to this discussion of general education merit a separate discussion: the emerging role of interdisciplinary courses and writing courses as points of entry into developing critical thinking skills.

Interdisciplinary studies have taken different forms over the past decade. In *Mapping Interdisciplinary Studies,* Klein (1999) writes, "The most prominent interdisciplinary practices in general education today are designing integrated alternatives to traditional distribution models, insuring breadth of knowledge, clustering and linking courses, building learning communities, and incorporating diversity, new interdisciplinary knowledges, and new pedagogies" (p. 11). Each approach to relational learning works toward the same goal of integrating knowledge from different disciplines by bringing it to bear on characteristically complex real-world problems.

Real-world problems are notoriously messy: What are the pros and cons of a managed health care system? How should we think about the politics of information technology such as privacy on the Internet or international copyright infringement? How should we prepare for an increasingly interdependent global economy and work to avoid cross-cultural misunderstandings? Why should the National Endowment for the Arts receive public support? Learning communities push against the traditional model of general education by challenging university curriculum committees to rethink the role of interdisciplinary studies. In the past, such courses and programs have been orphans on traditional campuses; if a course is not owned by an academic department or college, it has a short half-life. Department chairs and deans may resist when faculty propose such courses because of conflicting resource pressures, but learning communities raise the visibility for interdisciplinary courses and have some surprising outcomes.

Elements of Successful Interdisciplinary Courses

Successful interdisciplinary courses share three characteristics: they are thematically organized, team-taught (or designed), and competency based. Thematically organized courses such as those described in the Portland State University Studies Program pose complex questions, exploiting the creative tensions between different disciplinary ways of knowing.

Team-taught courses allow faculty members to model the experience of learning from peers. Carol Schneider, president of the American Association of Colleges and Universities, and Robert Shoenberg (1998) describe the power of interdisciplinary experiences: "The instructor serves as exemplar of the person whose role is to find fresh and instructive connections, helping students learn how to test intellectual and practical usefulness—the explanatory power—of the connections they find" (p. 10).

Finally, interdisciplinary courses are developed with broad learning outcomes in mind. Portland State identifies competencies in the areas of communication skills, inquiry and critical thinking, research methods, computer literacy, diversity and multiculturalism, ethical issues and social responsibility, community building, and group process skills (*Portland State Advisor's Guide to University Studies,* 1997). These objectives are described quite differently from course objectives in the disciplines, where scope and sequence in a given field are primary objectives. Learning communities sit at the crossroads of discussions about student-centered and learner-centered curricula.

Many hard-fought battles have occurred over interdisciplinary courses in learning communities, especially around granting general education credit for such courses. During the course of these discussions, faculty from many different fields working together sometimes find that they have more in common with colleagues from different disciplines than with the more conservative members of their own departments.

An Example of an Interdisciplinary Learning Community

A well-designed learning community curriculum is crafted to tease students' imaginations and evoke curiosity about topics and issues that might have gone unnoticed and unremarked in a typical listing of general distribution requirements.

The University of Maryland's College Park Scholars Science, Discovery, and the Universe Program is designed to offer an interdisciplinary focus on astronomy and its long-standing role in the evolution of societies and civilizations from past, to present, and into the future. Participation in this program gives students a necessary start in understanding and becoming familiar with the technology that will be part of their life beyond college. Students in the program combine interests in science, religion, philosophy, history, and communications. The program is interdisciplinary in nature and seeks to draw students with an interest in astronomy from different majors.

Students in the program take two to three courses together in the first semester: the one-credit colloquium and a three-credit freshman writing course. They also choose one four-credit physical science lab course, which fulfills a general education requirement. Over the next three semesters, they select two additional courses from a recommended list of electives in humanities, literature, history, or arts that have a connection to the theme of the learning community. Students thus have the opportunity to proceed through their curriculum together, defining a sense of community that will enrich their university experience and likely lead to the formation of close personal friendships. Exhibit 4.1 provides an overview of the requirements for students in the Science, Discovery, and the Universe Program. Students who complete the two-year program by fulfilling all the requirements are eligible to earn a College Park Scholars citation, which appears as a notation on their transcript, similar to an honors notation.

The curriculum exemplifies how thematic, interdisciplinary programs are organized. Typically these programs are clusters of courses held together by one-credit seminars or special cross-disciplinary courses that might be taught by two or three faculty members. Many learning communities use one-credit seminars to create points of intersection between or among the clustered courses and provide a time for synthesis.

College Park Scholars began with one-credit colloquia as a launching pad for the program themes. Initially faculty directors invited experts from across campus to visit their colloquia and share their passions about their disciplines. The advantage here was obvious: first-year students had close contact with faculty from many different areas of expertise, sharing the rich fabric of the research activities of the campus.

EXHIBIT 4.1. STUDENT REQUIREMENTS IN THE SCIENCE, DISCOVERY, AND THE UNIVERSE PROGRAM, COLLEGE PARK SCHOLARS, UNIVERSITY OF MARYLAND.

CITATION REQUIREMENTS
To earn a CPS–Science, Discovery, and the Universe Citation, you must complete 17–23 credits with an overall average GPA of 3.0 in designated CPS courses, including ENGL 101. If you are exempt from ENGL 101, you must complete 14–20 credits. These credits must be satisfied during the two-year period of the CPS Program (4 semesters).

REQUIRED COURSES
Fall 1998 (Semester 1)
CPSP 118D Colloquium: 1 credit; ENGL 101 Composition: 3 credits (if not exempt); CORE Physical Science Lab Course: 4 credits

Spring 1999 (Semester 2)
CPSP 118D Colloquium: 1 credit; ENGL 101: 3 credits (if not completed in Semester 1); Supporting Course (see below): 3–4 credits

Fall 1999 (Semester 3)
CPSP 218D Sophomore Project: 1–3 credits; Supporting Course (see below): 3–4 credits

Spring 2000 (Semester 4)
CPSP 259D Sophomore Project: 1–3 credits; Supporting Course (see below): 3–4 credits (if not completed in Semester 3)

Supporting Courses (Total of 6–8 credits)
Complete two courses from the following list (or any other course approved by the CPS-SDU Director) by the end of Semester 4. All courses are 3 credits unless otherwise noted. CORE designation is in parenthesis.

AMST 211(HO) Technology in American Culture
CLAS 170 (HL) Greek and Roman Mythology
CMSC 102 Information Technology
CMSC 106 (4) Introduction to C Programming
CMSC 107 Introduction to UNIX Operating Systems
ECON 200 (4)(SB) Principles of Micro Economics
ECON 201 (4)(SB) Principles of Macro Economics
ENGL 277 (HL) Mythology: An Introduction
GVPT 100 (SB) Principles of Government and Politics
HIST 110 (HL) The Ancient World
HIST 157 (SH) American History since 1865
JOUR 100 (SB) Introduction to Mass Communication
MATH 140 (4) (MS) Calculus 1
MATH 220 (MS) or higher Elementary Calculus
MUSC 140 (HA) Music Fundamentals
MUSC 210 (HA/D) The Impact of Music on Life
PHIL 101 (HO) Introduction to Philosophy
PHIL 250 (HO) Philosophy of Science
SOCY 100 (SB) Introduction to Sociology
SOCY 105 (SB) Introduction to Contemporary Social Problems

Source: Science, Discovery, and the Universe Program, College Park Scholars, University of Maryland. Used by permission.

Writing Courses

The learning communities models described in Chapter Two illustrate the growing practice of linking one or two courses with a first-year writing course. Learning communities often use writing courses as a foundation to promote student learning and foster intellectual engagement in the disciplines. Writing and writing competence has always been a high-priority learning outcome for general education, and over the past two decades, research in composition has had a strong emphasis on writing across the curriculum (Herrington and Moran, 1992).

As the field of composition and rhetoric matured, so did the recognition that students would not achieve fluency and rhetorical competence with only one semester-long course in freshman writing. Rather, infusing writing across the curriculum and inserting writing as a tool for learning in all disciplines became a high priority in the 1980s (Anson, 1988; Herrington, 1981). Light (1992) demonstrated that requiring writing in a course increased students' involvement in the disciplinary courses and contributed to stronger learning outcomes. Writing has also been clearly linked to student cognitive development and intellectual maturity (Shapiro, 1985). When students are challenged to write in their courses, they are forced to grapple with a complex intellectual task that pushes them to higher levels of intellectual maturity.

Writing courses provide an ideal opportunity to create thematic links among courses that fulfill general education distribution requirements, and students in learning communities are encouraged to take advantage of the writing course link. When learning communities are thematically defined, students get a cluster of classes that together create curricular coherence by bringing together several disciplinary perspectives on a theme or topic.

Writing courses can fulfill this function and still preserve their primary purpose. Typically composition courses include instruction in rhetorical theory about audience and purpose, organization and style, and delivery. Frequently students engage in exercises that begin as journal entries and progress to fully developed papers. A second characteristic of writing courses is instruction in the writing process: the process of idea generating, drafting, reviewing, and revising.

Choosing a Topic

Many freshman writing courses are designed around a schedule of assignments constructed to accommodate unspecified content, thus making writing courses a natural vehicle for integrating learning community courses together. For example, students may be asked to analyze a persistent or particular problem in a field and develop research papers that build on the same topic. Students in learning communities have ready access to faculty from different disciplines who could help them identify successful topics for these papers and steer them in the direction of particularly relevant sources.

Both the content and the process of a college-level writing course that is not a literature course usually require students to arrive at their own topics for papers and their own areas of study. Almost any student will admit that coming up with a topic is one of the hardest parts of writing a paper. Most freshman writing instructors concur, confirming that they spend as much time counseling students on how to narrow and focus a topic as they do on correcting first drafts.

It is also a problem for writing teachers to assemble the expertise they need to read papers developed from an unlimited number of content areas since typical research papers allow students to pursue their own areas of interests. A single writing teacher may be faced with reading papers on jazz history, on cloning, and on the legal implications of intellectual property rights for Web-based technologies—all written in response to one assignment on written argument. No single writing instructor can be expected to be able to support students on all of those topics equally well. Furthermore, unless a student happens to select a topic in an area of the teacher's expertise, the student is left to spend a lot of time trying to identify relevant and reliable sources of information.

What distinguishes a first-year writing-composition course from other writing courses is that it introduces first-year college students to a different way of thinking. Writing and thinking are inextricably linked (Shapiro, 1984), and the introduction to writing that is required in most colleges and universities is, at its best, an introduction to critical thinking. Critical thinking takes place when students are challenged to analyze a communication situation, analyze the audience and the purpose of a piece of writing, and construct a rhetorical argument or response that takes the perspective of the "other" into consideration even as it constructs a strong argument from evidence. Typical writing assignments in a freshman writing class include description, comparison and contrast, evaluation, and argument. All of these assignments require students to become more proficient in appropriate discipline-based methods to arrive at a position and support it with evidence (Walvoord and McCarthy, 1991).

Most freshman writing assignments require that students spell out or identify their audience and their purpose. Writing instructors who have taught students in learning communities and nonlearning communities writing courses often comment that students in learning communities have a clearer understanding of the multiple meanings of audience. One hypothesis suggests that students are more likely to test their ideas with their classmates, with whom they share several classes. Another is that students in learning communities who take classes clustered around a theme are exposed to different disciplinary perspectives on a particular issue and better understand how to interpret an event or issue using different lenses. In any case, writing courses form a natural bonding place for learning communities. Students are encouraged to use the subject matter from their content classes to provide the content for the papers they write in a process-oriented writing class.

Teaching Assistant–Instructor Professional Development

A corollary advantage of using writing courses as the linking course among different disciplinary courses is that the writing instructors themselves benefit from having direct access to the disciplinary faculty of the cluster. A student who wants to pursue a particular topic that is not familiar to the writing instructor can appeal to a collaborating faculty member for advice and support.

Typically writing instructors in research universities are graduate assistants, and their experience across disciplines is limited. Exposure to faculty outside their departments gives them a professional advantage over their colleagues. Two examples illustrate this point. After only one year as a teaching assistant in the College Park Scholars Program, one freshman writing teaching assistant landed a lucrative evening job teaching an MCAT (Medical School Admissions Tests) course to biology students. Another found his way into a job as a technical writer-editor through an engineering faculty contact.

Tompkins and Mader (1998) note that the opportunity to teach as part of a learning community broadens professional growth of graduate students. They see this as a chance for graduate students to gain a wider perspective on the workings of the university because they are part of interdepartmental instructional teams. They observe, "By expanding the scope of teaching assistant's experience across the university, Learning Community Faculty Development reaches into the future, affecting future faculty for years to come" (p. 23).

Writing Links

Many learning community models organize linked courses that include a writing component. Learning to write requires overlapping instruction, sometimes found in writing courses, sometimes in writing-intensive courses, or linked courses. (A detailed syllabus illustrating such a pairing of a sociology course and a writing course can be found in Anson and others, 1993, pp. 129–140.) Learning to write also requires practice; one freshman-level course cannot be expected to finish the job. However, writing across the curriculum has proved that disciplinary faculty are uneven in their confidence about coaching students in writing in their disciplines (Walvoord and McCarthy, 1991). Writing faculty, however, are quite expert at coaching students in the writing process, and the collaborations between disciplinary faculty and writing faculty take on a new dimension when the courses are linked. When faculty from both courses read and respond to student papers, students take their writing assignments more seriously because they know they will have multiple readers. There is research waiting to be done on the effectiveness of this approach, but students and faculty who have participated in the earliest models are positive about the long-term results with respect to the development of student writing and thinking (Walvoord and McCarthy, 1991).

Using writing as a linking course has some obvious advantages, but because it is also one of the fundamental studies courses and so central to general education outcomes, it also creates some logistical problems if it becomes a required part of the learning community model. What happens, for example, when students who sign up for a cluster with a writing course test out of the required writing course through placement exams or high scores on a college entrance exam? How will these students benefit from the advantage of the integrated writing experience? Should they be required to take the course even if they are exempt from it if they want to be in the learning community? Composition departments have been trying to make a case for universally required writing courses for years. Learning communities add a new spin on that debate. Should the program exempt any student from freshman writing if it is indeed a prelude to the more complex levels of critical thinking required in college? Another part of the rationale for linking learning communities through writing courses is that students benefit from taking that introduction to writing (and thinking) as early in their college career as possible. But most English departments cannot afford the resources to teach all or most sections of freshman writing in the first semester. Every campus will have to address these issues and others from within their own campus culture. The learning community model raises them to the campus level for debate and discussion.

Freshman Seminars

In a 1997 study, the National Resource Center for the Freshman-Year Experience found that over 70 percent of American colleges and universities offered a first-year seminar. Of those, 14 percent of institutions linked or clustered those seminars with other courses in learning communities (Gardner and others, 1999). This concept of the interrelatedness of issues in a general education curriculum is generally characteristic of learning communities, whether the learning community is a simple cluster of courses, as in FIGs, or a more elaborate citation- or certificate-driven program, where students who complete the sequence requirements earn special recognition on their transcript.

Seminars or colloquia differ from freshman writing courses in that they are typically one-credit courses that meet only one hour a week and have a more loosely defined curriculum. One-credit courses are not usually considered robust enough to earn core credit. In some learning communities programs where participation extends beyond the first semester, students are required to take a one-credit seminar in each semester of participation. The accumulated credits of coursework may be viewed as a full course, albeit an elective.

Many campuses have opted for a one-credit orientation course for freshmen that introduces them to the university: academic life, the library, student services, peer counseling, and study skills workshops. These courses are usually led by undergraduates or adjunct faculty, and are structured to create a kind of home base for first-year students. Learning communities have infused these one-credit courses with a pivotal role of integration. Faculty who teach these seminars are often the lead faculty for the learning community. In the seminar, they can provide the nexus for the thematic crossing of paths among the linked courses. Seminars are the crossroads courses, where faculty can invite colleagues from different disciplines to debate in front of the students, and students can watch and participate in the critical analysis of hypotheses using different critical methodologies.

Indiana University Purdue University Indianapolis (IUPUI) developed first-year seminars as a central component of their learning communities (Evenbeck and Williams, 1998). The first-year seminars are intended to introduce students to the expectations and practices of the academic community and, using the small-group model, build a strong sense of community through interactions between peers and instructors. Faculty and student support personnel form instructional teams comprising a faculty member, an academic adviser, a librarian, a student mentor, and a technical support person. One of the challenges of this program is to create stronger ties between the first-year seminars and disciplinary courses, and break away from the traditional study skills seminar model. The instructional team approach offers a way to move in this direction.

Experiential Learning: Undergraduate Research and Service-Learning

Learning communities can push the boundaries of disciplines and foster interdisciplinary connections for both students and teachers. And they can serve another important function in undergraduate education: they are an ideal site for integrating experiential learning into the curriculum. The term *experiential learning* covers a wide array of strategies that involve students in learning opportunities that go beyond traditional lectures, reading assignments, and essay writing. As far back as John Dewey, we have understood that students learn best and retain most when they are active participants in their own learning.

Two models of experiential learning, undergraduate research and service-learning, have expanded the options for institutions and faculties looking for ways to transform higher education into a more participatory learning experience for undergraduates. Both put students to the test by engaging them in problem-posing and problem-solving activities that force them and their faculty mentors to make connections between what they are learning in their classes and how that knowledge and information can be applied to real-world questions and situations.

Undergraduate Research

The Boyer Commission on Educating Undergraduates (1998) found that during the first two years at college, undergraduate research experiences are constrained and limited by several realities. First, since undergraduates, especially first- and second-year students, are not trained in sophisticated research methodologies, faculty are hesitant to involve them in serious research. Second, even when a faculty member requires a research paper in an undergraduate course, the choice of topics and sources of information are generally prescribed to fit a certain course or topic. Students undertaking such projects typically view them as a necessary evil and, beyond striving for a high grade, rarely invest much of their ego in the outcome. In fact, the research paper typically assigned to students in a traditional course has more in common with high school assignments than with what should be qualitatively different college-level learning. The third element that limits opportunities for learning in project-oriented research is the absence of an audience that goes beyond the instructor.

The idea of promoting research-based experiences for college undergraduates, particularly those at research universities, is not new. University-sponsored research internships, in which undergraduates work on a project directly tied to a faculty member's research program, are perhaps the most widely used vehicle for exposing students to the research environment. The University of Michigan Undergraduate Research Opportunity Program (UROP) is an excellent example of a campuswide commitment to undergraduate research. It has the advantages of using existing faculty resources and affords students a rewarding view of knowledge creation at the cutting edge. In exceptional cases, students may develop an extended involvement with a project; they may be included as a coauthor on a publication or may be inspired to pursue a related career path. This program has played an important role in the retention of minority students (Sandra Gregerman, personal communication, Feb. 13, 1999).

We have come a long way from Astin's 1993 report that suggested that faculty research priorities have a negative impact on undergraduates. The recent thinking in the field clearly promotes expanding research opportunities for undergraduates. However, even if faculty were inclined to work with undergraduates, the entry barriers are high. The inexperience of undergraduate students, their relatively short-term availability for extended projects, and their crowded schedules of coursework and activities act as negative indicators for involvement in serious research on faculty-initiated projects.

Learning communities offer creative and exciting opportunities to reshape undergraduate curriculum to include undergraduate research. The Boyer Commission Report (1998) noted several outstanding models of undergraduate research, many of which come out of a learning community context. The Undergraduate Research Opportunities Programs at MIT and the University of Michigan are examples of research-based learning communities. Duke University's Freshman Focus clusters and the University of Utah's linked courses (LEAP: Liberal Education Accelerated Program) are offered as examples of a reinvention of undergraduate education. Stanford's Sophomore College engages students in seminar-type studies with faculty, and the University of Maryland's World Courses build large lectures with discussion sections around the interaction of faculty from three disciplines, demonstrating the nature of knowledge and inquiry by allowing students to observe and participate in cross-disciplinary dialogue.

Students benefit from undergraduate research experiences in a variety of ways. They learn how to frame meaningful questions and evaluate sources and evidence, gain experience with technologies of presentation and data sources, and use current computer technologies. These are skills they will use in college and beyond. Not only those undergraduates planning to go on to graduate school benefit from undergraduate research experiences. All undergraduates benefit, and it is a waste of precious resources to deny or limit their experiences during the short time they have access to the universe of research on campuses.

Discovery Projects

An innovative undergraduate research approach based in a learning community setting is the Discovery Projects at the University of Maryland, originally developed for sophomores in the College Park Scholars Program (Shapiro, 1997). The freshman year is seen as a critical transition to college, with stresses of adjusting to change, communal living arrangements, and completing fundamental studies in English and mathematics. During the sophomore year students are consolidating their resources and preparing for study in the major. Yet it is a time during which most campuses do not provide the types of orientation support or targeted courses or seminars that characterize the freshman year.

College Park Scholars has a strict citation requirement that students engage in an experiential learning project in order to earn the transcript citation. With support through a grant from Funds for the Improvement of Post Secondary Education in 1996, the program developed a sophomore-level capstone research experience, Discovery Projects.

Discovery Projects began as an experimental assignment in the Science, Technology, and Society Program. A history professor, Robert Friedel, assigned students to choose an invention and research the patent and the inventor by using the voluminous resources at the Lemelson Center for the Study of Invention at the Smithsonian Institution Museum of American History. Working closely with the center's archivist, Friedel helped students locate primary sources such as inventors' notes and sketches, early prototypes, even personal journals. Students picked an invention—the curling iron, the snow board, Tupperware—and were let loose in the archives. Their products at the end of the semester were not traditional research papers. Rather, the goal was to assemble an "invention discovery kit" that included copies of original documents that they classified and labeled. The kits became artifact archives for later papers or were offered to local public school libraries as resource kits for teachers and students.

Discovery Projects are another example of how the faculty themselves function as a creative learning community. When Shapiro and Friedel shared this idea with other College Park Scholars faculty directors from different programs at a faculty retreat, they caught a measure of his excitement. They collectively brainstormed ways of generating similar projects in their fields and stimulated each other to design remarkable research assignments for their students. College Park Scholars in International Studies worked with professional archivists in the National Archives, where they pored through boxes of old letters and photographs, recently declassified memoranda, and Central Intelligence Agency (CIA) reports, audiotapes, and old newsreel footage. One student learned of bungled plots to assassinate Fidel Castro in the 1960s and listened to tapes of CIA debriefings that only recently were declassified. Another student discovered boxes of letters from African Americans to the secretary of state in the 1930s requesting permission to fight in the Ethiopian-Italian War.

Learning communities faculty design these projects in ways that connect the assignment to the theme of the program but also give students the widest possible latitude in topic choice. The faculty then select sites for research. Through the learning communities program, students participate in workshops on different research methodologies. In Maryland's program, students practice skills of searching, recording, classifying, analyzing, and assessing information—stopping just short of writing a paper. These research projects are targeted to sophomore students, with the goal of creating a sense of excitement around discovery.

Faculty were at first skeptical about assigning research projects without a final paper. But the student engagement in the process of research more than made up for the lack of a written product. The faculty role in these projects was to establish the professional links and points of entry that their students needed to be able to move into on-site study. From the National Institutes of Health (Life Sciences), to the National Zoo (Environmental Studies), to the National Gallery and the Kennedy Center (Arts), students from the different programs discovered how knowledge is created, valued, and preserved.

As part of the evaluation of the Discovery Projects, Callahan and Colson (1998) conducted a pretest-posttest study on a set of student essays. They found that students who participated in the project realized measurable improvement in four categories: writing competence, finding information, awareness of the research process, and ability to make choices.

Service-Learning

The concept of service-learning has emerged as a powerful, valuable vehicle for experiential learning in college. Service-learning intentionally connects a socially valuable, public service activity with a particular academic course content toward the goal of intellectual growth. Service-learning has come to be understood as a new way to integrate experiential learning into an academic curriculum (Jacoby, 1996).

Service-learning is built on five basic principles that can be used to construct an experiential curriculum: community voice, orientation and training, meaningful action, reflection, and evaluation (Mintz and Hesser, 1996). Many students enter colleges and universities having completed some community service requirement for graduation from high school. Service-learning opportunities in college engage students in meaningful community-based activities that are tied in some critical ways to the disciplinary or thematic content of individual courses.

Service-learning opportunities take students out of the classroom and into a real-world context, where they can apply their new understandings while gaining some practical, situated experiences. It requires that students have mentors or supervisors who guide them through the experience and help them make connections between what they learn actually doing this work with what they are learning in class or in their research. Students in the life sciences or environmental sciences, for example, may work on ecology projects in the community, and students in social sciences may work with social service agencies, mentoring unwed mothers or building houses for Habitat for Humanity. Each of these activities becomes a purposeful learning experience when the instructor incorporates readings, discussion, and reflections about the experience in lessons, lectures, or assignments.

The difference between volunteer work and service-learning is in the intentional connections between the learning and the service. It is the difference between curricular and cocurricular, between mainstream and peripheral obligations or responsibilities, between examined and unexamined experience.

As with other curricular innovations, not all faculty or students are equally motivated by service-learning curricula, and sometimes service-learning proponents meet considerable resistance on a campus or in a program. Yet evidence is emerging that for many students, service-learning experiences enhance their purpose around their educational objectives and lead to a deeper level of understanding of course content and intellectual maturity around substantive issues, clearly desirable goals of higher education (Enos and Troppe, 1996).

No single service-learning model or experience will work for every discipline, every course, or every student. In fact, discussion and debate are ongoing about how to define service-learning and build academic experiences around community service, particularly around how to balance the needs of the community with the overriding goal of academic and intellectual growth. As faculty grapple with the right mix, the right guidelines, and the appropriate venues for service, they are increasingly aware of the potential for realizing their own goals through these service experiences. Jacoby (1996) explores a number of different models and methods for implementing a service-learning component on a campus and cites evidence "that service-learning that is connected to specific course content can increase student's learning of course content" (p. 323).

Service-Learning in Multiple Disciplines

In the summer of 1996 the University of Maryland's College Park Scholars Program took an important step toward expanding the mission of the program to include service-learning. As part of the experiential learning component of the curriculum, the program inaugurated the first Day of Service, arranging for all six hundred incoming freshmen to spread out into the community in teams of fifteen to twenty to perform a variety of volunteer service duties as part of the new student orientation. The day-long event was an ambitious kickoff to the new service-learning component of the curriculum. By involving the offices of student affairs, commuter affairs, resident life, and undergraduate studies, and the cities of College Park, Takoma Park, and Washington, D.C., the program provided a catalyst for an innovative learning and community-building experience that ultimately led to a permanent curriculum component of the program and gave a boost to the campuswide service-learning initiative.

The Day of Service became the first step toward a curricular innovation that expanded the definition of experiential learning in this learning community. Experiential learning is one of the key elements of this residential learning community, and during the first year, the learning experiences were tied to the colloquia through a number of short field trips and off-campus site visits.

The service-learning curriculum offered students the hands-on, resumé-building experiences they wanted and allowed faculty to tap mentors both on and off campus to share the supervisory responsibility. In many cases, the schools, parks, nongovernmental organizations, and nonprofit organizations had organized volunteer programs in place that afforded students excellent experiences. The role of the program faculty was to make sure the placements and the reflection on the work related to the academic content of the thematic program.

Some of the learning communities followed the Day of Service with extended opportunities for service-learning in their areas. American Cultures students worked with the Maryland English Institute's Speaking Partners Program, which matches American volunteers from the university with foreign students who want to improve their English. Environmental Studies students worked with a local school and local science center, assisting high school students in designing and developing three kinds of organic gardens at the center. Science, Technology, and Society students took responsibility for leading after-school club meetings of Hands on Science with the goal of increasing their awareness of and appreciation for science and technology by learning how to teach it to others. Topics included aerodynamics and airplanes (paper airplanes), air and space, the planets and space, technology and communication, surfing the Internet, and e-mail. The Advocates for Children Program provided reading and mathematics tutors to an elementary school that had below-average reading scores. The faculty director, Albert Gardner, commented, "The partnership with Paint Branch Elementary School brings all of our colloquium discussions into very sharp focus. The process of teaching others is itself a very powerful learning process for our scholars" (personal communication, Dec. 8, 1998).

In all of these programs, the activities were more than merely volunteer community service. The faculty who chose to incorporate service-learning in their curricula participated in professional development workshops and attended campus presentations that coached them on how to build in opportunities for reflection and discussion as part of the colloquia syllabus.

Service-learning is emerging as one option for experiential learning where students meet community needs while developing their own critical thinking skills and understanding of an academic area. Learning communities are optimally situated and organized to explore this curricular innovation.

Conclusion

The Wingspread Report (1993) called on all of higher education to direct itself to three fundamental issues: taking values seriously, putting student learning first, and creating a nation of learners (p. 7). Learning communities embody these three principles. At their best, they become the incubators for campus reform.

Learning communities do not replace or create a new core curriculum. Rather, they represent a new way to think about accomplishing the overriding goals of general education while helping students link their learning to career and future aspirations. Parents as well as students are demanding a more meaningful higher education, and the definition of *meaningful* needs to be broad enough to accommodate both the inclinations and perspectives of the faculty and the very real expectations of students, their parents, and society at large. Learning communities take into consideration the cognitive developmental stages of college freshmen and provide a loosely structured framework to help students fully understand their choices. They can be seen as new curricular structures that not only have the potential to change the way traditional core courses are delivered but can transform the way traditional general education programs are conceived.

CHAPTER FIVE

RECASTING FACULTY ROLES AND REWARDS

Faculty and students are at the heart of any learning community. Whatever infrastructure is put in place to shape a learning community—linked courses, residential or thematic communities, architecturally coherent shared spaces, extra- or cocurricular activities, and service-learning—none of these is sufficient to support a learning community without the active involvement and participation of faculty.

Paradoxically, faculty are both the first and the last to initiate change in institutions of higher education, particularly in research institutions. As they develop new theories, generate new data to substantiate models, or encounter innovative ideas through interactions with their colleagues at professional conferences, they are more readily willing to integrate these new understandings into their research, scholarship, and teaching. In fact, it is new knowledge and new connections—breaking virgin ground in academic disciplines and content fields— that define the traditional work of faculty.

However, faculty members in general are frequently slow to accept changes that appear to alter traditional relationships between faculty and administration, faculty and students, faculty in their own departments, other departments, and the university community at large. In this respect, learning communities introduce serious challenges to the usual way of doing things. Partnerships with student affairs, the introduction of interdisciplinary courses, promoting active learning, and rethinking the intended outcomes for undergraduate education combine to shake up the predictable order and offer new paradigms for defining faculty work. Exhibit 5.1 contains University of Maryland faculty member Albert Gardner's reflections on teaching in College Park Scholars.

As higher education institutions move toward a greater level of accountability for undergraduate education and as higher education moves into closer partnerships with K–12 colleagues and the employers who hire college graduates, faculty, through their own disciplinary associations and institutional committees, are searching for ways to become more responsive to broader public expectations. Learning communities create new pathways for faculty to interact with each other and their students. They have become a leading edge in higher education reform.

Attracting and Recruiting Faculty to Teach in Learning Communities

At their best, learning communities capture the imagination of creative faculty members who see the potential of radically changing expectations of undergraduate student learning. One secret of generating a positive buzz on campus when introducing learning communities is to involve in the early planning faculty members who are among the most respected teachers and scholars on campus or who are involved with on-campus teaching-learning initiatives: teaching circles, peer review projects, teaching improvement centers, or instructional technology efforts. Attracting star-quality faculty to learning communities in the beginning makes the job of recruiting other faculty in later stages much easier. Recruiting this level of faculty takes planning and forethought and is intrinsically related to the institutional reward structure.

In the earliest conversations around learning communities at the University of Maryland, College Park, the dean of undergraduate studies brought together deans of the four colleges with the greatest number of undergraduate majors and asked each to nominate faculty to be part of this experiment. Working through the deans and department chairs, four lead faculty were identified and given course release or summer stipends, or both, to participate in planning the learning community. They were encouraged from the beginning to have direct contact with their deans, assemble an advisory group of faculty from related disciplines, and meet regularly with each other as they developed the plans for the curriculum and activities that would define their programs. This autonomy was both appropriate and reassuring to the faculty directors. They understood they were being asked to forge new alliances using traditional processes, all the while keeping the learning communities linked securely to collegiate homes and creating multiple vested interests. As the process unfolded, it became an honor to be invited to join the ad-

EXHIBIT 5.1. ALBERT GARDNER'S REFLECTIONS ON BEING A FACULTY MEMBER IN COLLEGE PARK SCHOLARS, UNIVERSITY OF MARYLAND.

When I heard of the proposal for the College Park Scholars Program I reacted with some skepticism. My egalitarian inclinations resisted the identification and privileged treatment of a selected university group. But as I listened to the emphasis on student-faculty contact, extracurricular activities, interdisciplinary learning and shared residential arrangements, I found the concept rather attractive. After all, some of these characteristics of a learning community had been part of my teaching for many years but were not built into a defined structure. Once I understood the structure of College Park Scholars I realized, with ecstasy, that this program was what I had been preparing for, waiting for, looking for, and hoping for all of these many years.

While many of us teaching in the university might not have known that such a possibility existed, we did know that it was students and subject matter that drew us into this work. It soon became evident that I was no longer cast off by myself doing classes à la "MWF 10:00–10:50," I was now living (at least spending a lot of time in the residence hall) and learning with . . . students, staff, and faculty members. We, all of us, were in this together . . . our focus, our mission was to enrich both the education and the life of undergraduates . . . that was why we, all of us, were in the program.

That is what sustains us, that is what inspires us. In such an atmosphere it just gets better and better: new ideas, new opportunities, new challenges. The latter are the true rewards of the program, along with the privilege and pleasure of working with dedicated students, staff, and faculty.

What kind of a faculty member seems best suited to be the director of a thematic program or to be a regular participant in such a program? Ready, willing, and able to:

- Place most efforts on teaching and involvement with students
- Work with staff from resident life and from the central CPS office
- Participate in extracurricular activities with students
- Integrate multidisciplinary learning in one's classes
- Support and encourage service learning activities and other experiential opportunities
- Manage a budget and address the details of registration, curriculum planning, course scheduling, and supervision of graduate assistants
- Counsel students on personal and academic matters, make referrals, suggestions and write letters of recommendation
- Plan and deliver imaginative and productive academic and extracurricular activities and experiences
- Provide resources for students (professors, specialists, sites, laboratories, libraries)
- And more

Source: Albert Gardner, College Park Scholars, University of Maryland. Used by permission.

visory board of the learning community, and those who served on these boards became articulate advocates for the program in their departments and across the campus.

Another approach is to invite faculty and administrators from across the campus to form work groups organized around the critical tasks in implementing learning communities, such as curriculum, faculty development, marketing and recruitment, and evaluation. Invitations to join these work groups typically come from the administrator, dean, or faculty member selected by senior administration to lead the project. Work groups are an effective way to broaden campus involvement and support for learning communities.

A second principle for attracting faculty to the learning community is that the assignment must be finite. Faculty may become part of learning communities for as little as a semester, when their course is linked to one or more collateral courses, or join up for several years, depending on the configuration of the learning community. Because College Park Scholars was planned as a two-year program, it was recommended that faculty directors assume their responsibilities for three to four years, giving them at least one complete cycle of students through the two-year program and allowing them to modify and improve the learning community through the benefit of their experience as they entered the second cycle. After two years, most of the College Park Scholars programs began to draw in more outside faculty, either as associate directors or as advisory board members, setting in place a mechanism for a knowledgeable second generation of faculty who could take over when the first generation cycled out and returned to their regular teaching and research roles. The new directors were expected to shape their programs differently. In this respect, the advisory boards offered an unexpected advantage: in several cases, the new directors came from the advisory boards of the original programs. The sustainability of learning communities is directly dependent on recruiting quality faculty to the project, so advocates for learning communities must pay attention to creating a process that encourages faculty to cycle in and cycle out.

On many campuses, however, a multiyear faculty commitment is not feasible or desirable. It may be more difficult, for example, to get a long-term commitment at a large research-oriented university than it is at institutions where teaching is the primary mission. Departments may be willing to pledge long-term commitment of courses to learning communities but prefer to assign faculty on a semester-by-semester basis. The importance of strong, visionary campus leadership cannot be underestimated when addressing the question of recruiting faculty to learning communities on any campus.

There are other ways of recruiting faculty into learning communities than by attracting them to the notion of teaching in a learning community to fulfill a promise of the profession. One way is to tie the learning community to departmental objectives and agendas. Within the institutional context, departments typically set targets for retention, attracting new majors, strengthening premajor preparation, and raising academic standards for incoming students. By developing learning communities, departments can address these pressing priorities and assign faculty to play major roles in delivering departmental instruction to undergraduates in a new way. Departments that promote learning communities and collaborate with other departments in interdisciplinary offerings may be able to attract and retain more majors. For these reasons, the campus should provide tangible rewards for those who make learning communities a reality.

Rewarding Faculty for Their Work in Learning Communities

Successful learning communities need a way of recruiting, training and developing, and retaining strong faculty leaders if they are to have institutional longevity. Toward that end, the institution needs to develop creative ways of rewarding the kinds of faculty behaviors that sustain learning communities. The faculty reward structure is only partly within the control of an individual institution. Disciplinary faculty members affiliate in important ways with their colleagues in their disciplines across the country and around the world through national and international professional associations. Nevertheless, a campus reward structure is critical to the success of campus learning communities. A learning community project must appear sufficiently attractive to generate faculty investment. Campus-based compensation and rewards come in many forms: course release, compensated time for planning and faculty development, public recognition and awards, summer stipends, base-salary adjustments, supplemental travel money, and so on. At some point in the planning, the campus must make a commitment, through internal reallocation or supplemental external funding, to fund the operation of learning communities and to reward faculty for moving forward on learning communities.

For College Park Scholars, the division of academic affairs began by offering faculty one month of summer salary to develop collaborative programs and recruit and orient new students. Program faculty participated in summer orientations for freshmen and service-learning projects with students and spent time writing and revising recruiting materials and colloquia curricula. The time commitment for faculty directors was considerably more than the typical teaching load for one course. Designing new interdisciplinary courses, working with faculty across disciplines, planning extracurricular activities, accompanying student groups on field trips over weekends and into the evening, and participating in informal residence hall roundtable discussions constituted a heavy demand on faculty time, which appears to be typical of many learning communities. For that reason, deans from participating colleges were required to invest in some tangible way to support these activities. Colleges that wanted to participate in the College Park Scholars program were asked to commit approximately $10,000 to $12,000 (one graduate assistant, course release for two courses, or half-time released faculty) to the enterprise. Once the programs were fully enrolled, the campus and the colleges collaborated to provide a graduate assistant for each faculty director. In order to be able to deliver the enriched experiences, the campus also allocated between $5,000 and $10,000 in instructional improvement grants to be used for curriculum development and honoraria to guest speakers, and to buy time from collaborating faculty or departments for workshops or colloquia during the year.

Regardless of the campus or context for introducing learning communities, the principle of tangible rewards and recognition is important. For example, as part of the regular annual report process, the executive director of College Park Scholars asked each faculty member to provide guidelines for his or her college or departmental teaching award competitions and wrote nominating letters to chairs and deans. Several of the directors have won campuswide recognition in this way, and the publicity around that recognition, in the college and across the campus at large (through student newspapers, alumni magazines, and other avenues), helped establish the reputation that faculty participation in College Park Scholars was warmly recognized.

Another example of less costly but creative campuswide recognition came in the form of a gracious gesture by the president of the university. At the end of the first year of College Park Scholars, the campus president invited the faculty directors to have wine and cheese in his office on a Friday afternoon in May. As the faculty directors and teaching assistants sat around in his office, the president asked questions and listened intently to the descriptions of their year's experiences—both highs and lows. In unrehearsed conversation, the learning community faculty described the past year as "the best teaching experience I've ever had!" It became clear to those in the room that learning communities had the potential to transform not just the student experience but the faculty experience as well.

This conversation with the president was a critical moment for the future success of the learning community on campus. The simple act of publicly and personally appreciating these faculty members' willingness to take on a new challenge was a remarkably effective strategy to raise the profile of the enterprise on campus. Leadership most definitely matters.

Finally, in order to sustain the involvement of senior faculty members in the learning community, it is important to have a way for faculty to cycle out and back to their departments, giving them some time to catch up on their research and writing agenda that necessarily took a back seat to undergraduate student teaching-learning activities. Although the University of Maryland, College Park, has not yet institutionalized a way to ease the transition of faculty back into their traditional departmental responsibilities, a campuswide committee is looking into a recommendation that they receive some form of a semester of reduced load to catch up on their research and writing. High-level policy committees need to examine the reward structures at different institutions.

A campus that is serious about attending to undergraduate education will have to institutionalize the roles and reward for faculty who dedicate themselves to this exciting but labor-intensive work.

Defining Different Roles for Different Ranks of Faculty

As a learning community program expands on a campus, it is important to establish a solid scaffold at many levels of instruction to support the project. Curriculum development and enhancement, student mentoring, program evaluation, and revision are best done as team efforts, involving different teachers at different ranks. Part-time instructors, graduate teaching assistants, undergraduate teaching assistants, student affairs advisers, and peer leaders can provide the support structure necessary to sustain a learning community.

Part-Time Instructors and Graduate Teaching Assistants

It is not unusual to find instructors and graduate students playing a large role in learning communities. Learning communities are a site for creative curriculum development, and some of the most creative teaching on a campus goes on in instructors' classes. On many campuses, instructors are on untenured lines or hired on a contractual basis, and they carry a heavier teaching load than faculty who have a dual responsibility for both research and teaching.

Learning communities can be seen as a working laboratory where faculty at all ranks can experiment and explore creative pedagogical strategies and models. They create a venue for professionalizing and publicly recognizing the role of undergraduate teaching and pedagogy. The greater the visibility of the learning community on a campus, the more opportunities exist for celebrating and rewarding the critical role that instructors play in the delivery of quality undergraduate education.

Graduate students too are recognizing that a rich teaching portfolio is an advantage as they chart their futures in higher education. They will be expected to combine their understanding and mastery of the best teaching methodologies with cutting-edge research if they are to be competitive on the academic job market.

According to Tompkins and Mader (1998), "Working with people in other departments gives [graduate students] a broader sense of the possibilities for faculty interaction across and within units. . . . By expanding the scope of teaching assistants' experience across the university, Learning Communities Faculty Development reaches into the future, affecting future faculty for years to come" (p. 23).

The experience of teaching and collaborating with master teachers in learning communities is a valuable credential worth the extra time that this work requires. Although graduate assistants need to be protected from exploitation and be encouraged to remain focused on their primary responsibility of completing their degree, most graduate assistants find the learning community experience to be time well spent.

When describing the experience of teaching in learning communities, graduate students often mention the professional identity that they acquire as they collaborate on interdisciplinary curricula and interact with faculty and administrators from across the campus. Graduate students who are involved in teaching teams in learning communities benefit from the natural mentoring component that pervades the experience (Levine, 1998, p. 24).

Peer Leaders and Undergraduate Teaching Assistants

Another category of teacher-mentor appears in some learning communities: upper-division undergraduate students, juniors and seniors, who have been identified as strong role models and peer leaders. In this respect, academic affairs is following the lead of student affairs, where the development of undergraduate leadership capacities has been going on for a long time. Residence hall assistants (RAs), peer advisers, and trained hot-line counselors have been ongoing participants in the redefined mission of the student affairs division on many large campuses. Developing teaching-learning capacities of mature undergraduates as part of a learning community seems to be a natural outgrowth of both the collaboration with student affairs and the focus on a community of learners.

These undergraduate teaching assistants or peer leaders typically participate in a supplemental course or training seminar that prepares them to assist and support the program faculty by leading workshops, offering tutoring sessions, establishing communications avenues (listserves, e-mail lists), and leading discussion sessions. Campuses that already have undergraduate peer leaders have a natural source of support for learning communities. Campuses that do not yet have this model in place may find that "graduates" of campus learning communities who have had strong, positive experiences working closely with faculty could become a rising class of responsible peer leaders.

The University of Maryland offers a credit-bearing undergraduate teaching assistant training course, "Guided Experiences in College Teaching," that is offered through the department of curriculum and instruction in the College of Education. Juniors and seniors of any major who are interested in becoming undergraduate teaching assistants (UTAs) first connect with the lead professor in the course in which they hope to assist and get faculty sponsorship. After that step, together they register for the UTA course and attend an orientation meeting that explains the mentor relationship and mutual responsibilities. The three-credit course includes assigned readings, papers, projects, and a journal that are assembled into a teaching portfolio at the end of the course. Students attend class concurrently with their UTA assignment, working through myriad issues that actually arise. They are assistants for their mentor professors but also serve as reflectors of current practice, giving the professors feedback from the students' point of view and working with their cooperating professor to address current student and course issues. The UTA classes address a variety of topics through relevant readings, discussion, and guest speakers—for example:

- Best and worst teachers, setting goals
- The purposes of education
- The craft of teaching
- Building a framework for planning and teaching
- Learning styles and teaching styles
- Critical thinking and developmental theory
- Types and levels of questions
- Assignments and classroom activities
- Planning for instruction: consideration of goals, methods, assessment, and reflection
- Cooperative learning: role of lead teacher, UTA, students, managing groups
- Classroom climate and culture considerations
- Evaluating and responding to student work

Readings for the course include *Scenarios for Teaching Writing* (Anson and others, 1993), *Classroom Assessment Techniques* (Angelo and Cross, 1993), *Cooperative Learning: Warm Ups, Grouping Strategies and Group Activities* (Johnson and Johnson, 1990), and *Pedagogy of the Oppressed* (Freire, 1974). Both faculty and students find this structured UTA experience to be a valuable opportunity to focus on student learning and understand much more directly what goes on in college-level teaching.

Another approach to training peer teachers is to include them in regularly scheduled faculty development activities for learning communities. At Temple University, undergraduate peer teachers partner with faculty to teach the freshman seminar course linked to several of Temple's learning communities. Faculty and peer teachers attend a presemester training workshop that focuses on the goals and objectives of the seminar, teaching strategies for first-year experience courses, and resources for faculty and students. During the workshop, peer teachers and faculty are given ample time to discuss their particular sections and plan their syllabi.

Faculty Development in Learning Communities

Recruiting faculty into learning communities is the first step in establishing sustainable communities on a campus. Building a campuswide learning community takes an investment in faculty development that ultimately redefines the roles and work of faculty, allowing people the time to develop trusting, reliable relationships. These synergistic relationships do not happen automatically when faculty are tapped for a role in a learning community. Tompkins and Mader (1998) describe the evolving understanding and concomitant planning for faculty development as "a sort of Odyssey without an Ithaca" (p. 17). They identify several different models used at Temple University to mentor new faculty into the learning community ethos: faculty development workshops; reliance on information technology (Web and e-mail); departmental activities (such as practicums for writing instructors); and mentoring, pairing of teachers, and collaborations within departments, between departments, and with other collegial units, such as residence life, graduate students, and centers for teaching excellence (pp. 19–24).

In the same way that the campus needs to prepare students with new expectations for their college experience by building in a transition (orientation week and other activities), it needs to acknowledge the importance of orienting faculty to the new roles expected of them. Faculty might have an affinity for teaching undergraduates or for experimenting with innovative curricular models, but much of the development of the sense of community comes from faculty exploring with each other and defining together their own expectations for this emerging structure. The more opportunities a campus can provide faculty for this work, the more successful and effective the resulting community will be.

A discussion of faculty development in learning communities necessarily encompasses two stages: defining the new roles and preparing faculty to fill them. Faculty who are recruited to teach in a learning community must be given an opportunity to help define their new roles, which might include:

- Learning to work across disciplines and divisions
- Managing writing links in a curriculum

- Designing an interdisciplinary seminar or colloquium experience for freshmen
- Setting high standards across disciplines for student work
- Academic advising
- Other, less traditional roles (facilities planning, recruiting students)

Working Across Disciplines

Regular learning community faculty meetings or workshops can be used to explore and develop the new alliances among disciplines. The entire premise of academic learning communities is that they exist as interdisciplinary programs, and one of the first important tasks of the program leadership is to open some gateways between disciplines in a nonthreatening way. At these workshops, faculty have time to discuss uses of collaborative teaching and learning methods and share examples of integrated curriculum design. Faculty workshops promote the role of both disciplinary and cross-disciplinary perspectives in learning communities.

Managing Writing Links

One of the most common forms of learning communities is to link content courses to writing courses. Anyone who has tried to integrate writing across the curriculum on a campus knows that the first fear of faculty who do not teach writing is that by buying into the link with writing, they might be required to assign papers. In fact, although learning communities typically do require students to write more in all classes, faculty development activities can help ease faculty into an understanding that "writing-to-learn" does not have to mean many more hours of paper grading.

Learning communities can invite the director of the freshmen or university writing program, as well as English teaching assistants and instructors in learning communities, to describe the generic first-year writing curriculum for other program faculty. Such discussions can teach those responsible for writing courses what campus faculty need from a writing course, and learning communities faculty gain an understanding of how the development of student writing takes four years and a whole campus to achieve.

Designing an Interdisciplinary Colloquium or Seminar

A continuing conversation among learning community faculty revolves around the nature of the interdisciplinary colloquium or seminar that is part of many learning community models. In many cases, this seminar is the heart of the learning community experience and sets students' experiences apart from freshmen enrolled in randomly selected core courses. Although guidelines for these courses are usually set out in the beginning of the planning, the implementation takes many forms.

In the early planning stages of the College Park Scholars Program, each faculty director had different ideas about what he or she might do in the colloquium course, and the discussion of the purpose and nature of these colloquia became a continuing series of conversations that lasted the better part of two years. Initially they explored the goals of the seminar. That conversation has to take place among the participating faculty, even if those who initiated the learning community movement on the campus had a particular vision in mind. Unless and until the faculty of the program reinterpret the nature and purpose of the colloquium in their own terms, it loses its strongest potential to influence change.

Faculty addressed the issue of defining the credit-bearing colloquium courses. Should a learning community colloquium be one credit or three credits? Will students see the course as important if it is only one credit? Three credits may pose a scheduling or workload burden for students in intense majors (such as engineering, education, journalism) with many requirements. Can students fulfill general education requirements with the interdisciplinary seminar, or does it have to become an elective? Can some faculty do it one way and others another way? In all discussions, faculty returned to the basic question of the purpose of the seminar-colloquium:

- To introduce students to faculty in related fields
- To excite students about special topics
- To support students in the transition to college

The learning community seminar is one of the key curricular vehicles that allow faculty to shape the student experience. If we expect faculty to take ownership over the learning community program, it must be the faculty who shape the nature of the seminar course.

Setting Standards for Student Work

Faculty are not accustomed to thinking beyond their own courses and their own disciplines, yet the reality of a learning community forces disparate disciplines to come together to define shared expectations of student performance. And students hold faculty accountable for having defensible standards and expectations. As far as they are concerned, there is only one academic culture: college—not separate cultures of mathematics and science versus history and art. If different faculty from different disciplines design radically different experiences for their students, the students will challenge faculty to defend these programs. Creating a community of learners necessarily brings students together in the residence halls or in common classes, where they can compare and contrast their different experiences. They will let faculty and program leadership know when their experiences do not match their initial expectations.

Faculty who are developing standards for students in their learning communities need the opportunity to talk about the different work associated with their courses and disciplines. Are mathematics and science courses graded more rigorously? Are they more difficult? Does the campus have "weed-out" courses? Should it? Is there more subjectivity in the humanities and social sciences than in the hard sciences? Are some majors being held to more demanding expectations? If so, what should be done about that?

Here, more by chance than by design, learning communities can launch a debate that delves deep into the heart of the definition of higher education. How do colleges ensure quality outcomes for students? Can performance standards be articulated? How do faculty know that students have reached those expectations? These questions frame some of the most critical questions facing higher education today: How do colleges decide what their graduates should know, and how do they know that students know it?

Faculty in Maryland's College Park Scholars Program struggled with these fundamental questions, recognizing full well that the answers have implications for all of undergraduate education. Each faculty member was asked to consider the following questions:

- How challenging should we make our courses?
- In a semester, how many hours does a student in your program spend in learning community-related classes?
- How many hours are spent out-of-class (reading, writing papers, studying for exams)?
- How many hours does a student spend on extracurricular or related activities (i.e. field trips, special programs)?
- What are the grading requirements for your courses?
- Describe the reading requirements for your courses? Can you provide an estimate for the approximate amount of reading required per week (in hours/pages)?

Academic Advising

Advising issues are inextricably integrated into discussions of general education and core graduation requirements, and they take on a unique spin in learning communities. Typically students who have declared their majors are advised in their major colleges, and those who have not declared majors are counseled by trained advisers for general education. Learning communities are particularly good sites for the kind of intellectual exploration that characterizes general education advising at its best. Although a number of campuses employ professional advisers, learning communities create new roles for faculty that overlap with existing protocols and may require some negotiation around new roles.

Faculty are not always properly trained or prepared to advise students who have not yet decided on a major. For this reason, it is important to make early connections between learning community faculty and the advising community on campus. Since different colleges and universities have different models of undergraduate advising, we can only begin to suggest ways for that collaboration to take place.

Faculty who assume leadership roles in learning communities need to know who will advise their students (faculty, professional advisers, or peers). They should know whether students receive midsemester grades during their first year and what those grades are. The more information that flows to the learning community faculty, the greater will be the support that a learning community can provide for the students. Faculty should also be familiar with the campus support services: writing centers, math tutoring, learning assistance centers, and career centers.

Students in learning communities sometimes have closer ties to their faculty directors, and the faculty in learning communities provide another level of advising and mentoring. Yet a smooth working relationship between informal faculty advisers and the regular advising function of the institution should never be assumed. For this additional resource to be advantageous rather than disadvantageous for the students, learning community faculty and administrators must develop a close relationship with advising and assistant deans, working with them to give consistent messages to the students they have in common.

On research campuses especially, advisers are constantly trying to inform faculty about advising issues. Learning communities offer the campus an opportunity to institutionalize that information exchange. Students come to their first-year orientation with a host of questions that are familiar to dedicated undergraduate advisers:

- How do I know what to take with what?
- Should I take psychology and sociology together, or are they too similar?
- If I want to be a doctor, does it matter if I take world history or a language?
- If I want to go into international business, what humanities course will be the best choice to fulfill that core requirement?

And the most open-ended question of all:

- What if I don't know what I want to be? What is the best combination of general education that I can take?

As part of faculty development for faculty in the learning communities at the University of Maryland, College Park, faculty were given two kinds of support for their new role as supplemental advisers to the students in their communities: technical support and support for student majors. This came in the form of a liaison to registration—someone who was proficient in the computer registration system and could trouble-shoot for students who were having scheduling problems. The major adviser always had the last word over final schedules for students. Outreach to the advising community paid off, because advisers understood the importance of the community-building colloquia courses, even if they looked like exchangeable electives. Participants became part of the same team—the student's team—rather than competing (and potentially conflicting) sources of information. Coordinating the advising for learning community students is a critical element in creating a successful program. In every instance, students' needs are put first, and it is not assumed that program faculty understood the nuances of the advising role without help.

Other Roles

In addition to these more traditional academic roles, learning communities faculty may find themselves involved in some completely new areas: planning facilities (such as classroom environments, computer labs, and student lounges), recruiting students, and decision making for program growth. Faculty in learning communities may be asked to help design spaces for their community. For example, classrooms may need tables instead of desks to make the learning space more conducive to group work. Faculty may be asked to join admission representatives on visits to high schools. Program leadership should consider in-service workshops to help faculty prepare for these new roles, with experts from other campus departments, such as facilities planning and admissions, speaking to these topics.

Resources for Faculty

It would be naive to assume that university faculty are prepared to step up to these newly conceived roles in learning communities without some help. That help can come in different forms—from faculty orientation and team-building activities to extra resources for extracurricular activities.

Faculty Orientation and Regular Faculty Meetings

Bringing faculty into learning communities means more than merely recruiting excellent teachers to teach some sections of linked courses. The institution needs to recognize that a new program needs different accommodations. One is release time for faculty to become oriented to the goals and purposes of the program.

Developmental theory and learning theory can and should be applied to faculty, as well as to students joining a learning community for the first time. Perry's (1970) model describing the intellectual development of college students has been broadened by subsequent developmentalists, including Gilligan (1982), to offer a framework for understanding how all of us approach new situations and new expectations. When we approach a new situation, we are grateful for advice from those who went before. We look for role models. Typically we ask, "What is the right way to do this? Are there any rules I should know? How will I know if I have succeeded?"

Yet when a campus decides to experiment with forming learning communities, there may not be anyone on hand who brings that level of experience to the group. Under those circumstances, the campus needs to provide some support for the prospective learning community faculty to interpret the goals for the project. Some seek out models and experts on other campuses.

Faculty Orientation Workshops. Most campuses that initiate learning communities find that some planned faculty development activities need to be put in place in advance of the arrival of students to prepare learning community faculty for their new roles. Temple University encourages all learning community faculty to attend one of three full-day workshops and offers a stipend for participation. Through the use of faculty panels, guest speakers, and team meetings, the new learning community faculty are mentored into the program by more experienced faculty. Temple University has established as a priority the importance of creating learning communities for faculty at the same time the faculty are creating learning communities for their students (Levine, 1998).

Early in the start-up of the College Park Scholars Program, some initial orientation meetings where held during which faculty directors explored with each other what was and was not possible. It was at these early orientation meetings, which occurred almost a year before the first students were admitted, that the project's mission and goals were discussed and debated. These early conversations raised the broad philosophical questions that led to further discussions of implementation and interpretation of the program's purposes, and probed the degree of support that would be forthcoming from the campus administration. By the third year of the program, those weekly meetings became bimonthly, but only when the faculty felt reasonably comfortable with their roles as learning community directors.

The earliest conversations among faculty may alternate between being provocative and discursive to more problem focused, specific, and practical. Agenda items for these meetings might include:

- Expectations for faculty
- Measuring success
- Identifying on- and off-campus resources
- Students' expectations
- Accountability
- Adequacy of facilities
- Campus expectations for the program

A campus that appreciates the possibilities for faculty collaboration in learning communities will take time to build the faculty community before it presumes to build a student community. Faculty orientation and regularly scheduled meetings become the process vehicle that spawns many of the innovations and creative programming that come to characterize the learning community.

Listserves. Listserves offer another conduit for connecting faculty. Faculty interaction and dialogue do not have to be limited to face-to-face meetings. With technology and ease of electronic communication, listserves and e-mail reflectors can serve an important role in keeping faculty connected as they work through their day-to-day teaching experiences. Listserves are also a valuable tool for faculty to use as they begin to foster community in their classes. For example, faculty in Learning Communities at Frostburg State use interactive listserves and Web pages to engage students in active discussions around topical postings.

Cocurricular Activities

One of the characteristics of learning communities that sets them apart from business as usual at a university is the heavy emphasis on cocurricular learning experiences. Through their participation in learning communities, faculty are empowered to think broadly about the kind of experiential learning that would complement and reinforce their academic goals. Under the best of circumstances, a campus administration supports learning communities by providing resources for faculty to implement these ideas. In a learning community, it is not uncommon for an entire class to attend an on-campus lecture or dramatic production and reflect on the experience in their seminars, colloquia, writing courses, or specially designated sections of a relevant course.

Faculty in learning communities also find they can draw on the expertise of their colleagues across campus in different departments to supplement the theme of a particular interdisciplinary unit for their students. This type of activity is not limited to learning communities, but it has been our experience that faculty cross-fertilize their ideas when they meet together regularly.

This cross-fertilization happened dramatically in College Park Scholars at the beginning of the first year, when the faculty directors came together to plan some group activities for their students. Not surprisingly, there was a broad interpretation of what was meant by "extracurricular academic activities," and that discussion alone was quite revealing. At one extreme, program directors and student affairs professionals described the importance of creating a sense of community early in the program. They recommended and helped facilitate activities that brought faculty and students together informally—cookouts in the quad, movie nights pegged to topics being covered in one or more of the colloquia, coffeehouse nights with student performers, and leadership activities in the area of service to the university and the community.

At the other end of the spectrum was the approach of reaching out to academic departments across campus in search of expertise to enrich the colloquia syllabus. For example, the Science, Technology, and Society program invited world-famous experts from around campus to lecture on timely issues. The director wrote to prospective students about this aspect of the program:

> This year, our Fall 1994 semester involved about thirty presentations by College Park Faculty and off-campus experts on various topics that related to issues in science, technology, and society. Some of the topics discussed included Cryptography, Energy, The Nation's Health, Scientific Literacy, The Plasma State and Fusion, How Theories Are Selected, Smart Structures, Nuclear Fear, Chaos Theory, History of Diesel Power, Biotechnology, Turbulence, History of Aeronautics, Elementary Particles and Forces, and Philosophers of Science. Students chose six of the presentations to attend, hosted one of the speakers at dinner, and worked in small peer groups to prepare a summary of the presentation. During the spring 1995 semester, the colloquium involved six separate workshops. Students chose one workshop to attend and followed the topic for four weeks. This format allowed for a more in-depth study of one topic. The topics the first semester included: "Creation of the Information Culture," "Science, Religion and Belief," "The Built Environment: Plan and Design for an Urban Society," "Choices, Value and the Environment," "Diversity

in Science and Technology," and "Science Policy Questions for the 21st century" [Letter to incoming students from Professor Charles Striffler, UMCP May 1995].

Faculty from across the campus were involved in these lectures and workshops, and students in the program had direct exposure immediately to the some of the greatest minds in their fields—the very heart of a university experience.

Conclusion

One of the unexpected benefits of learning communities is that the faculty learn as much the students. They learn about their colleagues' work from other disciplines, nonacademic campus resources that support student learning, the broad mission of student affairs, and powerful collaborations that enable them to experiment creatively with new teaching and learning models. Learning communities have had a profound effect on almost every campus on which they appear. They challenge old paradigms and create a platform for new voices.

Learning communities have the potential to transform undergraduate education because they offer alternative models for defining professional roles along side the traditional ones. Today universities and colleges are struggling to adapt to a changing population of students in a changing social and political environment. As we move from teaching institutions to learning institutions, traditional faculty roles will change too. In learning communities we can see some of the most promising and positive directions for that change.

CHAPTER SIX

BUILDING ADMINISTRATIVE PARTNERSHIPS

A learning community that begins in the classroom can extend beyond classroom walls, challenging the separateness of the curricular and cocurricular. This integration requires collaboration among the administrators, faculty, and staff responsible for the academic and social dimensions of the undergraduate experience.

Building Partnerships

In spring 1998, the American Association for Higher Education (AAHE), in partnership with the American College Personnel Association (ACPA) and the National Association of Student Personnel Administrators (NASPA), issued the report of the Joint Task Force on Student Learning (1998). The task force concluded that the most successful approach to meeting the challenges to higher education is to move forward with powerful partnerships that share responsibility for student learning. It cited the considerable research undertaken since the mid-1980s that has provided valuable insights into the learning process of college students.

Powerful Partnerships (Joint Task Force on Learning, 1998) concludes that the task of transforming institutions to meet the challenges to higher education must begin with collaborations for change: "People collaborate when the job they face is too big, is too urgent, or requires too much knowledge for one person or group to do alone" (p. 1). The first step in identifying resources for learning communities is to draw in the two most powerful segments of the campus: academic affairs and student affairs.

The realization of collaborative and meaningful partnerships between academic and student affairs is more easily stated as a value or goal than as an institutionally supported practice. In 1987, Ernest Boyer, in his widely cited work *College: The Undergraduate Experience in America*, wrote about divisions on a campus and conflicting priorities that endangered the social and intellectual quality of the undergraduate experience. He identified the separation between academic and social life as a significant problem facing colleges and universities and was troubled by the willingness of faculty to distance themselves from student life outside the classroom. Boyer challenged educators to seek answers to the question: "How can life outside the classroom support the educational mission of the college?" (p. 5).

Since 1987, campuses have begun to explore opportunities to enhance both the academic and social dimensions of the undergraduate experience. Many campuses are improving the quality of academic and social life for their students through learning communities. Because these communities are built around shared intellectual experiences, their principles and values translate to out-of-classroom learning activities and residential life. For this to happen, however, academic and student affairs need to create partnerships that will allow the free-flowing transfer of learning experiences between the classroom and the out-of-classroom dimensions of undergraduate life.

Identifying the Obstacles

On most campuses, establishing such partnerships requires undoing a history of separateness and redrafting an organization chart previously based on specialization and clearly defined boundaries. Communication and cultural gaps also must be negotiated. Schroeder, Minor, and Tarkow (1999) cite several barriers to forming partnerships, including a clash of values and cultural differences between academic and student affairs, the organizational structure of student affairs, and a reluctance on behalf of student affairs to initiate partnerships. Other barriers are issues of territory and boundaries, a lack of awareness of each other's goals and initiatives, and limited resources.

Cultural Differences. Cultural differences between academic and student affairs can be a barrier to effective partnerships. Students are asked to move swiftly, and on their own initiative, between the interrelated cultures of the classroom and greater campus community. On many campuses, however, the maintenance of these cultures is separate functions. They are not the seamless environments and organizational structures that we would like to assume are invisible to students. In fact, on many campuses, the "two sides of the house" mentality is very real and represents significant, visible barriers to student success.

Implementing learning communities requires an assessment of the campus's faculty, student, and administrative culture. This understanding begins with a basic awareness of the important differences between the cultures and how these differences affect the relationship between academic affairs and student affairs.

According to a classification offered by Love, Kuh, MacKay, and Hardy (1993), three distinct faculty cultures exist on campuses: the academic profession, institutional type, and discipline. These cultures produce some fundamental differences in terms of how faculty and student affairs approach their work. For example, faculty tend to value autonomy over collaboration, whereas student affairs professionals tend to value collaboration over autonomy.

Another difference involves labels used to describe the primary functions of each group. Faculty are considered "educators," while individuals in student affairs are often considered "professionals" or "practitioners." Learning communities provide a structure for bringing these individuals together as educators to assume a shared responsibility for promoting student learning and development.

Learning communities programs recognize that learning involves both formal and informal learning experiences. However, faculty and student affairs cultures tend to view learning differently. Faculty tend to view learning as the formal learning that occurs in the classroom and as a direct result of their instructional activities. Student affairs practice is guided by the principle that learning can take place informally, beyond the classroom and intentional instruction. Faculty tend to promote learning as an individual exercise, while student affairs professionals typically promote learning as a more social, interactive activity (W. Zeller, personal correspondence, Dec. 1998).

The Joint Task Force on Student Learning (1998) report calls for faculty and student affairs to work collaboratively to create opportunities for informal and incidental learning to occur. This requires various outside-the-classroom activities that enhance formal learning experiences and bring faculty and students together under a variety of settings and circumstances. Faculty, student affairs, and staff need to be committed to programming that has clearly defined educational and social purposes.

Territory and Boundaries. Barriers to effective partnerships often develop out of issues of territory. The classroom has always been considered the sole domain of the faculty, while the extracurricular and the living environment (on residential campuses) is considered student affairs territory. Learning communities merge the formal curriculum and the informal curriculum, and seek to introduce and orient students to their roles as college learners and members of a campus community. They offer campuses a structure to develop seamless environments for learning and climates that promote students' intellectual and social development.

Lack of Awareness. On many campuses, academic and student affairs engage in short- and long-term planning with little to no awareness of the other's planning process or outcomes. For learning communities to succeed, planning processes need points of intersection. When academic and student affairs begin to share conversations about goals and priorities, common agendas can begin to replace a culture of the "right hand not knowing what the left hand is doing."

Faculty, administrators, and residence life professionals at Temple University recently came together to discuss opportunities for residence-based learning communities. Plans for new residence facilities had prompted Learning Communities leadership to consider ways to incorporate residence-based learning communities into its established program. The Learning Communities program formed a campus work group, cofacilitated by a faculty member and student affairs administrator, to explore the potential of living-learning programs. Committee members also included a college dean, the housing director and one assistant director, and the university writing director.

The work group's first activity was to educate the campus community about the learning activities already taking place in the residence halls, such as studio space for architecture students and performance floors for music majors. The work group then sponsored a two-day series of workshops and participated in a campus colloquium to discuss goals and models of residential colleges and living-learning programs. The work group hopes to use the general interest in living-learning communities that emerged from the workshops to develop a pilot project.

Although the planning process is still in the infancy stage, the group has made its first strides by simply talking about efforts already under way and increasing mutual awareness of each other's goals and agendas. The next challenges are to broaden campus participation in the planning process and to gain senior administration support for a pilot initiative.

Limited Resources. Even when there is cross-campus support for learning communities, limited resources and competing priorities can create barriers to full collaboration between academic and student affairs. Carefully coordinated and ongoing short- and long-term planning activities can help avoid such barriers. In addition, shared conversations about goals for the growth and expansion of learning communities are critical, with evaluation and assessment information driving the dialogue. Even when campuses develop collaborative processes that involve both academic and student affairs in learning communities planning, achieving goals may be difficult. The end-of-the-year report for 1996–1997 for the Bradley Learning Community at the University of Wisconsin-Madison described problems within its university systems that created barriers for the learning community.

The Bradley Learning Community is a residential program that in many ways cuts against the grain of traditional housing programming (Brower, 1997, p. 15). Housing is credited with strong and consistent support of efforts to develop the Bradley Learning Community and other special programs at the university. However, the current housing system and its processes for selecting, hiring, and training staff make it difficult to reward individuals who are committed to unique programs like learning communities. It is also difficult for the housing office to continue to give special attention or additional resources to one or two programs, leaving other initiatives feeling slighted or left out.

Why Partnerships Are Critical

In 1994 the American College Personnel Association (ACPA) published *The Student Learning Imperative,* a document written to create discussion on how student affairs professionals can promote a campus environment that promotes both student learning and personal development. The *Imperative* stressed that learning and student development are "inextricable, intertwined, and inseparable" (p. 37). The authors acknowledged that higher education has traditionally separated learning into the domain of academic affairs and development (cocurriculum, student activities, and residential life) into the domain of student affairs. They called for a linking of the two domains through partnerships between academic affairs and student affairs. The report redefined student affairs professionals as educators working with faculty, students, and academic administrators as partners in the transformation process to "create conditions under which students are likely to expend time and energy in educationally-purposeful activities" (pp. 37–38).

In 1997 the American College Personnel Association (ACPA), in partnership with the National Association of Student Personnel Administrators (NASPA), published *Principles of Good Practice for Student Affairs,* intended for use as a companion piece to Chickering and Gamson's *Seven Principles for Good Practice in Higher Education* (1987). (See Exhibit 6.1.) Principle 6 of the ACPA/NASPA document emphasizes the need for student affairs professionals to forge partnerships that advance student learning. The *Principles* characterized the partnerships as interdepartmental and as extending across campus to include students, faculty, academic administrators, staff, and even individuals outside the university. This practice can

EXHIBIT 6.1. PRINCIPLES FOR GOOD PRACTICE IN HIGHER EDUCATION.

Seven Principles for Good Practice in Undergraduate Education	Principles of Good Practice in Student Affairs
1. Encourages student-faculty contact	1. Engages students in active learning
2. Encourages cooperation among students	2. Helps students build coherent values and ethical standards
3. Encourages active learning	3. Sets high expectations for students and student affairs practitioners
4. Gives prompt feedback	4. Uses systematic inquiry to improve student and institutional performance
5. Emphasizes time on task	5. Provides leadership and efficient use of resources to help achieve the institution's mission and goals
6. Communicates high expectations	6. Forges educational partnerships
7. Respects diverse talents and ways of learning	7. Builds supportive and inclusive communities

demonstrate an institutional approach to learning by "fostering inclusiveness, bringing multiple perspectives to bear on problems, and affirming shared educational values" (p. 6).

Student affairs professionals, motivated by documents such as the *Student Learning Imperative* and *Principles of Good Practice,* and by what they know to be sound educational practice, are reaching out to faculty and academic administrators in efforts to become integrally involved in the central mission of their institutions. The type of connections and partnerships that student affairs leaders and scholars describe can be accomplished only through structures that intentionally merge the academic and social functions of the undergraduate experience. Learning communities offer such a structure. They promote learning environments that unite the ways that students learn, within and outside the classroom, and they create a forum for the merging of the strengths, values, practices, knowledge, and expertise of all educators.

Learning communities provide opportunities for organizational seamlessness and the sharing of resources and expertise. Planning for learning communities requires consideration of broader educational outcomes: knowledge acquisition, identity development, dealing effectively with others, and strengthening critical thinking, moral reasoning, and leadership skills. By sharing resources and ideas, academic and student affairs can apply different and new perspectives to the discussion of ways to achieve these and other educational outcomes.

Creating Partnerships

The Joint Task Force on Student Learning (1998) noted that "learning is strongly affected by the education climate in which it takes place: the settings and surroundings, the influences of others, and the values accorded to the life of the mind and to learning achievements" (p. 9). The architects of the report advised that creating this type of educational climate requires that faculty and staff work together to (1) build a strong sense of community among all institutional constituencies, (2) organize ceremonies to honor and highlight contributions to community life and educational values, (3) publicly celebrate institutional values, (4) articulate how each administrative and academic unit serves the institution's mission, and (5) share and use information on how units are performing in relation to this mission (pp. 9–10). Planning for learning communities is an ideal setting to create an educational climate that promotes student learning and development. In addition, as partners in the learning community planning process, academic affairs and student affairs are modeling the collaborative behavior that must be present to help build campus community.

At the University of Missouri-Columbia, student affairs leadership and personnel joined in partnership with the College of Arts and Sciences to develop and implement a FIG learning communities program. Schroeder, Minor, and Tarkow (1999) identified strategies they used to build educational partnerships between academic and student affairs:

- Identify a common purpose.
- Engage in joint planning and implementation.
- Link a variety of resources.
- Coordinate in- and out-of-class learning experiences.
- Define desired outcomes, and develop assessment strategies to evaluate the impact of learning communities.
- Think and act systemically.
- Involve senior administrators.

Identifying a Common Purpose. When academic and student affairs meet to discuss goals for students and the desired outcomes of a learning communities initiative, the gap between the two divisions begins to fade. What emerges is a conversation about shared objectives (Banta and Kuh, 1998). Shared outcomes might include improving student receptivity to diverse ideas, student tolerance and acceptance of others from different backgrounds, and the quality of student living environments, with living space as sites of intellectual as well as social activity. Another might be to increase retention, quantity and quality of student interaction with faculty, student involvement, and student identification with the institution.

Engaging in Joint Planning and Implementation. From the planning stages through implementation and assessment, learning communities work groups should include faculty, academic and student affairs administrators, and students—especially the front-line practitioners who are most likely to be involved with students daily. An important setting for this collaboration is the faculty and staff development required to build and sustain learning communities.

Faculty development activities are an ideal setting for joint conversations on goals for student development and for student affairs and faculty to develop a common language on student learning. Learning communities aim to support students in the academic and social transition to college. Faculty find themselves on unfamiliar ground when the conversation shifts to developmental outcomes. However, as participants in collaborative conversations about learning communities, they often find themselves fascinated by insights into student development theory. For student affairs staff, this is an opportunity to share expertise and knowledge.

Linking Resources. The FIG Program at the University of Missouri-Columbia is supported by funds provided by the chancellor, provost, and vice chancellor for student affairs. Academic departments also offer some fiscal and personnel support for affiliated learning communities. At Missouri and other campuses where learning communities include a residential component, residence life has dedicated living and gathering spaces for use by learning communities faculty and students.

Coordinating Learning Experiences. Learning communities faculty, in partnership with student affairs, can develop a range of activities—field trips, social events, community service projects—to support student learning and development. The Life Sciences program of College Park Scholars, for example, offered students an opportunity to go on a wilderness trip to a peat bog nature preserve as a culminating activity of the colloquium in life sciences. Led by both the director, a professor of entomology, and the residence life community director, the students studied the unique natural environment and also set up the camp, cooked, and cleaned. When they returned to campus, they wrote about this experience in both their colloquium and their freshman writing classes.

Defining Outcomes and Developing Assessment Strategies. Evaluation is critical to the maintenance and ongoing development of learning communities. Administrators need to document the impact of participation in learning communities on students, faculty, and student affairs, and use the information to make decisions on ways to improve the program. The evaluation plan should also include ways to describe the role of partnerships between academic and student affairs in developing and implementing learning communities. This information should be shared across campus and with the broader academic and student affairs communities.

Thinking and Acting Systemically. Learning communities are designed to introduce students to their roles as members of the intellectual and social communities that make up the undergraduate experience. Their learning experience needs to be structured in such a way that they see the academic and social dimensions of college as integrated. This requires collaborative partnerships that make invisible to students the boundaries between academic and student affairs.

Involving Senior Administrators. For partnerships between academic and student affairs to succeed, senior administrators in both academic and student affairs must be visible and vocal champions for innovation and change. They need to be committed to forming and sustaining educational partnerships (Schroeder, Minor, and Tarkow, 1999). Administrative leaders are crucial to the success of these partnerships. They take the lead by rethinking how their institutions are organized and by creating environments out of which more innovative structures can emerge, structures that promote collaboration between academic and student affairs (Joint Task Force on Student Learning, 1998).

Identifying the Partners

If campuses recognize and apply good practices for learning, such as the ten learning principles put forth by the Joint Task Force on Student Learning (1998), and set out in Exhibit 6.2, they may be able to create the partnerships and structures that promote more powerful opportunities for student learning. Creating learning communities out of these collaborative partnerships requires identifying the players critical to the success of the initiative.

Leadership

Commitment is essential from those in the institution who are ultimately accountable for measurable outcomes such as enrollment, persistence and retention, graduation rates, or placement of graduates in jobs or graduate schools. Learning communities can lead to improvements in such outcomes. Administrators who

EXHIBIT 6.2. LEARNING PRINCIPLES AND COLLABORATIVE ACTION.

1. Learning is fundamentally about making and maintaining connections: biologically through neural networks; mentally among concepts, ideas, and meanings; and experientially through interaction between the mind and the environment, self and other, generality and context, deliberation and action.

2. Learning is enhanced by taking place in the context of a compelling situation that balances challenge and opportunity, stimulating and utilizing the brain's ability to conceptualize quickly and its capacity and need for contemplation and reflection upon experience.

3. Learning is an active search for meaning by the learner—constructing knowledge rather than passively receiving it, shaping as well as being shaped by experiences.

4. Learning is developmental, a cumulative process involving the whole person, relating past and present, integrating the new with the old, starting from but transcending personal concerns and interests.

5. Learning is done by individuals who are intrinsically tied to others as social beings, interacting as competitors or collaborators, constraining or supporting the learning process, and able to enhance learning through cooperation and sharing.

6. Learning is strongly affected by the educational climate in which it takes place: the settings and surroundings, the influences of others, and the values accorded to the life of the mind and to learning achievements.

7. Learning requires frequent feedback if it is to be sustained, practice if it is to be nourished, and opportunities to use what has been learned.

8. Much learning takes place informally and incidentally, beyond explicit teaching or the classroom, in casual contacts with faculty and staff, peers, campus life, active social and community involvements, and unplanned but fertile and complex situations.

9. Learning is grounded in particular contexts and individual experiences, requiring effort to transfer specific knowledge and skills to other circumstances or to more general understandings and to unlearn personal views and approaches when confronted by new information.

10. Learning involves the ability of individuals to monitor their own learning, to understand how knowledge is acquired, to develop strategies for learning based on discerning their capacities and limitations, and to be aware of their own ways of knowing in approaching new bodies of knowledge and disciplinary frameworks.

Source: American Association for Higher Education, American College Personnel Association, and National Association of Student Personnel Administrators, 1998.

support the infrastructure allow faculty and staff to implement successful learning communities.

Similarly, school and college deans and department chairs interested in recruiting and, more important, retaining their majors after the first year are also stakeholders in learning communities. Deans play a key role in the development of learning communities because faculty who wish to be involved often need the approval of their deans. Faculty may be attracted to the concept, but teaching in learning communities represents a nontraditional way of spending time that may be seen as taking away from research or the staffing of critical departmental courses.

In the case of residential communities and learning communities programs that promote significant extracurricular activities, faculty participation cuts into regular teaching schedules unless learning communities are part of their load. In some cases, teachers in learning communities may need release time from other assignments such as courses and committees if they are going to function as lead faculty in a learning community.

Department chairs are another critical link in the successful implementation of learning communities on a campus. To obtain authentic faculty participation, faculty need to be supported by their chairs, celebrated for their roles in creating community for the students in a department, and encouraged to spend time networking across campus with their colleagues in other departments. Strong chairs are not threatened by this role and, in fact, welcome the opportunity to leverage resources through cooperation with other departments. Faculty who have support from their chairs are much more comfortable spending the time networking across campus. Otherwise they are justifiably concerned that they need to be more visibly present in the their departments. Learning communities should not be set up as competing with departmental teaching or resources; rather, they can be seen as complementing and promoting departmental goals and priorities.

Residence Life Staff

The benefits of learning communities for residence life are considerable because of the enriched living environment that grows in a residential learning community. Opportunities are developed for more meaningful collaboration between academic affairs and housing that often leads to new and different responsibilities for both faculty and housing administrators.

At the University of Wisconsin-Madison, the assistant director of housing–residence life is a member of the Bradley Learning Community steering committee. The assistant director's role is to represent housing administration from the planning stages through implementation and to help build collaborative relationships among faculty, staff, and students. In addition, the person in this position voices the needs of the Bradley Learning Community, as well as those of the other residential learning communities programs, to other housing administrators and staff (K. Reuter-Krohn, personal communication, Jan. 17, 1999).

The experience of the College Park Scholars Program at the University of Maryland is a good example of the necessary compromises that must be crafted between program leadership and residence life to create learning communities. When the university began planning the College Park Scholars Program, it asked three questions:

- What kind of space would be available for academic purposes (faculty office space, classroom space, study space, computer labs, and so on)?
- How would residence life personnel (resident directors, resident assistants) participate in the project?
- Would the learning community be open to nonresidential students, or would the experience be limited to residential students only?

Each of these questions led to a host of controversial issues that no one had confronted quite so directly, although the groundwork had been established by the emerging philosophy of the new student affairs learning imperative (American College Personnel Association, 1994).

Residence life had always provided study lounges in the residence halls and, more recently, had joined with the academic computing center on campus to provide computer labs in the residential halls. However, the learning community model was something new. Academic affairs was proposing that more spaces (residential spaces that are direct revenue-generating student rooms) be transformed into faculty offices and, in some cases, redesigned as seminar rooms, classrooms, music rooms, and libraries. The extent to which these proposals were welcomed and ultimately accepted for the College Park Scholars Program is a demonstration of how powerful the learning community concept proved to be at the university. After lengthy discussions, it became clear that a residential learning community depends as much on physical community space as on the intellectual resources of faculty in academic departments and the logistical support provided by registrars, administrators, and academic advisers.

But space alone is not the only contribution that came to the College Park Scholars learning communities from residence life. The learning community residence hall director was selected with great care by the Division of Student Affairs and Residence Life and met regularly with the faculty involved in the project to help plan a supportive staffing arrangement. Since a large part of the role of residence life staff is to provide programming for students in the residence halls, it seemed natural that the programming be built around the learning community themes, priorities, and expectations. This expectation was neither obvious nor easy to fulfill.

Residence life professionals study and implement the most creative, developmentally appropriate, high-quality extracurricular experiences for their residential students. Typically faculty are unaware of the developmental complexity and variety of extracurricular learning experiences that constitute the residence life character development curriculum for undergraduates. Everything from judicial processes and fairness to privacy and tolerance of difference comes into play in a fully developed residence hall program. A goal of College Park Scholars was to meld the curricular and cocurricular, the intellectual and the moral, into a coherent whole. From the beginning it was essential that faculty and residence life professionals clearly understood and respected each other's expertise.

The residence directors at Maryland invited faculty to interview the candidates for the undergraduate RA positions and informed the RAs that their programming responsibilities would be fulfilled in collaboration with their faculty learning community director. For example, when the Life Sciences Program prepared a Halloween program that included pumpkin carving and a midnight lecture on bats, the RAs acted as program assistants to the faculty member, helping with logistics, publicity, clean-up, and follow-up with students. Such RA-faculty collaboration has become one of the strongest elements of the residential learning community at College Park Scholars.

The third issue that arose early in the collaboration between academic affairs and residence life occurred around the issue of nonresident (commuter) students and their participation in residentially based learning communities. Here again College Park Scholars found themselves in uncharted territory. If a learning community is an academic initiative, supported through the office of academic affairs and the college deans, it stands to reason that students who pay tuition and qualify should be eligible to participate. However, one of the most important tenets of safety and security in residence halls is that no unauthorized nonresident should be allowed unlimited access to the building. Building security is perhaps the single most pervasive value and responsibility of a campus that houses students. Legally and ethically, University of Maryland residence life could not compromise the safety of the residential students by opening the halls to nonresidents.

This issue created one of the most serious stumbling blocks to College Park Scholars' residentially based learning community. The solution, a costly one, was to outfit the building with key-card access at the entrances and the elevators. Although the card readers at the entrance were programmed to allow entry to all learning community students, elevator use was limited to residents only. This compromise did not solve all the problems and took almost a year to work out, but the willingness to seek a solution was clear evidence that the campus had made a serious commitment to the success of this program.

Admissions Personnel

Learning communities are strong recruiting devices for attracting students to a university. For this reason, partnerships between learning communities programs and admissions are logical and beneficial to both. Admissions staff can promote the learning communities program through open houses, publications, and recruiting events. They have the resources to disseminate the concept widely by distributing program literature to large numbers of potential learning communities participants.

Recruiting students into the program is the most important job in the first few years of program development, and the admissions office is a gold mine of expertise, strategies, and resources. College recruiting is a competitive business, and all admissions directors benefit from opportunities to create unique learning programs designed especially for incoming students.

Orientation Staff

Orientation often represents the first opportunity for students to hear about learning communities on campus, and it is essential that the orientation staff be brought into the planning early. When students arrive on campus for their first orientation session, they expect to leave with their schedules, their adviser assignments, and possibly the names of their roommate(s). At this time, learning communities need to be introduced in ways that make them attractive and not confusing for new freshmen. This is no small task since everything is confusing for new freshmen.

New students receive a great deal of information during orientation. Material on learning communities needs to be accessible and easy to read and understand. The orientation learning communities pitch should make it apparent to students that learning communities represent the best way for them to make the transition to college.

Orientation staff play a critical role in recruiting students into learning communities. Once students are signed up, orientation staff assume quite a different role, facilitating the sense of community from the beginning of a student's experience. During orientation, learning communities students often meet other members of their cohort, including their teachers. It is an important opportunity for faculty and students to begin shaping expectations for the community. Orientation activities should model the type of seamless learning environment that learning communities seek to create during the academic year. This requires involving faculty, student affairs educators, and peer leaders in the planning and delivery of orientation activities.

Academic Advisers

Love and Tinto (1995) described three ways that advisers participate in learning communities. First, they can contribute to faculty and program leadership conversations on how communities will be structured, specifically in regard to curriculum. Advisers regularly meet with students to discuss academic and career goals. They are familiar with students' course-taking patterns and know the courses that present difficulties for students. Advisers are both specialists and generalists. They know the requirements of individual majors and are familiar with academic requirements across campus. Advisers can also make recommendations to learning communities leadership and planning committees on pairings of courses that will benefit and appeal to students.

Second, advisers assist students with selecting and registering for learning communities. Academic advisers are often the first people with whom new students come in contact, usually during orientation or other presemester activities. Advisers meet with students to discuss academic goals and select courses, and on many campuses they play a crucial role in recommending and placing students in learning communities. When the learning communities offerings are finalized, advisers should meet with faculty to discuss the themes, learning objectives, and planned activities for each community.

Third, advisers can participate as members of the learning communities faculty team. On many campuses, academic advisers participate in the learning community as instructors, often teaching an integrated seminar or freshman-year experience course paired with department-based courses. Advisers by training are qualified to help introduce students to the skills and resources they will need to succeed in college and beyond. They also help students better understand the relationship between courses they are currently taking and their broader academic and career goals. Academic advisers in learning communities help bridge the academic and social divide by connecting academic advising to students' classroom learning experiences.

Student Affairs Staff

Like advisers, student affairs educators can also participate as members of the learning communities teaching team. On many campuses, the division of student affairs has a tradition of offering and teaching student success, or freshman-year experience, courses. When campuses begin to consider learning communities, student affairs educators play a central role in linking existing student success courses with emerging learning communities.

Student affairs professionals can also assist faculty in planning cocurricular activities for learning communities participants. By design, learning communities support students in their academic and social transition to university life. Students enter college with concerns about meeting people, managing their time, and earning good grades. In learning communities, they instantly find a cohort of peers struggling with the same worries and fears. To survive, students need a support network to help them address their academic and social concerns. Faculty are most comfortable in helping students understand what is expected in the classroom. Learning communities force faculty to become more engaged with their students' lives. Supporting student development outside the classroom and helping students form positive social relationships is unfamiliar territory for faculty, but is considered the traditional domain of student affairs. Student affairs can partner with faculty to plan various activities designed to help learning community members connect with their peers and others in the university community.

Learning communities promote greater student involvement in the campus community. One way this is achieved is by connecting learning communities participants to student organizations. Learning communities students are captive audiences. Learning communities faculty can invite student leaders to recruit members by speaking to new students about the benefits of joining student organizations. The resultant increase in membership in campus organizations will benefit and strengthen the learning communities program as well. It is not unusual for learning communities students to emerge as campus leaders. Within the first three years that the College Park Scholars Program evolved at the University of Maryland, College Park, current and former CPS students were elected president of the student government association and president of the Black Student Union.

New Roles

The creation of new cultures for teaching and learning may also lead to new roles to help direct these learning partnerships. Zeller (1997) described the emergence of the learning specialist, a role that requires expertise and experience in the "creation of learning systems and in managing the learning process" (p. 2). Learning specialist is a hybrid position, combining the skills and competencies of academic and student affairs. On some campuses, the coordinator of a learning communities or living-learning program might be considered the learning specialist, as coordinators and directors of learning communities are often charged with managing a new learning system.

In Zeller's model, the learning specialist is responsible for developing enriched learning environments, creating more comprehensive pedagogical techniques, addressing individual learning style differences, and creating peer instruction models that maximize learning and retention for students. In addition, this specialist is a learning systems expert who has the knowledge and skills to work within four distinct cultures: that of faculty, students, student affairs, and the newly created learning culture.

On several campuses, the development of learning communities has created the need for learning specialists or other new professional roles. For example, Portland State created a student affairs fellow position as part of University Studies, its interdisciplinary general education program. At Portland State, student affairs reports to the provost. This reporting line was a result of a deliberate decision by Portland State University to align academic and student affairs better. Even so, the two divisions still functioned as two very separate entities. When the University Studies program made the decision to focus on the whole student, it became logical and necessary to consider student affairs as a partner in the program (V. Torres, personal correspondence, Oct. 5, 1998). For example, during training for freshmen inquiry faculty, the two student affairs fellows lead a two-hour session on the use of developmental theories in teaching. The session was created to directly apply to the goals of University Studies.

The fellow position, which began as an assistant professor position with teaching responsibilities within University Studies, has evolved. The position, originally funded by University Studies, is now two positions, with one located in the division of student affairs. The fellows serve on the University Studies committee, the group that makes policy recommendations for the program, and teaching continues to be a primary responsibility. One fellow is one of the cluster coordinators for the leadership cluster. Cluster coordinators are point persons for a group of theme courses that satisfy the junior-level requirements of the University Studies program. Student affairs is involved in teaching the gateway sophomore inquiry course, which leads in to the leadership cluster. The cluster coordinators communicate with cluster faculty to maintain some cohesion among the courses.

Conclusion

By design, learning communities are organized to help students build networks of support that begin in the classroom and extend across campus. Administrators and faculty need to model collaboration and demonstrate how learning from each other can lead to more powerful intellectual and social experiences. To build successful learning communities programs, community must be created out of partnerships of faculty, students, administrators, and staff.

CHAPTER SEVEN

PUTTING ADMINISTRATIVE STRUCTURES IN PLACE

In learning communities work, "creating" learning communities has a dual meaning: the operational process of creating communities through scheduling courses and enrolling students and the developmental process of building community among the students and faculty that constitute each learning community.

Creating Communities: Scheduling Courses

Understanding the logistics of installing learning communities into the undergraduate curriculum is one of the most important aspects of program development. In some ways, the scheduling and logistics of learning communities is the easiest part and in other ways the most difficult. Scheduling decisions, for example, may appear easy when compared to issues of faculty buy-in and reward structures. However, any crossing of boundaries at an institution invariably results in turf battles, including decisions about the times that courses are offered.

In conversations about establishing learning communities programs, we hear such advice, as, "The registrar is any learning communities program's best friend," or, "If you do not understand and respect the work of registration and scheduling personnel, you cannot successfully enroll students in learning communities." Other campuses have found that offering learning communities does not guarantee participation, particularly among a freshman population often skeptical to try something new or different.

Temple University believed that offering learning communities was as simple as, "If we build it, they will come." After Temple received a grant from the Pew Charitable Trusts in 1993, the provost and vice provost for undergraduate studies appointed a faculty fellow for learning communities and then formed several committees of faculty and administrators to begin the process of creating learning communities. The goal was to develop learning communities offerings for the fall 1993 semester. The curriculum committee went right to work and developed an inventory of learning communities. The first sets of offerings linked two or three courses around simple curricular themes. For example, the Business learning community paired a statistics, law, and composition course. An International-Spanish learning community paired intermediate Spanish with a philosophy and Latin American studies course. A community designed to explore America's role in the global community paired an anthropology, sociology, and math course.

The faculty and program leadership were quite pleased with the intellectual opportunities these communities would offer currently enrolled students and entering freshmen. The students, however, did not quite see things the same way. The program leadership found it difficult to get the word out to students about the benefits of learning communities. When they attempted to register freshmen in communities, they encountered enormous problems with the registration process. Program leadership was left wondering: "How difficult could it be for students to register for the two or three courses, each with its own registration number, that formed a community?" or "What exactly did academic advisers mean when they reported that most freshmen simply do not register for philosophy or intermediate foreign language courses in their first semester?" The lessons learned in the first year of the program led to the development of learning communities registration policies and procedures that were implemented in the second year.

Establishing a Planning Cycle

Establishing a regular planning cycle is essential in sustaining learning communities initiatives. Most campuses already have a calendar or schedule for creating semester schedules, and most schedules are usually completed six to eight weeks before the information becomes available to students. Learning communities staff need to be aware of university deadlines for submitting semester schedules and departmental processes for scheduling courses and assigning faculty.

In addition, learning communities staff need to be aware of procedures and time lines for disseminating information to students. Admissions counselors begin recruiting potential students in the fall, almost a year ahead of when these freshmen or transfer students actually arrive on campus. Before admissions recruiters leave campus to meet with prospective students, they need literature on learning communities, including an update on any upcoming changes for the program. Another important point for disseminating information to potential learning communities participants is new student orientation. Planning for orientation is a year-round process. Learning communities staff need to be involved in the process and work with orientation staff to make sure there are ample and appropriate opportunities for orientation participants to learn about learning communities.

A checklist and calendar for academic planning should include the following components:

- Time frames for departments to schedule courses and assign faculty for an upcoming semester
- Deadlines for department and college submission of schedules to the registrar
- Deadlines for collegial or university review for approval of new courses of new programs
- Deadlines for submitting text for campus publications, undergraduate bulletins, and semester schedule registries
- Deadlines for reserving campus facilities—classrooms and residence hall space, for example
- Time frame for meeting with other offices that will assist the program in disseminating information to students: admissions counselors, academic advisers, or orientation staff

Designing and Scheduling Learning Communities

The major activity in the learning communities planning cycle is the process of designing and scheduling the communities for which students will register. Once decisions about models and course pairings have been made, learning communities need to be scheduled. To schedule the courses that will constitute the communities, program leadership needs an understanding of how the course scheduling process works at the department, the school or college, and the university as a whole.

Working with Departments. Working with departments to schedule courses as part of learning communities is an annual process. Program leadership needs to understand how and when departments establish a semester schedule. On many campuses, scheduling is an electronic process done in the departments with varying levels of collaboration with the university registrar. There are specific deadlines for creating, adding, and deleting courses, and departments have different policies for assigning faculty or graduate assistants to courses. It is essential that learning communities personnel understand these processes and time lines.

Several issues typically need to be addressed when working with departments to schedule classes. One is how courses will be used or created. Jundt, Etzkorn, and Johnson (1999) discuss four typical approaches to scheduling learning communities courses. The first approach is *reserving an entire course* for learning communities participants. In linked course or cluster models, learning communities typically consist of two or three paired courses with enrollments of about twenty to thirty students. These sections are reserved for learning community use only.

The next three approaches are alternatives for scheduling learning communities in which participants are enrolled in courses that also enroll nonparticipants. One approach is *reserving a recitation or discussion section for the course.* This works well with a large lecture course. Learning communities students enroll in the lecture course as a subset of the entire course enrollment and coregister for a recitation reserved specifically for students in a particular learning community.

A related approach is to *create a subsection* in a course. This makes it easier to register and identify as a cohort the learning communities students enrolled in the large course. Another scheduling technique is to *lower the total course enrollment* to the maximum number of nonparticipants and allow advisers or learning communities staff to add learning communities students to the course until the class is at full capacity. This approach involves more hands-on maintenance of registration activity, but works well on campuses with manual registration systems.

In some learning communities models, courses are established specifically for use in communities. Others, such as the linked course or FIG approach, rely on existing sections in the course inventory. Another alternative is to give students some limited choices of courses to link themselves—some from one group and some from another. Regardless of the model, there are several issues to take into consideration:

Preferred size of the course. Are the numbers of seats in each course consistent with the other courses in the community? If the numbers of seats need to be decreased, will the department faculty still be able to meet their teaching load objectives? If the numbers of seats need to be increased, what are the pedagogical or curricular implications?

Scheduled course meeting time. Block scheduling works best in learning communities; it provides faculty and students with more time to plan and engage in collaborative learning and community-building activities. Students' registration preferences need to be considered. On campuses where large numbers of students work or commute, afternoon classes tend to be underenrolled. Scheduling learning communities courses in popular time blocks simplifies the process of encouraging students to participate. Academic advisers, most often the campus experts on the course-taking preferences of undergraduates, can be of use here.

Course location. Many learning communities programs have a campus home that includes classroom meeting space. On other campuses, space is at a premium, and learning communities courses meet in regularly assigned classrooms. Whenever possible, faculty should attempt to schedule learning communities courses in close proximity; some faculty teams prefer to teach their courses in common space. They can work with the registrar or person or office responsible for room scheduling to designate specific classroom space for learning communities use.

These decisions are reached in conjunction with department chairs and often require conversations with department chairs across different academic divisions or schools and colleges.

The School or College. Many learning communities programs are established in collaboration with school or college deans. Colleges look to develop learning communities to accomplish several objectives: improve retention, enhance achievement, recruit majors, or improve student satisfaction. When departments invest their best faculty and resources in learning communities, they may find they end up recruiting new majors from a larger pool of undecided freshmen. Learning communities are also an effective way to support students' transitions to the major. Learning communities help students and faculty establish college or program identities. Academic program and college goals need to be considered alongside the broader university goals for establishing learning communities.

On campuses where course scheduling and registration activity is decentralized, typically a dean or associate dean within the college has scheduling responsibility to make decisions about course inventories, teaching loads, and enrollment goals. The learning communities leadership needs to be aware of college policies and procedures concerning course inventories and should meet regularly with school or college administration to discuss program objectives and course needs.

Some learning communities programs build learning communities using newly designed, often interdisciplinary courses. On most campuses, new courses must be approved through a formal, faculty-led course review and approval process that typically occurs at the department, school or college, and even university level. Learning communities leadership needs to be aware of the process: the information needed to submit a course for review and the time line for the approval process. For some campuses this is a major hurdle and time-consuming process. If some level of course approval is required, it is important to begin the process as early as possible so that all the approvals are in place when the semester course schedule is published.

The University. On most campuses, the registrar has responsibility for scheduling courses and producing semester schedules and clearly is an important participant in conversations about developing learning communities. Program leadership needs to be aware of the process and time line for building a semester schedule. In addition, important policies for controlling and monitoring learning communities enrollment need to be in place. If enrollment in courses will be limited to learning communities participants, there should be procedures in place to monitor class lists—for example:

- Using unique section numbers or course designation codes to distinguish learning communities sections
- Linking the courses in the community with a common registration number or code
- Requiring special authorization to enroll in a community to make sure that only students with approval can register
- Designing and distributing preprinted registration forms or special authorizations cards to all individuals responsible for registering students
- Monitoring class lists weekly to verify that students are properly enrolled in learning communities
- Reviewing registration error reports that list students with incomplete learning communities registrations

Consider how learning communities courses will be listed in printed schedule materials. Listing learning communities courses among regularly scheduled offerings might be confusing to both prospective learning communities students and students not eligible to participate. However the learning communities offerings are listed, the information should be easy for potential participants to locate and understand.

If the learning communities initiative includes a residential component, residence life needs to be involved in the scheduling and planning process from the beginning. If a campus intends to house its learning community students together in a residential house or hall, considerable planning needs to occur before the campus expects to enroll students to ensure that the residential facilities and residence life planning can accommodate the new initiative. Planners need to work along several time lines:

A construction time line if any building or renovation will be done to the residence halls to prepare for faculty offices, program spaces, classroom spaces, or theme-related spaces (dance studios, soundproof music practice rooms, or computer labs)

A housing selection time line if any upper classmen are going to be displaced to accommodate new first-year students

A personnel hiring time line if faculty are to be involved in screening the residence hall director or RAs who will be assigned to thematic floors or halls

Residential living-learning programs offer their own challenges to campus planners because they add a significant level of complexity to the project. Nevertheless, the payoffs for students, faculty, and residence life are significant.

Registering Students

Registering students in learning communities can be a complicated process if program leadership does not meet with registration personnel early in the planning process. The registrar or a representative from the registrar's office should be included in initial and ongoing discussions on how to establish learning communities. Conversation about registering students in learning communities needs to address the following questions:

Will enrollment in learning communities courses be exclusive (that is, only learning communities participants can enroll in a designated learning communities section)?

What, if any, registration procedures are necessary when learning communities students constitute a subgroup of enrollment in a larger course?

Will registration for one course in a community automatically trigger enrollment in the other courses in the pair or cluster?

Course Registration Procedures

Most campuses adopt specialized registration procedures for learning communities, but if these procedures are too elaborate, they can be confusing to students and frustrating for academic advisers and registration staff.

Learning communities registration processes need to be efficient and convenient for all members of the university community: students, faculty, academic advisers, and registration personnel. If learning communities courses are designated with special section numbers or codes, this information needs to be widely publicized. In addition, learning communities registration processes should be virtually invisible to students; that is, they should be able to register for learning communities at the same time and in the same manner that nonparticipants register for courses. If a learning community does not constitute students' entire schedules, students should be able to register for communities at the same time and in the same manner they register for other courses.

At LaGuardia Community College, liberal arts students come to campus for preregistration advisement. They are given descriptions of the eight to ten clusters available for the semester and select one at this time but must return to campus at the start of the semester to register for the cluster. LaGuardia does not have any special registration procedures for its cluster participants. Program directors believe that special procedures would eliminate some problems, such as students' not registering for a cluster because they are under the impression that participation is optional, but the larger campus community tends to oppose special treatment for any group of students.

Registration procedures need to be consistent with existing modes of registration, especially if the campus uses technologically advanced systems such as telephone or Web-based registration. Regardless of the design, the registration process should be user friendly for students, academic advisers, and registration personnel. In addition, it may be useful for a program representative to explain learning communities registration policies and procedures when students arrive on campus to register.

In some cases, particularly when significant numbers of entering students enroll in learning communities, the registration and advising segment of orientation activities is structured around the learning communities program. At the University of Washington, students are given binders that include information on FIGs when they come to campus for orientation and are asked to complete the registration worksheet (see Exhibit 7.1) indicating the FIG in which they would like to enroll. Advisers or student orientation leaders meet with students to approve their FIG choice and select additional courses for the students' schedules. Once students select their courses, they are given registration instruction sheets (see Exhibit 7.2) indicating how to proceed.

The FIG registration system relies on both telephone and manual registration systems. Students use the telephone registration system to enroll in the General Studies 199 section for their FIG, and then a program staff member manually registers them for the remaining FIG courses. Registering for one course by telephone introduces students to the registration system they will be using in future quarters. The manual registration component avoids students' having to deal with a confusing array of registration codes.

Registration processes also need to be consistent with the intended outcomes of learning communities, such as increased student-faculty interaction. The University of Southern Maine's Russell Scholars Program is not an honors program

EXHIBIT 7.1. FIG REGISTRATION WORKSHEET, UNIVERSITY OF WASHINGTON.

Freshman Interest Groups 1998 **Registration Worksheet**

Name _____ Student Number _____

Phone ( ) _____ E-mail _____

1. Which FIG? FIG # _____ and Title _____

2. Does this FIG include a MATH course? (FIGs 42-51, 61-74 and 76-88)

   ☐ NO YES It includes (check one of the boxes below):
   ☐ 111 ☐ 120 ☐ 124 ☐ MATH of choice: _____
   If YES, which of the following applies to you?
   ☐ I have taken the Match Placement Test and have placed into MATH _____
   ☐ I have college credit for MATH _____ through: AP Exam / transfer credit
   (circle one)
   Please note: You must present proof of your placement test score, AP exam score, or earned transfer credit when you register for a FIG which includes a MATH course.

3. Does this FIG include a FOREIGN LANGUAGE course? (FIGs 35-42 and 67)

   ☐ NO
   ☐ YES (circle or fill-in: FRENCH 110/ITAL 101/LATIN 101/SPAN 110/Choice: _____)
   Please note: If you are continuing your foreign language from high school you must have taken a placement test prior to your registration for that foreign language and you must present proof of your score when you register for your FIG.

4. Does this FIG include English 111? (1,2, 12, 24, 26 and 33)

   ☐ NO ☐ Yes **Please note:** If you took the English AP exam and received a score of 3 or above, you have credit for English 111 and have fulfilled the English composition component of the Language Skills requirement. Unless you select a FIG that does not include English 111, you will lose your AP credit.

5. Have you submitted your "Measles Immunity Verification" to Hall Health Center and been cleared to register?

   ☐ YES ☐ NO **Please note:** You will not be able to register until you have been cleared by Hall Health. You cannot submit this worksheet until you are cleared.

Having filled out this worksheet, what do you do now?
Present this completed worksheet to a staff member and obtain a FIG entry code.
Codes are available:
   Day One of Orientation from 3:30 pm to 5:00 pm in the Orientation lounge in the HUB.
   Day Two of Orientation from 8:00 am to 9:30 am in the Orientation lounge in the HUB.
   Day Two of Orientation from 9:45 am to 5:00 pm in 9 Communications, Undergraduate Advising.
   After August 20: come to the Undergraduate Advising Center 8 am-5 pm or call (206) 543-2551.

EXHIBIT 7.1, Continued

Freshman Interest Groups 1998   Registration Worksheet

FOR OFFICE USE ONLY
             Date _____ Approved by: JJ MJ KE JA MT (other) _____
FIG # _____ Space # _____ Course of choice? _____ SDB: _____

Source: FIG Program, University of Washington. Used by permission.

but rather a learning community that seeks out motivated students with above average to excellent academic backgrounds and interest in an intense educational
experience characterized by supportive relationships with mentors, teachers,
and peers. To be considered for membership in the Russell Scholars Program, students must complete a short application and participate in an in-person or telephone interview. Once selected, they are assigned Russell Scholars faculty mentors
who help them select courses and identify learning opportunities within the program and the overall undergraduate experience.

Citations and Transcript Recognition

In some cases, learning communities create a special citation to recognize students
who make a commitment and stay the course. These citation programs, like the
University of Maryland's College Park Scholars, have special requirements for admission, a predetermined curriculum, and sometimes a capstone experience.
Keeping track of every student's progress toward the goal of receiving a special
citation on the transcript is another area where it is important to tie into the records
and registrations office, undergraduate advising, and the office of undergraduate studies or general education. Different campuses have different processes for
adding transcript notations (such as an honors citation), and this can be a powerful lever for faculty to set high academic expectations of the students in their
learning communities.

Housing Assignments

Residence-based learning communities programs require coordinated course registration and housing assignment procedures. University of Missouri-Columbia
students are sent materials on FIGs and a form to request participation in March

EXHIBIT 7.2. FIG REGISTRATION WORKSHEET, UNIVERSITY OF WASHINGTON.

Freshman Interest Groups 1998	**FIG #: 1**
Registration Instructions	**Ancient Culture**
	Peer Instructor: Marnie Bergman

Congratulations on your decision to join a Freshman Interest Group this Autumn.

Registering for your FIG

To register for your FIG, all you need to do is call STAR and add one course: General Studies 199. Once you register for General Studies 199, the other courses in the FIG will be added to your schedule within two working days. Call STAR according to the instructions you have been given by your orientation leader and/or adviser. You may also consult the STAR Work Sheet on page 8 of the Time Schedule. The following is all the information you need to register for General Studies 199:

Once STAR prompts you to enter your transaction, press "A" for ADD, followed by the four-digit Schedule Line Number (SLN), followed by the star key (*), followed by the five-digit entry code, followed by the number-sign key (#). You'll know you've done it right when STAR tells you that General Studies 199 has been added to your schedule.

GEN ST 199 A1   SLN: 3908   ENTRY CODE: _____

Note: You have 24 hours to use this entry code.

Your Autumn Schedule

Your FIG consists of the following schedule of courses:

CLAS	430	AC	5	Greek and Roman Mythology MWF 9:30 TTH 9:30
ENGL	111	C	5	Composition: Literature MTWTH 8:30
HIST	111	AH	5	The Ancient World MTWTH 10:30 F 11:30
GEN ST	199	A1	1	University Resources, Information, and Technology M11:30

During the summer you may not drop any individual courses from your FIG.

In early September you'll receive your registration confirmation, which will note any changes to this schedule and include the locations of your classes.

Beginning your FIG in the Fall

The First FIG meeting will occur on Sunday, September 27, at 1:30 in Kane Hall (the day before classes start, right after Freshman Convocation). Please note that your attendance at this meeting is a requirement of the General Studies 199 course. Your FIG Peer Instructor will be writing you with additional information about this meeting soon after Labor Day.

If you have any problems registering or if, after registering, you still have questions, call 206-543-4905 or send an e-mail to figs@u.washington.edu.

Source: FIG Program, University of Washington. Used by permission.

at the same time housing contracts are mailed (F. Minor, personal communication, Jan. 20, 1999). In the early stages of the FIG program, students were first placed in FIGs and then assigned to rooms. The message to students was, "Apply to a FIG and we will tell you where you will live later." A mistake was not recognizing the important of residence location to new students. Now FIGs are located in specific buildings and floors, this information is included in mailings to students, and students are placed, by hand, in rooms. Although a manual assignment process seemed antiquated, initially it was the only way residence life could coordinate the housing assignments. Since the FIG program has grown considerably, Missouri-Columbia is now piloting an autoassign process, using a computer program to place students in both a FIG and a room.

Monitoring Enrollments

Monitoring learning communities enrollments is an important part of the registration process. In designing learning communities registration procedures, campuses should incorporate steps for verifying that only learning communities–eligible students enroll in communities and that those students are properly enrolled. At Temple University each course in a learning community has a unique registration number, making it possible for students to register for one course in a community but not the other. Throughout the new student orientation period, the Learning Communities program receives weekly enrollment reports flagging students who are inappropriately registered. Advisers then contact students to resolve registration problems: enrolling the student in the complete community or assisting the student in registering for appropriate nonlearning community courses.

Learning communities often have both maximum and minimum enrollment limits. When learning communities feature regularly scheduled courses, these limits are negotiated in conjunction with departmental guidelines for enrollments and teaching loads. New and developing learning communities programs have to pay particularly close attention to these limits, since it is costly for departments to run underenrolled courses. Ongoing enrollment monitoring helps programs make informed decisions about which communities to run and which to cancel.

Diablo Valley College implemented a "bail-out" procedure in the event one of the learning communities in its Block Interdisciplinary Program (BliP) was underenrolled. BliP faculty and the dean of instruction and assistant dean of instruction, or both, mutually agreed on the procedure, which was primarily based on the Diablo policy that the administration may cancel any class with an enrollment of fewer than twenty students.

The first bail-out procedure was to cancel any BliP that did not have twenty students two weeks prior to the start of the semester. The hope was that by canceling the BliP and offering these courses as individual sections, they would reach the twenty-student enrollment limit. This process, however, led to several lost sections that never reached enrollment minimums and were ultimately canceled.

A new bail-out procedure is now in place. In May BliP faculty visit "Orientation to College" events to recruit students for fall BliPs. If the BliP package of courses is attractive to students, the community typically fills by the beginning of June. BliPs that do not have twenty students at this time are cancelled, and classes are allowed to fill individually for the remainder of the summer. This procedure has reduced the number of lost sections (B. Koller, personal communication, Dec. 18, 1998).

Marketing the Program:
Recruiting Students to Learning Communities

The process of building community in learning communities begins with the recruitment of students to the program. Developing a marketing plan, particularly if participation in a learning community is not mandated for students, is an important step in program development. A marketing plan is defined as "a detailed description of resources and actions a firm needs to achieve its stated marketing objectives" (Boone and Kurtz, 1998, p. 192). Developing a marketing plan is an effective way for learning communities leadership to clarify program objectives, assess internal resources, and measure environmental risks and opportunities. Marketing plans typically address three questions (Boone and Kurtz, 1998, p. 192):

1. Where are we now?
2. Where do we want to go?
3. How can we get there?

A useful strategic planning activity for program leadership and learning communities work groups is the SWOT exercise (scanning internal and external environments for *s*trengths, *w*eaknesses, *o*pportunities, and *t*hreats). For example, a strength of the program might be a strong commitment from campus leadership; a limited budget or lack of dedicated space for learning communities classes and activities could be considered weaknesses. Strong faculty and student interest in the program is an opportunity; impending cuts in state higher education funding might be a threat. These nuts and bolts issues of marketing and recruiting are legitimate concerns for the success of learning communities and need to be addressed just as seriously as the academic and intellectual aspects of the community.

Where Are We Now?

In this phase of the marketing planning process, program leadership assesses the historical background of the initiative, reexamining the original set of goals and objectives for learning communities to revisit the expressed goals of establishing learning communities. An important next step is to identify the market or audience, which includes newly admitted students, prospective students, and various constituencies on campus.

Where Do We Want to Go?

Considerations here are not only the goals for the program but also the purposes of the marketing plan—for example:

• Generating interest among clearly defined populations
• Increasing program enrollments
• Increasing campus awareness of the learning communities initiative
• Communicating program expectations to students

Marketing objectives can be measured in either quantitative or qualitative terms. The marketing plan must be reviewed regularly, with adjustments based on successes, disappointments, or changes in the environment. During the first year of recruiting in the College Park Scholars Program, for example, the students received a questionnaire at the end of orientation asking them where they first heard about this learning community and whether the learning community had influenced their decision to attend the University of Maryland. The results of that survey helped the campus market the program the next year.

How Can We Get There?

This stage focuses on decisions about marketing strategies to promote the program. It needs to identify the multiple opportunities for promoting learning communities on the campus and among prospective students and identify the different individuals and offices that can help market the program.

Preadmission. If learning communities are advertised as the ideal way to make the transition from high school to college, admissions staff should be discussing the program with prospective students and their families. Working with the admissions staff is crucial to the success of learning communities, and bringing them into the earliest planning conversations makes a big difference in their willingness and ability to describe the benefits of such an innovative program enthusiastically.

Admissions office personnel are important partners in the success of learning communities and need to be aware of program news, particularly evidence of student satisfaction with the program. Admissions counselors can be strong advocates for the program with the prospective student population. If the campus expects entering students to participate in learning communities, admissions counselors need to communicate the goals and benefits of learning communities to students and their families. Learning communities information should be included in viewbooks, applications materials, and other admissions literature. On- and off-campus recruitment events should feature learning communities faculty and students, who are often the best promoters of the program.

Preenrollment. To guarantee student familiarity with learning communities before the orientation visit or registration, many programs distribute fliers or brochures. Mailings typically include response cards that students can return to indicate interest, a good way to increase student familiarity with learning communities and to measure interest in the program.

For residential-based learning communities programs, preenrollment housing mailings play an important role in the recruitment process. At the University of Wisconsin-Madison, students interested in becoming members of the Bradley Learning Community apply by ranking "Bradley" as the number one choice on the university housing assignment preference form (see Exhibit 7.3). Assignments are on a space-available basis, but students admitted to the university by April 1 and who rank Bradley as their first assignment have the greatest chance of participation.

For popular programs with a limited enrollment, students must know and understand the importance of deadlines. Parents and student can be understandably disappointed if they inadvertently miss an opportunity, and that disappointment can register against the learning community.

Orientation. Since most learning communities programs draw participants from new students, orientation is a critical point during which to promote the program. Once students have been admitted, program leadership should promote learning communities as places where students can connect to each other, faculty, and their new environment. Departments and colleges find that talking to students about learning communities during orientation gives new students, who might not be ready to focus on their majors, a way of thinking about constructing their schedules.

EXHIBIT 7.3. HOUSING ASSIGNMENT PREFERENCE FORM, UNIVERSITY OF WISCONSIN-MADISON.

UNIVERSITY OF
WISCONSIN
M A D I S O N
DIVISION OF UNIVERSITY HOUSING

11/29/1997   SEQ: 1

Assignment Preference Information
Academic Year 1998–99

ID Number: Name:

Do you smoke? ____ Yes ____ No

If you are a non-smoker, are you willing to live with a smoker? ___ Yes ___ No

ROOMMATE (In order for roommate requests to be honored, each of you must request the other on your form.)

Roommate's Student ID _____ Roommate's Name _____

HALLS (Please rank "8" choices with "1" being your highest priority.)

___	Bradley Learning Community	___	Ogg West
___	Chadbourne Residential College	___	Sellery A
___	Cole	___	Sellery B
___	Eliz Waters-Limited Visitation	___	Slichter
___	Elizabeth Waters	___	Sullivan
___	Kronshage	___	Witte A
___	Kronshage-Smoke-Free	___	Witte A-Substance-Free
___	Ogg East	___	Witte B

Student's Signature _____ Date _____

Return this form to: Assignment Office, Division of University Housing, 625 Babcock Dr., Madison, WI 53706-1213.

EXHIBIT 7.3, Continued

Step Two

How to Complete Your Assignment Preference Form

The Sample Assignment Preference Form illustrated below shows how you should record your preferences to maximize your chances of obtaining your assignment choices. Use the living options charts and hall descriptions on pages 10 and 11 to help you select your choices.

3/10/94

Division of University Housing
Assignment Preference Information
Academic Year 1998–99

ID Number: 444-44-4444   Name: Doe, Jane

Do you smoke? _____ Yes _____ No ❶

If you are a non-smoker, are you willing to live with a smoker? ___ Yes
No

ROOMMATE (In order for roommate requests to be honored, each of you
must request the other on your form.) ❷

Roommate's Student ID _____ Roommate's Name _____

HALLS (Please rank "8" choices with "1" being your highest priority.)

___ Bradley Learning Community ❹	___ Ogg West ❸
___ Chadbourne Residential College	___ Sellery A
___ Cole	___ Sellery B
___ Eliz Waters-Limited Visitation	___ Slichter
___ Elizabeth Waters	___ Sullivan
___ Kronshage	___ Witte A
___ Kronshage-Smoke-Free	___ Witte A-Substance-Free
___ Ogg East	___ Witte B

❺

Student's Signature _____ Date _____

Return this form to: Assignment Office, Division of University Housing, 625
Babcock Dr., Madison, WI 53706-1213.

---

① Indicating your smoking preferences is required. Non-smokers will be assigned with non-smoking roommates unless you indicate "Yes"—you are willing to live with a smoker. If a smoke-free hall is important to you, be sure to read the chart on pages 10 and 11 carefully to help you select smoke-free hall choices.

② Complete this section to list a roommate choice if you are indicating to us that being with a preferred roommate is more important to you than your hall choices. Leave this section blank if you do not have a roommate preference.

③ Rank 8 choices in order of priority with number "1" as your first choice and ranking all others "2," "3," "4," etc. It is important that you rank all 8 choices.

Your room assignment depends upon the number of spaces still available for your choices at the time the computer reaches you in the computerized sort.

④ If you list the Bradley Learning Community or Chadbourne Residential College as one of your assignment choices, you are indicating that you are interested in fully participating if assigned to either Bradley Learning Community or the Chadbourne Residential College, and agree to the additional charges.

⑤ Be sure to sign and date your form. You may want to make a copy for your records.

Source: Division of University Housing, University of Wisconsin Madison. Used by permission.

By design, learning communities alleviate many of the major fears entering students have about college and the undergraduate experience: Will I be just a number? How will I meet people? Will my professors know my name? What support resources are there if I need help in a class? Promoting student involvement in learning communities is an excellent way to demonstrate the institution's commitment to building a supportive learning environment for entering students.

New students typically meet during orientation with advisers to select courses. This is an opportunity for learning communities faculty, peer leaders, and former participants to speak to these students and distribute literature on the program. If the goal is for students to build their schedule around their learning community, both advisers and students need material to help them reach an informed choice about which learning community best meets a student's academic interests and needs. Some programs sponsor adviser training sessions, develop resource notebooks, or maintain registration hot-lines to help advisers solve student problems during registration.

Promotional Activities. Informative, student-friendly literature should be developed to describe the program to perspective students and their families, current students, or any other groups targeted as participants. Program literature should answer basic questions that students will have about learning communities:

- What is a learning community?
- Why should I enroll?
- What can learning communities offer me?
- How does participation affect my general education and major requirements?
- How do I enroll?

Recruitment plans should address involving current and former learning communities students and faculty in promotional activities because they are the best spokespeople for the program. Program literature should include quotations from former participants. What did they consider the benefits of participation? Why did they join a learning community? Why would they recommend it to other students? Former students can talk to prospective students at on- and off-campus recruitment events and network with new participants during presemester and start-of-term orientation activities.

Many campuses develop multiple pieces of literature—fliers, brochures, and posters—to use in recruitment. An increasingly popular publication used to familiarize students with learning communities is a program booklet—a specialized undergraduate bulletin that describes the program, lists available communities, and includes course descriptions and registration information.

William Rainey Harper College developed several recruitment pieces to attract learning communities participants from both incoming and currently enrolled student populations. A multicolor brochure with a pocket containing insert cards, known as class cards, that describe the program and the individual communities is distributed across campus at various locations where students congregate: the counseling center, general information desk, division office, library, and student activities areas (personal communication, J. Mott, Jan. 12, 1999). Copies are also given to faculty so they can recruit currently enrolled students. This brochure is used to recruit prospective students and along with a cover letter is mailed to district high school counselors and to the homes of students who visit Harper for new student orientation.

Because the multicolored folder and inserts are costly to produce, William Rainey Harper also developed a single-page informational piece that is distributed more extensively across campus. This sheet lists community offerings and is inserted, along with a general information insert card, into every new student's catalogue. During orientation students are asked to locate and review this material and indicate a learning communities preference before meeting with a counselor to plan their schedules.

At William Rainey Harper, program leadership assumes primary responsibility for developing recruitment materials, but faculty are asked to submit a paragraph of text promoting their courses and community. Faculty have final approval of the class card for their communities. When a student returns a reply card requesting information about a specific learning community, one of the instructors makes a personal call to that student.

Many programs are also developing Web sites. Web sites should describe the learning communities program and include information on how students can enroll. Most sites typically include a listing of offerings. Comments from current and former community members—both students and faculty—are a popular feature. Learning communities Web sites can also include links to other related sites. The home page for the Freshman Year Initiative (FYI) Learning Communities program at Queens College (http://www.qc.edu/Freshman.Year.Initiative) includes a link to the admissions page.

The Web site for the University of Missouri's FIG Program (http://www.missouri.edu/~figwww/) features a variety of useful information for student visitors. Students can discover what a FIG is, review answers to frequently asked questions, and browse through FIG offerings, including links to course descriptions.

Web sites can be designed for multiple audiences: students, faculty, and the general higher education community. The site for the learning communities program at the University of South Florida (http://www.usf.edu/~lc) includes a general overview of the program, announcements, and a semester schedule. Visitors to the site who are interested in learning more about South Florida's program can review the grant proposal outlining the implementation plan for the learning communities initiative. From the learning communities home page, faculty can go to the Information Literacy Across the Disciplines site, which presents material on the role of faculty teams in writing across the curriculum and includes information about on-line writing resources.

Web sites are an effective way to begin the process of community building among students and faculty. They can include links to course syllabi and to the home pages of teachers for the community. Teachers can post welcome messages to students, providing a preview of what students can expect from the learning communities experience.

Creating Community

Once students select their learning community, the process of creating community begins. Learning communities faculty and staff do not need to wait for the start of the semester to begin this important step in developing successful learning communities.

First Contacts

Outreach letters to incoming students by faculty and staff of the program send signals to students and their parents that this undergraduate learning communities experience will be something special. Maryland's College Park Scholars Program found that a personal letter from each director welcoming students to his or her learning community sends a powerful message to both parents and students about what students can expect when they arrive on campus. (Exhibit 7.4 shows two examples.)

A second opportunity to connect with students and bring them into a special relationship with each other and with the college or university is new student orientation. Typically student affairs or registration processes define the orientation schedule for new students. The paramount goal of orientation is to give the students time with their adviser to schedule their first semester of classes, with advisers making sure that they take courses at the appropriate level.

Much more than this minimal threshold of registration can take place in a carefully planned orientation. Learning communities faculty see orientation as a rich teachable moment. Entering students bring a sense of expectancy, curiosity, and anxiety that cries out for close contact with faculty. New students come to campus expecting to be "processed," especially on large campuses. If all institu-

EXHIBIT 7.4. LETTER ABOUT THE COLLEGE PARK SCHOLARS PROGRAM TO INCOMING STUDENTS, UNIVERSITY OF MARYLAND, COLLEGE PARK.

Date

Address

Dear

I thank you for your interest in our *Life Science Scholars* program. Our faculty have created an exciting new program for a select group of students who want a targeted learning experience in the life sciences—biology, chemistry, biochemistry, agricultural sciences, and psychology. Scholars will create a small-college community by sharing residence hall, a cluster of freshman courses, and a special colloquium to broaden awareness of life sciences. The College Park Scholars faculty will integrate the basics of biology, chemistry, writing, and speech communication in all aspects of the program.

College Park Scholars, who live on campus, reside in a remodeled wing of Cumberland Hall and have access to a computer room and ecological corner complete with an aquarium, observation bee colony, and changing displays. The program has a budget for such activities as field trips on a Chesapeake Bay research vessel, an environmental weekend in Garrett County, and special events including canoe trips, pool parties, and Oktoberfest. We also expect that the *Scholars* will be involved in community service, leadership, and internships.

The enclosed information provides an overview of our *Scholars Program.* If you have immediate questions, or wish to talk with any of our students or would like to visit with us please call Cathy Schwab at (301) 314-8375 or me at (301) 405-0528.

We will give you a call within the next week or so and offer any assistance you need applying for the program.

Sincerely,

John L. Hellman
Director, College Park Scholars
Life Sciences

Dear

Thank you for your interest in the College Park Scholars. Let me briefly introduce to you the main features of the International Studies program. The 20-credit units are spread over the first two years of your study and evolve around a specially designed colloquium each semester.

The current cycle focuses on the subject of "Domestic Diversity and International Conflict in the Post-Cold War Era." Essentially, we are trying to understand why ethnicity, or religion, or other minority attributes result in violence in some

EXHIBIT 7.4, Continued

societies, while in others, such genuine differences are managed and often resolved peacefully.

This year, we spent the first semester together, studying theories of negotiation and conflict resolution. The remaining three semesters are conducted in small sections. Each section covers a different case-study. This year students are looking into the Mayan Indian rebellion in Chiapas, Mexico; the impact of religion on the Israeli/Arab conflict; ethnic strife and democratization in Nigeria; and the transfer of Hong Kong to China. At the same time, students are learning specific skills, such as electoral monitoring, conflict resolution, lobbying, and second-track diplomacy.

Next year students will undertake the responsibility of organizing an international conference. During the program we involve the Scholars in proactive learning, and connect them through electronic mail to students and professors in the country of the case study. Their participatory research is channeled through access to information resources, and they work closely with our librarians using Internet, Peacenet, The World Web, and Lexis/Nexus.

We have a rich program of special activities, including visits to embassies in Washington, D.C., participation in congressional hearings, high table dinners, retreats, and more. We are also offering specially designed Studies Abroad programs during the summer break, for additional credits.

I would be glad to talk to you personally or over the phone and hear more about your personal interest and qualifications, as well as to provide you with additional information. Do not hesitate to call me at (301) 314-7711 or (301) 405-0529.

Sincerely,

Edward Kaufman
Director, College Park Scholars
International Studies

---

tions do is create schedules, they waste important opportunities to introduce students to what college is about. Orientation in learning communities provides a valuable opportunity to build on student expectations for something qualitatively different, developing habits of inquiry into the realm of knowledge making.

Learning communities faculty can use new student orientation to promote building the intellectual community. For example, the faculty director of the University of Maryland's College Park Scholars Environmental Studies (ES) Program was able to involve her learning communities students in an academic activity during orientation.

After much negotiation and haggling about the time of other orientation events, specifically the mathematics placement exam and the tour of campus, the environmental studies director was able to carve out a ninety-minute block of time for students to walk around campus testing water samples for a variety of pollutants. She posed questions for them to answer: How clean is the water in the outdoor water fountains? The residence hall bathrooms? The drainage pipes outside the chemistry lab? This mini–field trip established an inquiry-based context as an introduction to the undergraduate experience and contrasted dramatically to the bureaucratic shuffling that tends to dominate orientation. Ultimately, this innovative approach paid off. Parents reported that students who had experienced this atypical orientation returned home bubbling with excitement about beginning their program in the fall.

Moving onto Campus

Students' arrival on campus for the start of the school year can be a particularly valuable community-building opportunity for faculty and students in residence-based learning communities. The College Park Scholars faculty began an unusual practice of helping students move in on the first day. Although this was never a required part of the faculty role, it has become a tradition to find College Park Scholars faculty helping parents and students move boxes into elevators and assist with computer hookups. In fact, the computer technical assistance was so highly praised that residence life started a technical assistance program for all residence halls using student assistants to help new freshmen hook up their computers to the campus network, make recommendations about computer purchases, and address other technology-related questions.

Community Service

A number of campuses have discovered that one of the best ways to foster community is to give students an occasion to act together toward some greater goals. Service-learning and experiential learning are avenues for developing community among student and faculty at the beginning of a semester.

The University of Maryland's College Park Scholars Day of Service is planned collaboratively with the office of service learning on campus and the department of residence life for incoming students during the first week on campus. Over the summer, students are offered a choice of three types of service projects: working with people (children, disabled, elderly), physical labor (environmental work cleaning parks, painting, and sprucing up schools and playgrounds in preparation for the opening day of schools), or office work (preparing mailings, inventories, and general filing for nonprofits in the community).

Working alongside other students and faculty in the program gave new students a great advantage as school got under way. Students have reported that they made friends and potential study partners long before their classmates in other classes did. Moreover, the experience reinforced the Scholars' commitment to the values of community service. In many cases, students continued to do volunteer work throughout the semester at some of the sites they worked at during Service Day, and they became unofficial liaisons between the university and its neighbors.

Community Identity

Any marketing expert would say that it is important to create a "trademark identification" to motivate people to rally around a concept, product, or movement. This is evident in national campaigns such as "Race for the Cure" and the AIDS quilt, as well as very traditional product lines. The same holds true for learning communities. Arriving at a name for the program, a logo, and even a T-shirt design allow a campus to foster community identification, which makes it that much easier to build authentic community. Creating a logo will not create a community of learners; however, if a campus is putting considerable effort, resources, and planning into its learning community, it should go the extra mile for effective publicity and product identification.

Conclusion

All the logistics for setting up learning communities—admissions, registrations, orientation, and residence hall programming—must be revisited and in some cases reinvented by each campus in order to build successful learning communities programs. Those involved in the planning and development of learning communities can invite other campus constituencies with different areas of expertise to join in the shaping and evolution of the campus-specific learning community logistical processes. In that way the community has the broader effect of creating and strengthening campuswide connections for the good of all.

CHAPTER EIGHT

EVALUATING AND ASSESSING LEARNING COMMUNITIES

Assessing and evaluating learning communities requires a research approach that takes into account the multiple perspectives and academic and social interactions at work in these environments (Ketcheson and Levine, 1999). Assessment is traditionally defined as the gathering of evidence, which is used as part of the process of evaluation. Defined as "the systematic collection of information about the activities, characteristics, and outcomes of programs, personnel, and products for use by specific people to reduce uncertainties, improve effectiveness, and make decisions with regard to what those programs, personnel, or products are doing and affecting" (Patton, 1982, p. 15), evaluation is often categorized as either formative (focusing on process and aims to gather information for use at the program level for purposes of improvement and management) or summative (focusing on outcomes and collected evidence of program impact). Information gathered as part of summative evaluations is typically used for decisions about program continuation, growth, and level of support.

Planning and implementing evaluation and assessment activities needs to be part of routine, regularly scheduled decision-making processes, along with routine decisions such as budgeting and the scheduling of communities. The collected information can inform decisions about all aspects of program development: curricular offerings, marketing, program growth, resources, use of facilities, faculty development, community activities, and student support needs.

Developing a Research Plan

Evaluation of learning communities involves two closely related agendas: proving and improving (MacGregor, 1995). Evaluation for proving involves recording and describing the impact of learning communities for both internal and external audiences. Evaluation for improving is the gathering of information for use by those most involved in the program for purposes of problem solving and program enhancement. The coordination of these agendas must be at the center of planning an evaluation of learning communities (Ketcheson and Levine, 1999). The process and topics we examine here should be viewed as suggested guidelines for developing a framework; different learning communities will adapt to their own particular circumstances and needs.

A well-defined research proposal or plan should be the product of ongoing dialogue and collaboration between those conducting the evaluation and those most affected by the results, the stakeholders—the "people who have a stake in how the evaluation comes out" (Patton, 1982, p. 55).

A carefully constructed plan should address several questions (Bogdan and Biklen, 1998). What are you going to do and how are you going to do it? Responses include information on where you will conduct your study, who it will include, what data you will collect, and how you will analyze it. Other important questions to address in the planning stage are Why are you doing the study? and How is what you are doing related to previous research? The research plan should also take into account any ethical issues involved in the study and how they will be addressed. Finally, you should consider the potential contribution of your study to learning communities practice and basic research.

The goals for evaluation should be determined in conjunction with decisions about the intended outcomes of learning communities. If an intended outcome is greater student involvement with faculty, for example, this should be a focus of the research. The audiences for the research need to be considered. If the collected information is to go to external audiences, the planning process should encompass their reporting formats and deadlines.

Like any other new project, planning an evaluation strategy begins with collecting information. Researchers should consider the literature on evaluating and assessing learning communities, ask colleagues on other campuses about the successes and disappointments they experienced in their evaluation efforts, and share information about findings, as well as what they have learned regarding the evaluation process itself, with others in the field.

At the beginning, the research agenda should be flexible. Decisions about assessment and evaluation are likely to be amended as the work proceeds and the researchers learn more, through both formal and informal evaluation activities, about what students and faculty experience as members of learning communities. An effort should start small, with questions that will give important and usable information and can be easily answered within a reasonable time frame using methods or researchers available (Ketcheson and Levine, 1999).

Selecting research methods is one of the most challenging decisions in the research planning process. This decision requires a clear understanding of the areas to be studied, a working knowledge of the potential methods, and an understanding of the financial, human, and technological resources necessary to conduct these activities.

Researchers can develop a research plan in the context of other evaluation activities taking place on campus. For example, if the institution already collects information on the reading and writing skills of entering students, they can consider ways of linking those data to a learning communities study on the performance of learning communities participants and nonparticipants in first-year writing courses.

All planning should include individuals or units involved in institutional research who can help in the collection and analysis of data. Researchers can determine the appropriate roles for program leadership and stakeholders in the collection and analysis of findings and realistically consider the levels of expertise and time commitments necessary to conduct evaluation and assessment activities.

An integrated research approach that relies on both quantitative and qualitative research methods addresses a variety of research questions in rich contexts and from different perspectives (Shulman, 1988). Qualitative methods—interviews, document review, observation, focus groups, ethnographic research, and other analytic approaches—are more descriptive, so the perspectives of the stakeholders are essential. The research design is more flexible, and hypotheses are developed as part of the research process. Quantitative research relies more on experimental and quasi-experimental designs and seeks more objective, unbiased answers to research questions. Quantitative research design relies on a systematic explanation of why a particular phenomenon occurs—for example, why participants in learning communities earn higher grades in math than nonparticipants do.

Regardless of the methods chosen, ethical issues need to be considered. Ethical research treats subjects with respect and invites their cooperation in the study (Bogdan and Biklen, 1998). Institutions have guidelines on research involving human subjects. If there is a formal application and review process, required forms must be filed well in advance of the start of the study.

An ethical issue often overlooked in research is the extent to which subjects have already been studied and involved in research. On many campuses, learning communities classrooms are considered laboratories for change. Faculty and students model ways of teaching and learning in more collaborative ways. Other faculty on campus, visitors from other institutions, and researchers want to visit these classrooms. If intrusions to classrooms and access to program participants are not closely monitored, students and faculty can begin to feel like "guinea pigs" and may resent and resist future efforts to examine their work (Ketcheson and Levine, 1999, p. 104).

A final issue to consider when developing the research plan is the expected contribution to practice and the literature that will stem from this work. This may be the most important aspect of the evaluation planning process. The process should identify all potential audiences for the results of the evaluation and, from the onset of the study, consider how decision makers and stakeholders will use findings, both positive and negative ones, to improve the program. Finally, the plan should address ways to disseminate information and lessons learned.

Defining Research Questions

One challenge in evaluating learning communities is formulating research questions that can best inform practice. Our advice is to start small and add or delete research questions over the course of gathering information and revising the original evaluation plan. In developing questions, consider what types of information are needed to improve and manage the program in its different stages of development.

Early Stages

A question to consider in the early stages of program development is who enrolls in learning communities. Unless the program is mandated for particular groups of students, this information is vital for describing and comparing participants and nonparticipants and addressing concerns about self-selection. This is the stage to document how students are recruited and enrolled in the program, and to prepare demographic profiles of participants and nonparticipants. Demographic data on students are typically collected as part of the admissions or orientation process and are then maintained as part of ongoing institutional assessment efforts. Early and continuous collaboration with individuals responsible for managing student information systems and records is important here. For example, it might be possible to add several key questions related to learning communities to an ongoing institutional research project, such as an orientation survey or postregistration telephone survey.

Another question to consider as the program develops is what happens to students and faculty when they participate in communities. Does participation affect students' attitudes and expectations about the first year in college? Do faculty teach differently when teaching as part of a learning community? Data can be collected through written surveys; classroom observations; individual interviews; telephone surveys with participants, alumni, or parents; and focus groups. End-of-semester course evaluations are particularly useful. Most departments, schools, or colleges require course evaluations, but researchers should consider developing a form that can assess the particulars of the learning communities experience. The course evaluation should go beyond a critique of readings, assignments, and classroom instruction by asking students to evaluate the connections between their courses and ways they were asked to work collaboratively with their peers and teachers. Exhibit 8.1 is an example of the cluster evaluation form used at LaGuardia Community College.

Findings from initial evaluation activities can be used in many ways. Since the primary goal of evaluation is to collect information for use at the program level, findings should drive the planning process for the next stages of program development. Significant findings—for example, that learning communities are "the best way to make the transition from high school to college"—can be included in fliers or brochures distributed to prospective and entering students.

Next Stages

As cohorts of students and faculty experience learning communities, the research agenda will broaden to assess the evaluation process itself and plan for necessary changes in data collection or analysis. This is the time to revisit the original evaluation plan and consider adding or deleting research questions based on preliminary findings and patterns in the data. As the numbers of students and faculty involved in the program increase, the process will need to address issues of what happens to both current and former participants, which requires developing a system for identifying and monitoring cohorts of participants. It would be useful to meet with institutional researchers and the managers of student records early in the evaluation process to design a cohort database or identification system.

Research questions in this stage of the program might focus on retention, student achievement, and student satisfaction with the undergraduate experience. How does participation in a learning community affect student performance, as measured by grade point average, in the first semester? Do students who participate in learning communities persist to the second year at greater rates than nonparticipants? Are students who participate in learning communities more likely to join and become active members of student organizations than nonparticipants?

Many of the questions that will need to be asked routinely will likely be dictated by internal or external reporting requirements. How many students

EXHIBIT 8.1. CLUSTER EVALUATION FORM, LAGUARDIA COMMUNITY COLLEGE.

Liberal Arts Cluster Questionnaire
Fall 1998

I. Write out the title of the cluster you are in _____

II. Circle the number that best expresses your view of the statement.
   1. I like my introductory cluster experience
      Strongly Agree   **Strongly Disagree**
         1   2   3   4   5

   2. The writing skills learned in Composition I and Research Paper writing help in thee other courses in the cluster.
      Strongly Agree   **Strongly Disagree**
         1   2   3   4   5

   3. Writing topics in Composition I were largely related to the reading and discussions in the other cluster courses.
      Strongly Agree   **Strongly Disagree**
         1   2   3   4   5

   4. The research paper topic was largely related to the ideas and themes discussed in the other courses in the cluster.
      Strongly Agree   **Strongly Disagree**
         1   2   3   4   5

   5. The central ideas or themes of the cluster were discussed in all of the cluster courses.
      Strongly Agree   **Strongly Disagree**
         1   2   3   4   5

   6. Through discussions/activities in the Integrated Seminar (LIB110) I was able to better understand relationships among ideas presented in the individual courses in the cluster.
      Strongly Agree   **Strongly Disagree**
         1   2   3   4   5

   7. Being in the cluster helped me realize that there are multiple perspectives from which to view an issue.
      Strongly Agree   **Strongly Disagree**
         1   2   3   4   5

   8. Grouping courses around central themes and ideas is an improvement over taking separate, unrelated courses.
      Strongly Agree   **Strongly Disagree**
         1   2   3   4   5

EXHIBIT 8.1, Continued

9. Being part of a group of students in all the courses in the cluster helped to create close friendships and a supportive atmosphere for speaking in class without fear.

Strongly Agree   **Strongly Disagree**
    1   2   3   4   5

10. Being in the cluster gave me the opportunity to learn from other students as well as faculty.

Strongly Agree   **Strongly Disagree**
    1   2   3   4   5

III. Briefly respond to the following questions.

1. Identify the central theme or themes in the cluster courses.

2. How did the cluster themes relate to one another in all of the courses, for example, through discussions of texts, written assignments, and other activities? Be specific.

3. The purpose of the Integrated Seminar (LIB110) is to help you make connections among the different courses in the cluster. Did the Integrated Seminar do this for you? If so, how? Give an example.

4. Was your LIB110 team-taught (two faculty teaching the class together)? If yes, was this helpful to you? How?

5. What did you like best about being in the cluster?

6. What did you like least about being in the cluster?

7. Would you recommend the cluster experience to others? What would you tell them?

8. Do you have any suggestions on how the cluster experience could be improved?

Source: LaGuardia Community College. Used by permission.

participate in learning communities? What is the breakdown of participants by gender, race, and ethnicity? What are the percentages of participants by school or college or by major? An evaluation cycle can be established to collect information for both short-term reporting and long-term planning needs.

Follow-Up

Learning communities research plans tend to emphasize assessment of the learning communities structure, particularly student satisfaction during or immediately following the semester of participation. Limited resources, both human and fiscal, require campuses to make difficult choices about the scope of an evaluation effort. As a result, follow-up studies may be limited to retention or graduation statistics. How many learning communities participants are retained to a second fall semester, a third fall semester, or graduation?

A well-designed research plan includes a long-term, follow-up component. Data collection methods might include exit interviews with former learning communities participants, telephone interviews with alumni, or questionnaires mailed to graduating seniors and alumni. Research questions should allow the assessment of different ways that participation has affected students' total undergraduate experience. For example, reflecting back over their college years, how do former learning communities students describe the impact of learning communities on their undergraduate experience? Do students who participated in learning community peer leadership roles report greater satisfaction with their college experience? Do learning communities students graduate at higher rates? Is there a relationship between the courses that students take as part of learning communities and their choice of majors?

Learning communities evaluation may reveal that participation improves retention or grades and increases student satisfaction with the undergraduate experience, but does it improve learning? (B. A. Holland, personal communication, Dec. 1998). Learning communities intentionally reorganize the curriculum in ways that affect how students learn. A challenge facing researchers is how to assess actual changes in learning that occurs as a result of learning communities participation. What does "collegiate learning" really mean in a learning community setting? (Ewell, 1997). How does participation in learning communities affect students' cognitive and skill development?

According to Ewell (1997) our understanding has advanced on how learning occurs, how it can be promoted, and the structures that best support it. A research plan for learning communities should consider literature from the areas of human learning and development, teaching improvement, curriculum and instructional development, organizational restructuring and continuous improvement, and cognitive science.

Using Collaborative Approaches to Research

Learning communities promote collaborative learning partnerships between students and faculty and are ideal settings for collaborative research (Love, Russo, and Tinto, 1995). Moreover, a collaborative research process increases the likelihood that evaluation findings will be used to inform practice.

Other research initiatives taking place on campus and data already collected can be useful in the evaluation of learning communities programs. Many universities collect data on new students as part of the admission, placement testing, or orientation process. This information can be useful in describing participants and nonparticipants in learning communities. Involving other researchers in these efforts will add credibility to findings and help alleviate concerns about bias.

Classroom Research

The evaluation of learning communities must document the type of teaching and learning that occurs in learning communities classrooms. Classroom assessment and classroom research are learner-centered, teacher-directed information-gathering approaches that provide answers to questions about what is taking place in the learning environment of a specific classroom (Angelo and Cross, 1993; Cross and Steadman, 1996). According to Cross and Steadman, classroom research benefits "both teachers and students by actively engaging them in the collaborative study of learning as it takes place day by day in the particular context of their own classrooms" (p. 2). Classroom-specific research projects can provide faculty and students with meaningful and timely feedback on classroom learning. Collectively these projects can present a rich, descriptive picture of teaching and learning in learning communities.

Uses and methods of classroom assessment as part of faculty development activities should be discussed. Classroom research involves faculty in the systematic study of how their teaching affects students' learning (Cross and Steadman, 1996). For many faculty, these assessment and research activities lead to additional questions about how they teach and how students learn. Learning communities faculty development activities are an ideal setting in which to address these issues. Faculty engaging in classroom assessment activities should be asked to share their results with program leadership and other learning communities faculty. Electronic discussion lists, Web sites, and newsletters represent additional ways to share information and results.

Reflective Interviews

The Washington Center for Improving the Quality of Undergraduate Education used end-of-quarter interviews, called reflective dialogues, to help faculty understand and improve their experiences in learning communities (Smith and MacGregor, 1991). At the end of each quarter or semester, teaching teams met with members of the center staff to discuss the following open-ended questions (p. 27):

- What were your original expectations for teaching in this learning community program? Given those expectations, in what ways did the experience meet or not meet them?
- What else stands out, in terms of observations and discoveries? What did you notice about your students, your colleagues' teaching, and your own teaching?
- What issues need attention in the future: what might future learning community teaching teams consider? What might the institution consider and address?
- As a result of teaching in this program, what will you take forward in your work?

Through these conversations, the center and teaching teams gained valuable information on what happens in learning communities: what faculty learn from each other, what student learning looked like, and what worked and what did not in terms of curriculum design and student assignments. An important part of the evaluation process is the development of a feedback loop that brings information back to those who can find it most useful. The center compiled findings from these interviews into "learning community 'gleanings': a combination newsletter and resource directory, with a listing of bright ideas being developed in various learning communities, and a discussion of curricular and institutional issues facing many of these programs" (Smith and MacGregor, p. 28). Eventually many of the individual campuses participating in the center interviews began to use reflective conversations in their own ongoing assessment and planning practices.

External Evaluators

Although it can be costly, using external evaluators and consultants can add perspective and credibility to program evaluation. They can ask the difficult questions that program leadership and others invested in the program are unable to raise without introducing issues of bias. Faculty and student participants are more likely to be open and honest in discussing their perceptions of their programs with a researcher who is not a member of the program or campus community. Reports provided by external evaluators should supplement internally gathered information.

Sharing Results

An important aspect of the evaluation process is the sharing of results. Too often so much of the planning process is dedicated to evaluation and design that the importance of reporting results and sharing information is often overlooked. If the evaluation design relies on multiple researchers and methods of data collection, the program leadership will need to gather all reports and prepare information to be shared with multiple audiences. External evaluators will communicate findings with program coordinators. Then it is usually the responsibility of program leadership to share information with the program stakeholders and greater campus community.

Potential audiences for the findings should be identified as part of the evaluation planning process. Audiences include program stakeholders, additional internal audiences, and external audiences, which encompass other colleges and universities. But issues of data ownership and distribution need to be addressed. Throughout this chapter we have emphasized the importance of using evaluation and assessment information to drive program improvements. Assessment needs to be conducted in an open and nonthreatening atmosphere that minimizes the risk that information will be misused. Should this information be considered "program property," not to be shared publicly? This is a difficult question to answer, and how learning communities programs respond will vary by the institutional research culture and policies of different campuses.

Stakeholders

Findings should be shared with the people most invested in the success of the program: faculty, students, and prospective students.

Faculty. There should be ample opportunities for faculty to review and discuss the findings. If the program has a learning communities oversight committee, that group can review preliminary findings to interpret initial patterns in the findings, clarify conflicting or confusing patterns in the data, and offer suggestions for improving the research protocol. Their contributions will strengthen the overall program evaluation.

There are different ways of feeding the findings back into the program. Evaluation and assessment data should be shared with faculty as part of the learning communities faculty development process. Researchers can share their findings through reports, and panels of veteran learning communities faculty can comment on how their experiences teaching in learning communities relate to the reported findings. Results can also be communicated through program newsletters or research briefs. If the research finds that participants are retained at higher rates than nonparticipants, that information needs to be communicated to learning communities faculty in a research update. If the campus office of institutional research already produces research bulletins, the learning communities information can be included. If evaluation is conducted in collaboration with institutional researchers, they will likely encompass the learning communities findings in their published reports.

Students. Students tend to be the forgotten audience when it comes to sharing evaluation data. They are asked to complete surveys, participate in focus groups, and admonished to "act normal" when observers visit their classrooms, but they are often overlooked when it is time to share what has been learned. Student media outlets—for example, the student newspaper—can communicate the results. If the program has a gathering space for learning communities students, research briefs can be displayed and students invited to meet with program leadership to discuss the findings.

Prospective Students. Prospective students and their families, high school guidance counselors, and high school teachers are important audiences for evaluation findings. If learning communities is the campus's premier program for entering students, it should be publicized as part of the campus recruitment plan, with descriptions of the program, along with quotations from students and faculty, in the campus viewbook. Faculty with the opportunity to address prospective students can share evidence of how learning communities support student success, particularly during the transition to college.

Additional Internal Audiences

Evaluation and assessment data will most likely be involved in university decisions about levels of support for the program, including budget, personnel, and facilities resources. Program leadership may need to present findings to chief academic officers, university or system presidents, and other groups with decision-making authority, such as faculty budget or curriculum committees, deans, and the board of trustees.

Evaluation results should be tied to the annual review and planning process for the program. Are we meeting our intended outcomes? What are we doing well? What can we do differently? Program leadership should also consider findings when planning for the growth of the program. Can we efficiently enroll more students in learning communities? Do we have the resources to support additional faculty teaching in learning communities? Have we outgrown our dedicated classroom or residence hall space?

A central theme in this book is that building learning communities requires campus partnerships. Academic advisers, registration personnel, and orientation coordinators are just a few of the units participating in the development of the program, and each should engage in conversations on how the program is doing. Meeting with these groups annually to review findings and discuss ways of improving policies and procedures is vital to the program.

External Audiences

How the program is funded plays a major role in determining external reporting responsibilities. If all or portions of the program are grant funded, the granter will outline expectations for evaluation activities and reporting. A program that relies on state or federal funds needs to plan for a systematic reporting of findings.

If the learning communities program is part of campuswide or school-specific curricular reform efforts, evaluation information will likely be included in reports to accreditation agencies. Assessment activities will be aimed at collecting evidence of how learning communities initiatives have changed the teaching and learning culture on campus.

Another consideration is to share information with the greater higher education community. The number of established learning communities programs has increased dramatically, and agendas at national conferences are filled with sessions on learning communities. Individuals involved in the work of learning communities on their campuses would agree that sharing information with others was an important part of their planning process. The American Association of Higher Education (AAHE) sponsors several annual meetings—the National Conference on Higher Education, Faculty Roles and Rewards, and an assessment conference—with themes conducive to presentations on learning communities.

Other organizations sponsor annual national or regional conferences suited to presentations on learning communities, including the following:

- National Conference on the First-Year Experience and Students in Transition (also sponsors the National Conference on Students in Transition and FYE West meeting)

- National Association of Student Personnel Administrators (NASPA)
- American College Personnel Association (ACPA)
- American Association of Community Colleges (AACC)
- The Learning Communities Conference sponsored alternately by Delta College and William Rainey Harper College
- National Academic Advising Association (NACADA)
- Association of General and Liberal Studies (AGLS)
- American Education Research Association (AERA)
- Discipline-based conferences (College Composition and Communication)
- Regional events sponsored by the Washington Center for Improving the Quality of Undergraduate Education
- International Conference on Residential Colleges and Living/Learning Programs
- Association of College and University Housing Officers-International (ACUHO-I)

Conclusion

Although there is no one best way to evaluate learning communities programs, the following approach is broadly applicable:

1. Develop a research plan that addresses why you are conducting the evaluation, what you are evaluating, and how you are going to do it.
2. Involve program stakeholders—the faculty, students, and program leaders who have the most at stake in terms of the outcomes of the evaluation—in all stages of the evaluation process.
3. Review the literature on evaluation and assessment. Locate studies on program evaluation, particularly those dealing with the evaluation and assessment of learning communities.
4. Consider uses of multiple research methods that will allow you to develop a variety of research questions in the context of learning communities work.
5. Consider small, faculty-led classroom research projects as an effective method for describing what takes place in learning communities classrooms.
6. Carefully plan a schedule of evaluation and assessment activities to avoid program participants from feeling "studied out."
7. Start small, and broaden the research agenda as you work through the evaluation process.
8. Identify the audiences for your results and plan for the systematic sharing of findings.

Information gathered through these venues will serve as a valuable catalyst for future planning and decision making for the program. Regardless of the relative complexity or simplicity of the research plan and methods used, this information will constitute important evidence as to the effect of learning communities involvement on a variety of audiences.

CHAPTER NINE

HOW LEARNING COMMUNITIES AFFECT STUDENTS, FACULTY, AND THE INSTITUTION

We now turn our attention to the question many readers may have been asking themselves since they picked up this book or were introduced to the concept of learning communities: *How do we know learning communities work?* Does participation have a positive impact on student performance and persistence? Do students report that participation eases the transition to college? Do learning communities faculty teach in different ways than faculty who are not, and what impact does this type of teaching have on student learning? How do learning communities affect the greater campus community?

Although this chapter describes evidence that reflects the impact that learning communities participation can have on students, faculty, and the organization, it is not intended as a meta-analysis of research on the impact of learning communities. Although we occasionally cite some studies that have yielded statistically significant results demonstrating the positive impact participation has on students (see Exhibit 9.1), our objective is to describe the types of evidence that campuses have collected to document their learning communities efforts.

What Counts as Evidence

What counts as evidence to demonstrate that learning communities work? For some, the answer is simple: retention data. This is a critically important variable

EXHIBIT 9.1. SUMMARY OF STUDIES.

Bowling Green State University (Chapman Learning Community): Correspondence provided an overview of the assessment of Chapman Learning Community, including preliminary findings from interviews with over fifty students participating in this residential learning community.

Collaborative Learning Project: This research project was a collaborative study of learning communities at the University of Washington, LaGuardia Community College, and Seattle Central Community College. The study was conducted by a team of researchers, under the direction of Vincent Tinto, for the National Center on Postsecondary Teaching, Learning, and Assessment. A summary of the findings is presented in this chapter.

Daytona Beach Community College: This campus compiled four research studies to assess QUANTA, a year-long, interdisciplinary program in which students and faculty participate in three courses integrated around a common theme. The report contains information on the intellectual development of QUANTA students, retention data, student evaluations of the program, and attitudes of QUANTA alumni.

Illinois State University (Connections): Researchers at Illinois State conducted an assessment of student achievement and persistence at the end of the freshman year. The study also examined which students were more likely to participate in learning communities.

Indiana University Purdue University Indianapolis: Information on linked-course learning communities at IUPUI came from a research brief and related journal article (Borden and Rooney, 1998) summarizing a quantitative study on the impact of learning communities participation on semester grade point average and retention to next semester.

Temple University: Temple University enrolls the majority of its entering freshman in linked-course learning communities. Retention data and findings from focus group research are reported in this chapter. Lessons learned from a qualitative case study of three learning communities are also shared.

University of Maryland: Two separate reports examining the impact of participation on students in Maryland's College Park Scholars Program are discussed in this chapter. One study analyzed the effect of participation on achievement and commitment to math and science. A second study explored student satisfaction with this residential, interdisciplinary learning community experience. Reflections of program faculty are also discussed.

University of Miami: The results of several studies are included in this chapter. Focus group research was conducted with students participating in the fall 1994 Learning Community, "Influences of Psychology and Public Relations on Cinema and Society," and in the fall 1995 Learning Community, "Why Are Your Parents So Weird: 1960s." Focus group research was also conducted with students in the College of Engineering IMPACT learning community. Results of student and faculty surveys are also discussed.

EXHIBIT 9.1, Continued

University of Missouri-Columbia: The University of Missouri studied the initial and long-term effects of participation in Freshman Interest Groups (FIGs). The findings were reported in a series of student life studies abstracts.

University of Southern Maine (Russell Scholars Program): This study described results from the evaluation of the inaugural year of the Russell Scholars Program, a four-year program that includes a curricular and residential component and enrolls students in learning communities courses for four years. End-of-year survey results from samples of Russell Scholars participants and nonparticipants at the end of the first year are compared.

University of Wisconsin (Bradley Learning Community): The end-of-year evaluation report includes information from a student connection survey, a dissertation on student development, and surveys designed by the program expressly for this evaluation report. Grade point average and persistence rates are also provided.

Washington Center for Improving the Quality of Undergraduate Education: The Washington Center in an interinstitutional consortium, located at Evergreen State College, devoted to improving undergraduate education. The results of a study designed to measure the intellectual development of students in learning communities are described in this chapter.

for higher education policymakers and cannot be underestimated, yet to describe the outcomes of learning communities only in terms of attrition or persistence rates is to ignore the influence that participation has on the teaching and learning culture of an institution. Retention figures reflect these changes, but by themselves fail to explain how participation affects students' social and cognitive development or their involvement within the institution.

Evidence of the impact of learning communities should be rich enough so researchers can begin to unravel causes as well as results. By design, learning communities are flexible, allowing for the type of active and collaborative learning that should occur both in and out of the classroom in learning communities. Describing how this learning occurs and its effect on such outcomes as achievement, persistence, and satisfaction with the institution requires a flexible research design that relies on multiple methods of assessment and collects quantitative and qualitative information on the impact of participation on various constituents.

In the best case, a variety of evidence should be collected to present a rich, descriptive picture of what happens to students and teachers when they participate in learning communities. This description should address the nature and level of organizational change that has occurred in the process of designing and implementing learning communities, an outcome that is often much more difficult to document than the effect of participation on individuals.

One approach is to rely on multiple research methods, and often multiple researchers, to capture the diverse array of experiences and outcomes that are taking place. The most widely cited analysis of studies of learning communities was a collaborative research project, sponsored by the National Center on Postsecondary Teaching, Learning and Assessment, that examined learning communities at the University of Washington, LaGuardia Community College, and Seattle Central Community College (Tinto, Love, and Russo, 1993). Researchers framed the study around two basic questions: (1) Do learning communities make a difference? and (2) If so, how? A team of researchers relied on both quantitative and qualitative research methods to conduct the research at the three program sites.

The QUANTA Interdisciplinary Learning Community Program at Daytona Beach Community College combined four research studies to present an overall picture of what happens to students when they participate in learning communities (Avens and Zelley, 1992). From the beginning, the researchers closely linked assessment to program goals. One report summarized how learning communities participation affected students' intellectual development, the second reported retention outcomes, and the third reported participants' evaluation of the program. The fourth report was a study of alumni that summarizes former QUANTA students' attitudes toward the program. These studies demonstrate different approaches to collecting evidence. When combined, they present a rich, descriptive picture of the student experience in QUANTA.

As a general rule, the evidence collected should be closely related to the stated outcomes for learning communities participation. For example, if one goal of learning communities is to enhance students' academic success, the evidence should present a picture of what happens to students' academic achievement when they participate in a learning community. How do participants perform academically compared to nonparticipants? Evidence that illustrates academic success might include the following components:

Grade point average earned at the conclusion of learning communities participation and/or over time (first year, each year of attendance)

Total credit hours attempted and completed at the conclusion of learning communities participation and/or over time (first year, each year of attendance)

Grade comparison studies (how students' grades in learning communities sections of particular courses compare to those of nonparticipants in a non–learning communities section of the same course)

Performance results on departmental exams (whether students who take such courses as part of a learning community outperform nonparticipants)

Researchers at the University of Miami formed an evaluation plan centered around one question: What does success look like? (J. T. Masterson, personal communication, May 15, 1998). The evaluation committee identified six success indicators: improved retention, increased student bonding with faculty and peers, increased linkage among courses, improved writing skills, higher academic outcomes, and positive perception of learning communities. They then collected information from three perspectives: students, faculty, and parents. Data sources included:

- Student surveys at the beginning and end of semesters (learning communities students only)
- Individual student interviews
- Focus group interviews with learning communities students at the end of each semester.
- Relevant data from files of learning communities students and control group (grade point average, retention rates)
- 1997 enrolled student survey (learning communities and control group)
- Individual faculty interviews at the beginning of each semester
- Individual faculty interviews at the end of the semester
- Faculty surveys
- End-of-semester telephone interviews with parents

Campuses collect different types of evidence about the effect of participation on students and faculty. Some programs also collect information on how the program is perceived within the greater campus community. The type of evidence described in this chapter includes information on the following areas:

- The impact of participation on students (retention and achievement, intellectual and social development, and involvement)
- What can be learned from how students describe the experience (reasons for joining, benefits of participation, classroom experience)
- How participation affects faculty (whether teaching in a learning community influences faculty attitudes toward teaching or student learning)
- The context of the learning communities program within the institution

The information we look at next came from both extensive research projects that relied on multiple methods of data collection and small studies designed to capture one aspect of the learning communities experience or describe the effects of participation on a particular group. In some of the studies, data were collected by institutional researchers; in others information was gathered by practitioners who sought to learn more about the effect their programs were having on students and teachers. What the studies reviewed in this chapter have in common is that they all tell the story of what happens to students, faculty, and the greater campus community as a result of learning communities.

Impact on Students

To examine the role of learning communities on students' experience, we summarize studies that demonstrate that participation has a positive impact on retention and academic achievement or that participation has a positive effect on students' intellectual and social development, or both. Campuses have also collected evidence on how participation affects students' transition to college and their satisfaction with the undergraduate experience. Much of this evidence comes from how students describe their participation in learning communities, their reasons for joining, and the benefits of participation.

Achievement and Retention

Several studies illustrate that participation in learning communities has a positive impact on student achievement and retention (Tinto, Love, and Russo, 1993). Although we focus on evidence and not research design and methodology, it is important to note that retention and achievement studies typically control for background differences. In addition, results can be reported at different levels: for the overall program or for narrowly defined subgroups of participants.

Temple University. Temple University implemented learning communities in 1993 and began tracking retention rates in 1995. Learning communities students are categorized by cohort—the fall semester of participation. Initial studies revealed that participants in the fall 1994 and fall 1995 cohorts were retained to their second year at rates 2 to 3 percent higher than that of nonparticipants. The most recent study focused on the fall 1996 cohort, the weakest cohort in terms of entry characteristics (measured by SAT-Verbal, SAT-Quantitative, high school percentile, and first-semester grade point average). That study revealed that learning communities participants were retained to the second fall semester at a rate 5 percent higher than a comparison group of nonparticipants.

University of Missouri-Columbia. Researchers studied students' academic records to determine if participation in FIGs was associated with higher levels of academic achievement and persistence (Student Life Studies Abstracts, 1996). Students in FIGs coenrolled in three courses and lived together on the same floor of a designated residence hall. Using grade point average as an indicator of academic achievement, students in the 1995 FIG cohort earned a mean grade point average of 2.89 compared to a mean of 2.66 for nonparticipants. Grade point average differences were even greater after controlling for entering ability. The study also demonstrated that participants in FIGs had higher rates of retention: the FIGs students in 1995 had a one-year retention rate of 87 percent compared to 81 percent for nonparticipants. A longitudinal study of this same cohort demonstrated a 12 percent higher retention rate over nonparticipants after three years.

Indiana University Purdue University Indianapolis. Retention studies can reveal the impact of participation on subgroups of participants. A retention study of IUPUI's 1995 learning communities participants revealed that overall participation had a positive but not statistically significant impact on the grades and persistence rates of participants when compared to nonparticipants. The more interesting finding was that participation may have had a disproportional positive impact on African American males, the group with the lowest levels of persistence at the university. The retention rate for African American male participants was not only significantly higher than that of nonparticipant African American males, but was higher than that of all other IUPUI undergraduates as well (Borden and Rooney, 1998).

University of Maryland's College Park Scholars. For some campuses, the impact of participation on GPA is revealed over time. Students who participated in the University of Maryland's College Park Scholars Science, Technology, and Society and Life Sciences learning communities for only one semester were outperformed by a matched sample (Scholnick, 1996). After the third and fourth semesters of participation, however, the participants earned higher grade point averages in science courses and higher grades in math courses. For the program, length of participation is an important variable in describing the impact of learning community membership on student achievement. At the conclusion of the two-year program, the students in these two learning communities completed a more rigorous math and science curriculum and outperformed the match group of nonparticipants.

Researchers at Maryland were also interested in persistence rates. In terms of overall retention, students who persisted in College Park Scholars beyond one semester were retained at higher rates than the matched sample of nonparticipants (Scholnick, 1996). In this study, however, the researchers wanted to determine if participation influenced students' commitment to science majors. After the third and fourth semesters of participation in learning communities, College Park Scholars students were more likely to retain interest in science majors.

Intellectual and Social Development

Since Perry's early work (1970) researchers have been curious about the nature of students' cognitive and intellectual growth. In 1992 Light reported his findings about student engagement in learning in the *Harvard Assessment Seminars.* Several of these findings are particularly relevant for learning communities. Light found that "interactive relationships organized around academic work are vital" (p. 8) and recommends that colleges create opportunities to help students work collegially. A second finding was that students value writing skills, and those who reported the most improvement in their writing worked with their teachers and peers in particular ways. A third finding highlighted the importance of academic advising. Advisers can play an important role in helping students reach decisions that will shape their college experience.

To collect evidence on intellectual and social development in learning communities, researchers have asked a number of questions: How does participation affect students' intellectual and social development? Are students learning to think in different, more critical ways? Do participants report that they are more comfortable learning from peers or interacting with students whose backgrounds are different from their own? And, perhaps most important, are learning communities—which by design rely on collaborative, interdisciplinary learning and more integrated ways of knowing— more likely to foster students' cognitive development than traditional educational systems? Several studies relied on the Measure of Intellectual Development, adapted from Perry's scheme of development, to answer these questions.

Washington Center for Improving the Quality of Undergraduate Education. MacGregor (1987) used the Measure of Intellectual Development, developed by Knefelkamp and Widick, to assess student placement along the Perry Scheme of Development and progress following participation in a learning community. At the beginning of the semester, students were asked to write a "pre" essay, describing either the best class they had taken in high school or college or the last time they made a decision about something of major importance. As a follow-up, students wrote a "post" essay describing a class that would represent the ideal learning environment.

The study revealed that the "pre" means for learning communities groups were generally higher than those of comparable groups of freshmen. This was due in part to the slightly older populations enrolling at the participating institutions (Evergreen State College and community colleges) and students' self-selection into learning communities. Students often choose to participate in learning communities because they are seeking a learning environment characterized by active and collaborative learning, and the building of curricular connections (MacGregor, 1987). Overall the study found that 57 to 73 percent of the students advanced a third or more in terms of intellectual development.

Daytona Beach Community College. The QUANTA Interdisciplinary Learning Communities Program at Daytona Beach Community College is a two-year program that enrolls students in a year-long freshman learning community experience linking an English, psychology, and humanities course around a common theme. An objective of participation is to help students develop critical thinking skills and "an attitude of open-mindedness, curiosity, and creativity" (Avens and Zelley, 1992, p. 4).

Researchers measured participants' cognitive development using the Measure of Intellectual Development developed by Knefelkamp and Widick. They began with the hypothesis that "participation in this collaborative active learning environment will result in greater movement along the Perry Scale of Intellectual Development than is usual in traditional classes" (Avens and Zelley, 1992, p. 9). In this study, students wrote three essays over the course of the academic year in response to a question on classroom learning, decision making, or career plans. Essays were compared at the beginning and end of the fall term and from the beginning of the fall term to the end of the winter term, to determine if students showed movement along the Perry Scale. Seventy-six percent of the students experienced a change of one-third position or more, 50 percent progressed a position of two-thirds, and 10.5 percent made a positive movement of a full position or more. When compared to results from a study of national norms, QUANTA students showed a greater movement along the Perry Scale than did students in traditional classes.

University of Wisconsin (Bradley Learning Community). Researchers working with the Bradley Learning Communities program described what they called the "Bradley Buffer"—an effect of participation on students' transition to the university (Brower, 1997, p. 6). They believe that participation buffers students from the disappointments and setbacks common in the first year, for example, drops in measures of self-esteem and self-efficacy. The Bradley study revealed that learning communities students experienced less of a decline in academic self-esteem and self-efficacy than did other freshmen.

Student Involvement

Student involvement is the extent to which students become involved with various environmental variables—characteristics of institutions, curriculum, faculty, residence, financial aid, and peer groups—and how this involvement affects their development (Astin, 1993). Important evidence of student involvement can be developed from information on how students interact with their peers and teachers in and out of the classroom. Several of the studies summarized here revealed that learning communities students adapt more quickly to the college classroom environment. They are more likely to participate in class discussions, raise questions, and seek an instructor's assistance than are nonparticipants. They report greater satisfaction with their classes and teachers. They are also more likely to participate in a range of academic and social activities (Tinto, Love, and Russo, 1993).

Focus group research on participants in Temple University's Learning Communities revealed that students in learning communities begin to see their peers as partners in the learning process. According to one student, "When I have a problem with my work I can ask a classmate for help and find that they might have the same problem" (Levine, 1994, p. 4). Another student described the sense of camaraderie: "[When leaving class] we all walk out together. We talk about everything" (p. 4).

University of Missouri-Columbia. In a study of FIGs, researchers at the University of Missouri-Columbia (MU) compared the responses of participants and nonparticipants on the MU freshman survey (Student Life Studies Abstracts, 1996). The survey contained three scales: academic integration, social integration, and institutional commitment. FIG students reported significantly higher levels of academic integration and institutional commitment than nonparticipants and greater gains in communication skills and general education. They also indicated higher levels of social interaction, although this finding was not statistically significant. Researchers examined data from three scales of the College Student Experience Questionnaire (CSEQ), a measure of educational outcomes and program effectiveness that includes useful information on student involvement. FIG students reported greater interaction with peers. They were also more likely than nonmembers to report that the intellectual content of interactions with peers, as well as with faculty, was greater. FIG students reported higher levels of integration of course content.

In 1997 researchers conducted a follow-up study to investigate the longer-term effects of FIG participation (Student Life Studies Abstracts, 1997). The study was prompted by decreases in difference on some measures between FIG and non-FIG students from the fall to the winter semester. To investigate if gains disappeared in the absence of programs, researchers conducted a follow-up study with the same groups of students from the 1995–1996 study. The review relied on survey data and information from the university's student information system to examine differences between the FIG and non-FIG students. The survey included scales designed to measure academic integration, social integration, institutional commitment, academic involvement, depth and breadth of interactions with others, and gains in general education.

Overall, both FIG and non-FIG students reported greater involvement in the second year. On the library experiences, course learning, and student acquaintances scales, the differences remained the same, with the FIG students holding the advantage. The difference between FIG and non-FIG students decreased for the campus union, campus residence, academic integration, social integration, and institutional commitment scales. Differences in general education gains also decreased. Researchers attributed the decline in differences to increases in involvement, integration, and commitment for non-FIG students. Differences between FIG and non-FIG students increased on the experience in writing, clubs and organizations, and experiences with faculty scales.

The researchers concluded that FIG participation has an immediate impact on students and that some of the benefits carry over into the second year of college. Decreases in involvement and use of on-campus facilities may be a result of students' moving off-campus and spending less time on campus. In addition, involvement with various on-campus events and groups may be related to specific programming. So although the gains FIG students make do persist into the second year, researchers concluded that some differences between FIG and non-FIG students do not increase over time. Other differences, such as experiences with writing and faculty-student interaction, appeared to be influenced by prior FIG involvement and led to increased differences between FIG and non-FIG students.

University of Southern Maine. An end-of-year survey revealed that Russell Scholars participants spent more time participating in organized activities than nonparticipants and the greatest amount of time talking informally to other students. According to Johnson and King (1997), these findings were statistically significant. Participants were more likely to cite "to become actively involved in student life and campus activities" as a goal than nonparticipants. This was the least-cited goal for nonparticipants.

University of Wisconsin (Bradley Learning Community). An end-of-year evaluation of student participating in the Bradley Learning Community revealed that Bradley students reported greater satisfaction with the first-year experience than nonparticipants (Brower, 1997). They attended more "Wisconsin Welcome" (opening of the school year) activities and reported more frequent use of safety and transportation services. Bradley students were more likely to seek assistance from peer learning partners, the program's student residence advisers, and to contact professors. They were also more likely to become student orientation or Wisconsin Welcome leaders.

Bowling Green State University, Ohio (Chapman Learning Community). Interviews with over fifty students residing in the Chapman Learning Community revealed that students joined Chapman for the smaller classes and the improved sense of camaraderie: "All of us were going to be in the same boat" (D. Purdy, personal communication, Jan. 21, 1998). Students also commented that the variety of extracurricular activities offered through Chapman enhanced their overall view of Bowling Green State University and the undergraduate experience. They praised the enthusiasm, support, and guidance of Chapman faculty and would recommend participation to incoming freshmen.

How Students Describe the Experience: Student Voices

The statistical findings presented evidence of measurable quantitative gains of participation in learning communities. Our focus shifts now to evidence derived from student voice. These qualitative data present a rich, descriptive picture of what students experience in learning communities and how they describe the impact of this participation.

Reasons for Joining

If students are not required to enroll in learning communities, it is important to understand who participates and why. In smaller learning communities programs, where participation is limited to a segment of the student population, the impact of self-selection must be considered. Researchers at Illinois State University learned that highly motivated students were more likely to participate in the Connections learning communities program. They compared ACT scores and student-reported information such as high school grades and hours spent studying, and found that learning communities participants entered the university with better academic track records than did students in the general population (Harris and Dillingham, 1998).

It is also interesting to learn why students choose to participate and if their expectations for participation are consistent with their learning communities

experiences. At the conclusion of participation, information on reasons for joining can be compared to satisfaction with the experience to understand better the
impact of participation on students' expectations and attitudes—useful information in recruiting students to learning communities.

University of Miami. When asked why they enrolled in learning communities,
focus group participants at the University of Miami cited intellectual, social,
and logistical reasons (J. T. Masterson, personal communication, May 5, 1998).
The most commonly cited reason for enrolling was the belief that the courses
would be more interesting. Students were also drawn to the common connection
between classes, as well as the perceived opportunity to understand the subject
matter better. Other students responded that their participation was coinciden-
tal or that they joined communities because the classes fit their schedule or were
required.

Temple University. In focus group interviews, Learning Communities participants
who were asked why they joined answered that they sought to combat their fears
about attending a large university, ease their transition to college, and benefit from
the support of their teachers and peers (Levine, 1994). They wanted smaller classes
and better opportunities to meet people. Some students explained their reasons
for selecting specific learning communities. Three female students said they joined
a learning community that included a math course because they felt they were not
good at math. They thought that taking the course in a community would make
the work easier because of the amount of personal attention they would receive
from their teachers.

Benefits of Participation

Survey research, focus groups, and interviews are methods for collecting information on how students describe the benefits of participating in learning communities. This evidence can be used to assess differences between the intended
outcomes of participation and student-described outcomes of participation. The
information gathered can also be used in marketing the program to prospective
and newly admitted students. On an end-of-year evaluation survey, students in the
University of Southern Maine's Russell Scholars Program most frequently cited
social benefits as advantages of participation—for example, "I met a nice group
of people quickly who were really supportive," and "Some good friends were
made" (Johnson and King, 1992, p. 24).

Asking students if they would recommend learning communities to prospective students is a good way to uncover what students consider the benefits of

participation. Students in the University of Miami's learning communities said they would recommend participation because of the opportunity to form relationships with classmates and the increased opportunities for interaction with teachers. Participants in Miami's IMPACT learning communities for engineering students report that they would encourage others to join for the access to the IMPACT computer lab as well as for the hands-on experience.

University of Maryland (College Park Scholars Program). The University of Maryland conducted focus groups with College Park Scholars participants to explore students' expectations and attitudes toward participation. When they joined the program, students expected to find students like themselves who shared similar interests and academic focus. They expected smaller and more active classrooms and more extracurricular activities (Rohall and Morrison, 1996). This finding led the program to plan more activities that cut across the various themes and involved all the students.

Sometimes research reveals that learning communities offer students too much of a good thing. For example, while students often seek membership in a learning community to interact with students with similar interests, they sometimes report a need for greater interaction with students in other learning communities or programs. According to a student participating in the College Park Scholars Environmental Studies program, "Socially, I know everyone in my program. . . . Sometimes . . . I feel like we are segregated a lot, program to program. We don't have, as a scholars group, interaction with International Studies or Public Leadership or the Artists or anything like that. It's your program alone" (Rohall and Morrison, 1996, p. 5).

Daytona Beach Community College (QUANTA). The QUANTA Program surveyed QUANTA alumni and asked, "Looking back, what do you think was most beneficial about your QUANTA experience?" (Avens and Zelley, 1992, p. 38). The most commonly cited response was the sense of community—working in and belonging to groups and friendships formed. Other students discussed the interdisciplinary nature of the program and the connections between courses. For others, the benefit was growth in their abilities to think critically and creatively, an increased sense of self-confidence, and better interpersonal skills. Students commented that participation in QUANTA eased their transition to college and contributed to their motivation to continue their education. Students also recalled their experiences with their teachers. They thought the supportive attitudes of teachers was a benefit of participation and that QUANTA made learning more enjoyable. One student, in law school at the time he completed the alumni survey, wrote that QUANTA was the only learning environment that he felt stressed cooperation among students.

The Classroom Experience

Learning communities intentionally seek to transform the learning environment. Surveys and interviews conducted with participants provide important information on how students perceive what happens in learning communities classrooms. Assessment efforts of the programs described here revealed that students value the interdisciplinary nature of learning communities courses, the emphasis on the development of certain academic and interpersonal skills, and the interactions between teachers and students.

Daytona Beach Community College (QUANTA). QUANTA relies on a student evaluation survey to learn how students rank the outcomes of participation. In six of the seven semesters in which the evaluation was conducted, the highest ranked item was, "The QUANTA experience helped me realize that there are multiple perspectives with which to view an issue" (Avens and Zelley, 1992). There was further evidence that what students valued most was the interdisciplinary nature of the program. The students recognized the curricular relationships among courses, realized the benefits of learning from other students, as well as their teachers, and appreciated the use of active learning methods (Avens and Zelley, 1992).

Students' responses to open-ended questions provided more personal perspectives. Students used vibrant and clear language to discuss changes in their learning styles and new-found abilities to learn and have fun at the same time—for example:

> In QUANTA where we get to explore the basic tenets of the individual disciplines and simultaneously discover the "big picture" of complexity and interconnectedness, I have found a learning experience which not only is worth the effort, but is irresistible! My personal learning style has flourished in the setting of looking at subjects from multiple perspectives and interrelating these angles and the subjects. . . . I have learned that learning is a challenge and I want to continue the quest! [Avens and Zelley, 1992, p. 24].

Students also wrote about the teaching and learning environment they encountered in QUANTA learning communities

> In QUANTA I felt as if the teachers were my friends and if I would have had a problem they would of known about it and helped me out. This is the ideal setting that every classroom should strive for. It is so much easier to *learn* from a friend than *to get taught* by a teacher [Avens and Zelley, 1992, p. 25].

University of Southern Maine. The University of Southern Maine's Russell Scholars Program enrolls a select number of students in learning communities: approximately fifty first-year students and ten upperclass students. Students share living space and participate in the program throughout all four years of study at the university. In the first year, they are coenrolled in a writing course, a Russell Scholars Seminar, and a one-credit learning community laboratory. The majority of the courses are team-taught.

At the end of the inaugural year of the program, researchers conducted an evaluation survey with participants and a control group (Johnson and King, 1997). Students were asked what they gained from participating in their courses. Significant differences were found between Russell Scholars and the control group. Scholars were more likely to respond that the program helped them improve their writing and understand another point of view. They were also more likely to indicate that the program taught them how to think critically and to become more aware of their own strengths and weaknesses.

Russell Scholars participants expressed greater satisfaction than nonparticipants with their classroom experiences, were more satisfied with their interactions with faculty, were more comfortable speaking up when they had a problem, and were more likely to feel encouraged to participate in class discussions. They felt that professors encouraged students to share their feelings about important issues and that professors could be trusted to look out for students' interests. All of these findings were statistically significant (Johnson and King, 1997).

University of Miami. Focus group participants in the IMPACT learning community for engineering students were asked to compare their combined curriculum courses to single, non–learning communities courses. Students responded that interactions between students and teachers were better in the learning communities courses and that learning communities instructors exercised "greater flexibility in class examinations" (Hewlett Grant Assessment and Evaluation Committee, 1996a, p. 4).

Analyzing student participation by learning community can reveal that students' experiences differ across communities. For example, students who participated in Miami's "Why Are Your Parents So Weird: 1960s" learning community commented that the three courses related well to each other and that the flow of the courses was enhanced by professors' sitting in on each others' classes. They praised the combined curriculum and commented that integration aided in their total understanding of the subject matter. Students in the "Influences of Psychology and Public Relations on Cinema and Society" learning community, however, questioned the combined curriculum and commented that they felt as if they were enrolled in three separate courses. They reported that their classes were not really combined, and the only connection between the courses was a documentary film project that took place at the end of the semester (Hewlett Grant Assessment and Evaluation Committee, 1996b).

Impact on Faculty

When we began collecting evidence on the impact of participation in learning communities on faculty, we came across anecdotal data on how they described teaching in the program and on the administrations' overall satisfaction with initial program success, but we found little real evidence of change in terms of teaching practices or organizational attitudes toward teaching and learning. We found that similar situations existed on other campuses. Here we describe information on how faculty reflect on the learning community experience, particularly the impact on their teaching.

Temple University. A case study of three learning communities offered as part of Temple's Learning Communities Program included a discussion of the experiences of faculty. This portion of the study centered on the question, "How do professors and graduate assistants experience Learning Communities?" (Reumann-Moore, El-Haj, and Gold, 1997). The study revealed that the flexible design of learning communities allowed teachers to shape communities in ways that reflected their own interests and priorities. For one professor, the academic connection was the important aspect of learning communities. For this reason, he focused on building connections between his and the other course in the community.

All of the professors interviewed for this study reported that teaching in a learning community had changed their pedagogy or philosophy toward teaching and learning in some manner. Some professors reported that they gained more of a "student perspective" (Reumann-Moore, El-Haj, and Gold, 1997, p. 27). Others described an increased understanding of the impact of group work on teaching and learning. One professor commented that she always used group work but that "the smaller size of Learning Communities classes enabled her to initiate more group work and to do a better job of coordinating it" (p. 28).

Several faculty members came away from the Learning Communities experience with a renewed sense of excitement toward teaching. Others were so pleased with the success of their learning communities courses that they implemented changes in their teaching styles in their non–learning communities courses. For one professor, teaching in a learning community helped him "reinvent [his teaching] methodology" and gave him an "impetus to think more innovatively" (Reumann-Moore, El-Haj, and Gold, 1997, p. 29).

Although the interviewed learning communities teachers emphasized the positive aspects of this teaching and learning environment, they did raise concerns that the learning communities atmosphere can resemble that of high school—the so-called grade 13 dynamic. Learning communities intentionally seek to help students navigate the transition from high school, or prior learning experiences, to college. In learning communities classrooms, faculty often have to invest time in helping students with the socialization process of becoming a college student. Graduate teaching assistants seem less comfortable with this role and are sometimes unsure of how to help students with the transition to college.

Teachers also identified institutional barriers that affected faculty involvement in learning communities. Learning communities attempt to foster greater involvement between students and their teachers. On a campus like Temple University, where large numbers of students commute to school, this is difficult to achieve. Temple Learning Communities faculty cited the culture of commuting as a barrier to faculty involvement. In some ways, this related to the overall culture of teaching, particularly the pressures to publish and research: "The Temple dynamic is very difficult. There's this sense of you go to class and get out. It pervades everything. It pervades faculty. It pervades students" (Reumann-Moore, El-Haj, and Gold, 1997, p. 36).

University of Maryland. Evidence on the impact of learning communities participation on faculty or students does not necessarily need to be the product of elaborate research designs and large-scale assessment projects. The College Park Scholars Program learned about the impact of its program on faculty through faculty reflection pieces. At the end of their first year, faculty were asked to submit thoughts on their first-year teaching experience in the program. One faculty member who taught in and directed the Scholars Science, Discovery, and the Universe thematic program described the joy of being able to share her scholarship with a broader audience of students. Prior to College Park Scholars, only small numbers of students enrolled in the advanced astronomy courses she taught. In the initial year of the program, she was deeply involved in the National Aeronautics and Space Administration project anticipating a comet collision with Jupiter and infected her students with her enthusiasm. She wrote in her reflection piece, "This event moved the story of the O. J. Simpson murder trial off the front pages of the *New York Times!* After this, how could I return to teaching a class of six?" (L. McFadden, personal communication, Oct. 5, 1998).

University of Miami. As part of its assessment effort, the University of Miami's Learning Communities Assessment and Evaluation Committee interviewed or surveyed learning communities faculty at the end of the semester. Faculty were asked to comment on interactions with students, the links among their courses, and their overall perceptions of learning communities.

Faculty reported increased interactions with students both in and out of the classroom. A small number of faculty, however, reported frustrations in organizing student participation in out-of-class events. In terms of course links, most faculty reported that they enjoyed the opportunity to plan and work with colleagues from other departments. They commented that links were strengthened when they were able to attend each other's classes, exchange syllabi, and review curricular material from the other courses. Course links were more easily achieved when the linked courses were the same size. In communities where a small class was linked with a large lecture class, faculty found building connections among courses more difficult. Planning time before the start of the semester was rated as highly important, with faculty noting that they needed more presemester training and planning time. Other faculty concerns were teaching load, performance review, and departmental support for teaching in learning communities.

Most faculty expressed a willingness to teach in a learning community again. One faculty member summarized the contributions of the program to the university as follows: "I would like this to take root. With a large university it is possible for students to hide in anonymity. This shakes up that anonymity, it does away with that. It puts a face on learning, it makes it more personal" (J. T. Masterson, personal communication, Dec. 1998).

Impact on the Institution

We found even less evidence on the impact of learning communities on the institution than on the impact on faculty. Nevertheless, understanding how learning communities are perceived within the institution can be helpful in the development and maintenance of learning communities initiatives. The information can be used to build or strengthen the administrative partnerships that directly affect the organizational efficiency of the program and the experiences of students and faculty.

University of Maryland. In the first year of the College Park Scholars Program, researchers at the University of Maryland conducted a study to determine the impact of the program on the admissions pool. They were particularly interested in whether the availability of College Park Scholars increased the yield of admitted students who chose to attend the university. The study revealed that "the yield rate for the Fall 1994 admitted students who were invited to participate in

CPS was significantly higher than that of similarly qualified 1993 admits, who would have qualified for a CPS invitation, if the program had existed then" (Flannery and Snyder-Nepo, 1994, p. 1). Fall 1993 College Park Scholars–eligible admitted students had a yield rate of 19.3 percent compared to 36.3 percent for 1994, the first year of the program. Researchers concluded that College Park Scholars was an important factor in students' decisions to attend the university.

University of Wisconsin (Bradley Learning Community). In the 1996–1997 end-of-year evaluation report of the Bradley Learning Community, program leaders reported several ways that program operations clashed with important university systems (Brower, 1997). First, the program experienced difficulty with the established registration and academic advising systems in attempts to implement an interdisciplinary academic anchor course for learning communities. Second, they realized that it was becoming increasingly difficult for the office of housing to continue to give special attention to one or two unique programs such as the Bradley Learning Community. A major concern was with the faculty system, which they described as encouraging "discipline-specific scholarship" (Brower, 1997, p. 15) and not the type of teaching required in learning communities—teaching that asks faculty to become involved with students in less traditional ways.

Temple University. A case study revealed that members of the campus community found the learning communities office and staff accessible, committed, and supportive of learning communities faculty. Program leadership had formed positive working relationships with offices across campus and could extend the benefits of these relationships to learning communities faculty and students. Here is how one learning communities faculty member described program staff: "In general they're supportive in ways that are hard to articulate . . . little things like working out room problems, connecting us to people to speak with about such things. . . . If I need something, I know they'll do their best to help" (Reumann-Moore, El-Haj, and Gold, 1997, p. 36).

This study also revealed that the Learning Communities Program had built a network of support that spanned across schools and programs. In fact, many people described ways that the learning communities initiative supported their own work. One student affairs administrator described how learning communities support students in the orientation process. "[Teaching students] survival skills [is a goal of learning communities]. . . . Over a semester, LCs provide important pieces of orientation. . . . Students have access to information when they need it [such as information on strategies for note taking, studying for exams, pre-registration]" (Reumann-Moore, El-Haj, and Gold, 1997, p. 38).

Evaluating the Evidence

Evaluating evidence is always a tricky business and invariably constrained by institutional context. When evaluating the evidence on learning communities, we need to consider the Hawthorne effect. Are positive results simply a side effect of the attention paid to learning communities participants, particularly in the early stages of their development and implementation? Evaluators of the Bradley Learning Community at the University of Wisconsin determined that "if the success of Bradley has largely been due to the 'Hawthorne Effect,' as was identified in the 1995–96 End-of-Year Report, then our challenge will be to maintain our positive effects even as our 'specialness' diminishes" (Brower, 1997, p. 1).

A second consideration is the nature of the patterns or themes that emerge from the data. What is the bigger picture? In a collaborative study of learning communities at the University of Washington, LaGuardia Community College, and Seattle Central Community College (Tinto, Love, and Russo, 1993), several themes emerged from the findings. For all three programs, learning communities helped students build a support network of peers. According to one student at LaGuardia Community College, "That's why the cluster is really great, because right now [September] I've made a lot of friends. In another school if I had different classmates, it would have been harder. I've made a lot of friends that I didn't know before, so that's good" (p. 6).

Another theme from the collaborative study was that learning communities helped bridge the gap between the academic and social dimensions of college. The personal connections that students established with their peers helped them experience their classes in new ways. Students in learning communities were more likely to attend and participate in class. According to one student, "In the cluster we knew each other, we were friends, we discussed everything from all the classes" (Tinto, Love, and Russo, 1993, p. 9).

A third theme was that through learning communities, students gained a voice in the construction of knowledge. Students, as active participants in the learning process, were encouraged to share ideas and raise questions. One student at Seattle Central Community College explained the experience this way: "These classes incorporate into your life and into your learning. It becomes part of your thinking. It just keeps connecting, and connecting, and connecting" (Tinto, Love, and Russo, 1993, p. 10).

When evaluating evidence it is also important to determine how that evidence is being used. Consider the difference between summative evaluations, which collect information about a specific program in order to make generalizations about effectiveness, and formative evaluations, which focus on a specific context and are used to improve a specific program, policy, or group (Patton, 1990). Much of the evidence described in this chapter came from formative evaluation research. Campuses collected information on what happens in learning communities and then used what they learned to improve the program and the experiences of its stakeholders—students, faculty, administrators, and staff.

Finally, consider ways to generalize lessons learned on other campuses. Campuses can invest time and resources in helping faculty and administrators understand the philosophy, goals, and approaches to learning communities, but if program leadership cannot adequately respond to the question of whether learning communities work, potential supporters may become future skeptics. Evidence on the impact of learning communities needs to be shared with faculty, students, administrators, and staff so they can recognize not only potential benefits but also barriers and obstacles to success.

Conclusion

Do learning communities work? Based on our experiences with learning communities on our respective campuses and our review of studies of a range of learning communities on a variety of campuses, we say yes. We do not suggest that learning communities work in terms of addressing all of an institution's concerns, yet as the range of studies described in this chapter demonstrate, programs seek different kinds of evidence of success. Whether taken as presented—brief summaries of lessons learned by individual campuses—or considered as a larger picture of the overall impact of learning communities, the studies discussed in this chapter describe the effect that learning communities have on the achievement, retention, and involvement of students; the ways teachers teach; and the manner in which organizations respond to change.

CHAPTER TEN

CONCLUDING ADVICE AND REFLECTIONS ON CREATING LEARNING COMMUNITIES

Throughout this book we have taken an intentionally practical approach in our discussion of creating learning communities because we hope that the collective wisdom of current practitioners can inform the continuing development of learning communities on a variety of campuses. We have addressed the questions that we are asked about our own work: What are learning communities? What do effective learning communities look like? How are they implemented? What does success look like?

Here we review and summarize some of themes that emerge from the chapters and offer recommendations to educators in various places along the continuum of learning communities work, from the initial gathering of information, through planning, implementation, and evaluation. Then we model an assessment tool of reflective interviews. We asked ourselves four key questions and tried to answer them honestly, out of our own experience: What do we know now that we wish we knew then? What lessons could not be taught, but rather had to be learned through trial and error? What knowledge have we acquired along the way? and What one piece of advice would we offer to beginners?

Conclusions

In *College: The Undergraduate Experience in America* Ernest Boyer (1987) outlined eight tensions facing colleges and universities: the transition from school to college, the goals and curriculum of education, the priorities of the faculty, the condition of teaching and learning, the quality of campus life, the governing of the college, assessing the outcome, and the connection between the campus and the world. We have offered in this book learning communities as a model that satisfies the educational objectives set out by Boyer and others in more recent reports (Boyer Commission, 1998; Kellogg Commission, 1998; Schneider and Shoenberg, 1998).

Learning Communities Models

Learning communities intentionally restructure the curriculum in ways that bring students, faculty, and disciplines together in more integrated and meaningful ways. The common approaches represent different levels of complexity in terms of curricular design, faculty role, cocurricular opportunities, and peer leadership. In choosing a model, campuses must carefully assess the faculty, student and institutional culture, and resources and support for the project. Our advice is to start small and after some success consider ways to improve that model or to customize the program by using multiple models to meet the needs of different student populations.

Learning communities are often smaller than most other units on campus, which is why large universities, the ones most often characterized by fragmentation and separateness, choose to place learning communities at the center of the freshman year. Learning communities provide a structure that supports students in their transition from high school learner to undergraduate. They also can be used beyond the freshman year to achieve other educational objectives. As members of a learning community students can begin to reframe their role as learners: from passive to active learner, from learning independently to learning interdependently, from teacher as authority to community as source of authority (MacGregor, 1990). Learning communities seek to create a safe and supportive learning environment for this transformation to occur. To create learning communities, however, campuses must identify the levers for change, redesign the curriculum, and reframe faculty roles.

Transforming Campus Culture

All campuses have change levers that can help advance the learning communities agenda: mission statements, strategic planning documents, departmental reviews, cross-department or college initiatives, and external reviews. Language and practice emerging from these levers can be used to assess a campus's readiness for change. When a campus is ready to move forward with learning communities, an important first step is identifying the stakeholders—faculty, administrators, staff, and students—and giving them important and visible roles in the planning process and in identifying priorities.

As with any other change process that requires transformation and risk taking, there will be obstacles. An important point is to avoid having the project become associated with one individual. Those doing the planning should seek advice from others and be realistic about costs and resources. Learning communities require human, fiscal, and physical resources. If the initial communities are grant funded, the budget that is developed should be one that the institution can sustain at the end of the grant period. Consider funding approaches that rely on contributions from the different partners in learning communities: central administration, schools and colleges, departments, and divisions (such as student affairs). Understand the different categories of costs, from initial planning and marketing to ongoing costs of faculty development and program support.

Creating Curriculum for Learning Communities

Learning communities seek to create a coherent and integrated learning environment in which students can formulate a view of knowledge that transcends disciplinary boundaries. Five curricular elements—general education, interdisciplinary courses, writing courses, seminars, and experiential learning—provide opportunities for active learning and a deeper understanding of issues across subject matters. Some campuses, Temple, for example, install learning communities in an existing general education program, while others, such as Portland State University, choose to develop communities as part of general education reform. The degree to which these elements are present in learning communities will differ from model to model; however, the most effective learning communities take learning seriously and put student learning ahead of other outcomes.

Changing Faculty Roles

Attracting and recruiting faculty to learning communities requires capturing the attention of individuals willing to be risk takers and change agents. Bringing these faculty together early so they can initiate learning communities and begin to cultivate the pool of quality teachers needed to sustain the program is an important step. A compensation and reward structure needs to be developed that recognizes faculty work in learning communities. Different ranks of faculty will have different roles. For example, graduate students at Temple, responsible for teaching many of the freshman writing courses in learning communities, are recognized as learning communities faculty. Undergraduates, who often are involved in the teaching of seminars linked to learning communities, can also become valued members of teaching teams.

Faculty development is critical to the success of learning communities. Presemester workshops and regular faculty meetings are effective ways to address issues such as the expectations for faculty, assessment, understanding students, curriculum design, and resources. This type of faculty development enhances the teaching and learning environment throughout the whole campus, not just within learning communities.

Essential Administrative Partnerships for Successful Learning Communities

Learning communities educators recognize that learning occurs both in and out of the classroom. The most effective learning communities programs bring together all individuals vested in the intellectual and social development of students: faculty, staff, students, and academic and student affairs administrators. In Chapter Six we offered strategies for building effective partnerships between academic and student affairs: identify a common purpose, engage in joint planning, link resources, coordinate students' formal and cocurricular learning experiences, define and assess desired outcomes, think systemically, and involve senior administrators. Identifying and supporting the partners and their roles in implementing and sustaining learning communities are vital activities.

Logistics of Establishing Learning Communities

Other implementation issues include scheduling courses, registering students, monitoring enrollments, marketing the program, and creating community among participants. Scheduling occurs in close collaboration with departments and with schools and colleges. Considerations are course size, meeting times, and location in the context of the goals for the program. Registration procedures must be efficient and easy to understand for students, faculty, advisers, and registration personnel. They should include a way to monitor enrollments to guarantee that students are properly registered and courses have sufficient numbers to run.

"If we build it, they will come" is not always true for learning communities, particularly in the early stages of implementation. A marketing plan with promotional activities and literature must address a range of questions, from "What is a learning community?" to "How do I enroll?" The process of creating community begins before the start of the semester or quarter. Faculty can be invited to participate in orientation, the point at which many students select their community, and can be encouraged to send entering students contact letters describing their goals and expectations for the community.

Evaluating and Assessing Learning Communities

Decisions about evaluation and assessment need to be part of the regularly scheduled planning and decision-making process for learning communities. We advise developing a research plan, defining research questions, considering multiple methods of assessment and collaborative approaches to research, and sharing results with those who are most invested in the success of the program. Directors need to ask themselves what it is they want to know and how they will use assessment data. Who enrolls in learning communities? What bearing does participation have on student retention, achievement, and satisfaction with the college experience? A major challenge facing learning communities researchers, and higher education in general, is how to assess actual changes in learning. Does participation in learning communities affect students' cognitive development?

Impact of Learning Communities on Students, Faculty, and the Institution

Are learning communities effective? We began this book with a review of longitudinal studies and higher education reports that support uses of learning communities as effective ways to address the challenges facing colleges and universities. Another way to respond to the question, "Why learning communities?" is to offer evidence of the positive impact they have on students, faculty, and the institution. On most campuses learning communities students earn higher grades and are retained at higher rates than nonparticipants. They demonstrate greater progress in terms of intellectual development, indicate higher levels of involvement with peers and the campus, and express greater overall satisfaction with the college experience. Although there is less empirical research available on the impact of learning communities on faculty, those who teach in learning communities report changed attitudes and approaches toward pedagogy and stronger interactions with students and colleagues. Concerns included teaching load, competing pressures of teaching and research, and adequate time for planning and preparation.

Reflections

The evidence that we found most informative in improving our own programs and in preparing this book came from studies that asked students and faculty to reflect on their experiences in learning communities. These personal testimonials provided insights into what the learning environment looks and feels like to individuals who teach and learn in them. Following our own advice regarding the value of reflection, we conclude this book with reflections on our own learning communities experiences.

In preparing this final section, we each reflected on and responded to the following questions:

- What do I know now that I wish I knew then?
- What lessons could not be taught but rather had to be learned through trial and error?
- What knowledge have I acquired along the way?
- What one piece of advice would I offer to beginners?

We have focused on the essential and intuitive knowledge, grounded in personal experience, that anchors our understanding of creating learning communities. Our reflections are presented from two perspectives, and offered as candid responses to the questions we posed.

What Do I Know Now That I Wish Knew Then?

Nancy Shapiro: I wish I had understood the campus planning cycles better. Many of the ideas that I brainstormed with the faculty, which seemed so promising, created stresses on the system because I did not fully appreciate the deadlines for publications, advising, registration, budget, or construction. At the time, these deadlines seemed to be annoying details, compared to the grand mission of creating a brand-new academic program, but as we all know, the devil is in the details. New learning communities directors should count themselves lucky if they have access to someone who has mastered the multiple time lines of a campus.

Jodi Levine: The "then" for this question would be my first year in my new role as coordinator of learning communities. The coordinator's position was created to provide logistical support to the faculty fellow for the project. My experience in advising and registering students was valued, since in the early stages, the program experienced difficulties recruiting students and properly enrolling them in the courses that constituted the linked-course communities. I understood my charge to be to attract students, develop efficient registration procedures, and annually increase the percentage of entering freshmen enrolled in learning communities.

What I did not realize early on is that building learning communities and increasing student enrollments in those communities are two very different processes. Simply enrolling students in common courses does not create learning communities. Although retention rates improved and students expressed satisfaction with the experience, there was tremendous inconsistency in the quality and uses of curricular integration and collaborative teaching across our linked-course communities. Creating learning communities is an intentional process of redesigning curriculum and bringing faculty and students together to create coherent and collaborative learning environments. Recruiting students to the program and getting them properly enrolled in communities are important logistical aspects of the work; however, designing and creating learning communities needs to be at the center of the implementation effort.

What Lessons Could Not Be Taught But Rather Had to Be Learned Through Trial and Error?

Nancy Shapiro: Discovering the underlying natural (or unnatural) alliances on a campus was a process of trial and error. Every campus is unique, and I found an odd assortment of supporters for learning communities in the admissions office, the residence life office, the commuter affairs office, the dean of undergraduate studies office, the orientation office, the registrar's office, the office of minority affairs, and the university's budget office, among others. It was my job to bring these individuals to the table with regular faculty, some of whom did not even know such offices existed on our campus. The two cultures needed to be bridged, and part of the process was discovering the right people on our campus to build those bridges. Finding the expertise on a campus takes some trial and error.

Another discovery was that some faculty really did not understand what were reasonable and what were unreasonable expectations of the first-year student. When in our first semester of the program, several of the first-time faculty directors insisted on teaching three-hour seminars, the first-time freshmen students shrieked in protest. Although I had tried to warn these faculty that students would resist this graduate school model of instruction, it took the shock of reality to create a climate for change. This crisis precipitated what in retrospect was our most successful faculty development workshop, where specialists in student learning from a variety of campus departments spent a day conducting a high-level seminar for program faculty in the areas of student development and pedagogy theory. Our pedagogy workshops became a standard component of future faculty retreats and orientations.

Jodi Levine: Determining the courses for our learning communities was a process of trial and error. We first went with the staples of the freshmen year: college composition, basic math, introductory social sciences, and survey courses in popular majors. Sections of first-year writing courses were involved in over 90 percent of our links. Occasionally faculty and department chairs approached us with creative ideas about new links. Can we try an American studies course linked to a literacy course in which students tutor older adults learning to read? What about a pairing of an inquiry-based physics course with finite math? When departments showed interest, we were always willing to experiment. Sometimes, even with extra promotion (mailings to students and advisers, fliers distributed at orientation, posters around campus), these courses were insufficiently enrolled. On other occasions students shared faculty excitement for the interdisciplinary potential of a link and a community filled. Learning communities educators do not always have a crystal ball.

What Knowledge Have I Acquired Along the Way?

Nancy Shapiro: Over the course of my work with the College Park Scholars Program, I experienced an unfolding appreciation of the vast resources on a campus that so often lie untapped. Those resources include the hidden energy that is released in the collaborative partnerships between student affairs and academic affairs and the student leaders who emerge because they have a nurturing environment within which to mature through the critical transition year of college. Perhaps most important, I found these hidden resources in the faculty who came into the profession to be teachers and somehow got lost in the shuffle. Every campus has dedicated, committed, passionate, natural teachers who sometimes go unrecognized and unrewarded. A learning community on a large campus acts as a magnet that attracts a particular kind of teacher-scholar. Learning communities bring them together into a critical mass where they validate each other and shine. In that process, they create something intrinsically worthwhile and something that ultimately serves the larger purpose of the campus.

Jodi Levine: I have learned new ways to talk about teaching and learning. I have learned about evaluation and assessment—most important, how to use it to describe our work and improve our program. I have discovered the literature on collaborative learning and faculty development. More important than the knowledge I have acquired is the support network I have built. Through e-mail, telephone conversations, conferences, site visits, and regular exchanges of program materials, I have developed a strong sense of what effective learning communities look like. I have a new community of colleagues with whom I regularly share ideas and vent frustrations. And in writing this book I learned so much more about the wonderful learning communities programs at other institutions that I now have a wish list for ways to improve the learning communities at Temple.

What One Piece of Advice Would I Offer Beginners?

Nancy Shapiro: The perfect is the enemy of the good. Don't get discouraged. Collect the wise people of the campus to form your advisory group. Give away credit.

Jodi Levine: Listen to the advice of other learning communities educators who have gone before you, but do not be deaf to the voices of reason, support, and objection on your own campus. Valuable lessons can be learned from the experiences of other learning communities programs, but I can not stress enough the importance of developing and tailoring learning communities to fit the student, faculty, and institutional culture of your campus.

Some Final Thoughts: How to Get from Here to There

Anyone embarking on a new project needs a road map to help them start in the right direction, and we hope this book has offered that kind of practical advice. We have tried to create such a chart for our colleagues—collecting and sharing hard-earned lessons and serendipitous successes because, in the end, we believe that as more campuses explore the possibilities of such communities, more students will enjoy a deeply rewarding college experience.

There is nothing easy about trying to change a campus culture. It has been described, variously, as akin to turning a battleship or, less reverently, herding cats. Yet our own experiences, and those we have described here, demonstrate that creating learning communities is quite manageable, especially if those who enter the process do so with realistic expectations and play to the strengths of their own campus. Members of a campus community who come together to design a learning community will recognize themselves in Chaucer's classic description of the Clerk: "And gladly wolde he lerne, and gladly teche."

LEARNING COMMUNITIES CONTACTS

Following is a list of contact information for learning communities programs discussed in this book. The list was compiled in part from *The Learning Communities Directory*, The Washington Center for Undergraduate Education, L-2211, The Evergreen State College, Olympia, WA 98505. Phone: (360) 866–6000, Ext. 6611; Fax: (360) 866–6662. Used by permission.

Bowling Green State University
Thomas Klein
Chapman Learning Community
Bowling Green, OH 43403
E-mail: Tklein@bgnet.bgsu.edu

Daytona Beach Community College
Codirectors: Richard Zelley, Cindy Avens
Quanta Program
P.O. Box 2811
Daytona Beach, FL 32120–2811
Phone: (904) 255–8131, Ext. 3407
Fax: 904–254–3012

Delta College
Julia Fogarty, Learning Communities Coordinator
English Division (1031)
University Center, MI 48710
Phone: (517) 686–9017
Fax: (517) 686–0485
E-mail: jtfogart@alpha.delta.edu

Diablo Valley College
Bruce Koller
Block Interdisciplinary Program
321 Golf Club Road
Pleasant Hill, CA 94523
Phone: (510) 685–1230, Ext. 455
E-mail: bkoller@viking.dvc.edu.

Drexel University
Valarie Meliotes Arms
Philadelphia, PA 19104
Phone: (215) 895–2444

The Evergreen State College
Barbara Leigh Smith
Academic Vice President and Provost
Olympia, WA 98505
Phone: (360) 866–6000, Ext. 6400
Fax: 360–866–6823

George Mason University
Teresa Michals
Director of the Linked Courses Program
English Department
Fairfax, VA 22030
Phone: (703) 993–1193
E-mail: tmichals@gmu.edu

New Century College*
John O'Conner, Dean
MSN 5D3, 4400 University Dr.
Phone: (703) 993–1436
Fax: (703) 993–1439
E-mail: joconnor@ofs1.gmu.edu
Karen Oates
Phone: (703) 993–1436
Fax: (703) 994–1439
E-mail: koates@gmu.edu

Illinois State University
Tim Gordon, Connections Program
340 Fell Hall
Normal, IL 61790–4000
Phone: (309) 438–3859 or 8364
Fax: (309)-438–7644
E-mail: twgordo@ilstu.edu

Indiana University Purdue University Indianapolis (IUPUI)
Scott Evenbeck, Dean
University College
815 W. Michigan Avenue
Indianapolis, IN 46202
E-mail: evenbeck@iupui.edu

Iowa State University
Steve Richardson, Director
Center for Teaching Excellence
204 Lab of Mechanics
Ames, IA 50011–2130
Phone: (515) 294–2402
Fax: 515–294–8627
E-mail: stevenr@iastate.edu

LaGuardia Community College
Will Koolsbergen, Phyllis Van Slyck
New Student House
31–10 Thomson Avenue
Long Island City, NY 11101
Phone: (718) 482–5496

Maricopa Community College District
Chandler-Gilbert Community College
Barbara Shovers
2626 East Pecos Road
Chandler, AZ 85225
Phone: (602) 732–7028
Fax: (602) 732–7028
E-mail: shovers@cgc.Maricopa.edu

Gateway Community College
Elizabeth Skinner
Phone: (602) 392–5085
E-mail: skinner@gwc.maricopa.edu

*George Mason was considering changes to this program as this book went to press.

Glendale Community College
Nancy Siefer
Phone: (602) 435–3234
E-mail: siefer@gc.maricopa.edu

Paradise Valley Community College
Sally Rings
Phone: (602) 787–6574
E-mail: rings@pvc.maricopa.edu

Portland State University
Charles White
P.O. Box 751
Portland, OR 97207
Phone: (503) 725–5890

Queens College
Judith Summerfield, Director
Freshman Year Initiative
65–30 Kissena Boulevard
Flushing, NY 11367
Phone: (718) 997–4686
E-mail: judsum@aol.com

Seattle Central Community College
Ron Hamberg, Vice President for Instruction
1701 Broadway
Seattle, WA 98122
Phone: (206) 587–5481
Fax: 206–344–4390
Rosetta Hunter, Associate Dean
Humanities and Social Science
Phone: (206) 587–2036

Temple University
Jodi Levine
Learning Communities
113 Curtis Hall
1301 Montgomery Avenue
Philadelphia, PA 19122

Phone: (215) 204–1937
Fax: (215) 204–2516
E-mail: jodih@vm.temple.edu
Daniel P. Tompkins, Faculty Fellow
Phone: (215) 204–4900
E-mail: dtompkin@thunder.ocis.temple.edu

University of Maryland
Katherine McAdams, Director
College Park Scholars
Phone: (301) 314-2777
E-mail: kmcadams@deans.umd.edu
Nancy Shapiro
E-mail: nshapiro@usmh.usmd.edu

University of Miami
John Masterson
Vice President for Undergraduate Affairs
Coral Gables, FL 33124–4628
Phone: (305) 284–2006
Fax: (305) 284–6758
E-mail: masterson@miami.ir.miami.edu

University of Missouri-Columbia
Charles C. Schroeder
Vice Chancellor, Student Affairs
Columbia, MO 65211–0001
Phone: (573) 882–6776
E-mail: charles_shroeder@missuri.edu
Frankie Minor, Director, Residence Life

University of Oregon
Jack Bennett, Director of Freshman Interest
Groups
Office of Student Retention Programs
372 Oregon Hall
Eugene, OR 97403–1217
Phone: (541) 346–1080
Fax: (503) 346–5811
E-mail: jbennett@oregon.uoregon.edu

University of South Florida

Joe Moxley
FIPSE Project Director
Department of English
4202 East Fowler Ave. CPR 107
Tampa, FL 33620
Phone: (813) 974–9522
Fax: (813) 974–2270
E-mail: moxley@chuma1.cas.usf.edu

University of Southern Maine

Steve Romanoff
Coordinator, Russell Scholars Program
96 Falmouth Street
Portland, ME 04103
Phone: (207) 780–4473

University of Utah

Slava Lubomudrov
Associate Dean, Liberal Education
Salt Lake City, Utah 84112
Phone: (801) 581–3811
Fax: (801) 585–5414
E-mail: lubomu_s@gse.utah.edu

University of Washington

Michael Ann Jundt
Director of New Student Programs
Box 353760
Seattle, WA 98195–3760
Phone: (206) 685–2705

University of Wisconsin-Madison

Aaron Brower
Bradley Learning Community
Madison, WI 53706
E-mail: Ambrower@facstaff.wisc.edu

William Rainey Harper College

Jacquelyn Mott
1200 West Algonquin Road
Palatine, IL 60067–7398
Phone: (847) 925–6894
Fax: (847) 925–6054
E-mail: jmott@harper.cc.il.us

REFERENCES

American College Personnel Association. *The Student Learning Imperative.* Washington, D.C.: American College Personnel Association, 1994.

American College Personnel Association and National Association of Student Personnel Administrators. *Principles of Good Practice for Student Affairs.* Washington, D.C.: American College Personnel Association and National Association of Student Personnel Administrators, 1997.

Angelo, T. "The Campus as Learning Community: Seven Promising Shifts and Seven Powerful Levers." *AAHE Bulletin,* 1977, *49.*

Angelo, T. A., and Cross, K. P. *Classroom Assessment Techniques: A Handbook for College Teachers.* (2nd ed.) San Francisco: Jossey-Bass, 1993.

Anson, C. M. "A Multidimensional Model of Writing." In D. A. Jolliffee (ed.), *Writing in Academic Disciplines.* Norwood, N.J.: Ablex, 1988.

Anson, C. M., and others. *Scenarios for Teaching Writing: Contexts for Discussion and Reflective Practice.* Urbana, Ill.: National Council of Teachers of English,1993.

Arms, V. M. "A Learning Community for Professionals: The New Engineering Curriculum." *Metropolitan Universities,* 1998, *9*(1), 63–72.

Astin, A. W. *Achieving Educational Excellence.* San Francisco: Jossey-Bass, 1985.

Astin, A. W. *What Matters in College, Four Critical Years Revisited.* San Francisco: Jossey-Bass, 1993.

Avens, C., and Zelley, R. *QUANTA: An Interdisciplinary Learning Community (Four Studies).* Daytona Beach, Fla.: Daytona Beach Community College, 1992. (ERIC Document Reproduction Service No. ED 349 073)

Banta, T. W., and Kuh, G. D. "A Missing Link in Assessment." *Change,* 1998, *30*(2), 40–46.

Bennett, J. "Learning Communities, Academic Advising and Other Support Programs." In

J. H. Levine (ed.), *Learning Communities: New Structures, New Partnerships for Learning.* Columbia, S.C.: National Center for the First-Year Experience and Students in Transition, 1999.

Bentley, M. "Discovery Projects: College Park Scholars Conduct Primary Research." *Terrapin Parent* (University of Maryland, College Park), 1997, *11*(1), 1.

Bogdan, R. C., and Biklen, S. K. *Qualitative Research in Education: An Introduction to Theory and Methods.* (3rd ed.) Needham Heights, Mass.: Allyn & Bacon, 1998.

Bombardieri, M. "Colleges Seek Answers to Poor Test Scores: Free Workshops, Early Exams Eyed." *Boston Globe,* July 11, 1998, p. B1.

Boone, L. E., and Kurtz, D. L. *Contemporary Marketing Wired.* (9th ed.) Orlando, Fla.: Dryden Press, 1998.

Borden, V., and Rooney, P. M. "Evaluating and Assessing Learning Communities." *Metropolitan Universities,* 1998, *9*(1), 73–88.

Boyer Commission on Educating Undergraduates in the Research University. *Reinventing Undergraduate Education: A Blueprint for America's Research Universities.* Washington, D.C.: Carnegie Foundation for the Advancement of Teaching, 1998.

Boyer, E. L. *College: The Undergraduate Experience in America.* New York: HarperCollins, 1987.

Brower, A. "End-of-Year Evaluation on the Bradley Learning Community." Unpublished report, University of Wisconsin-Madison, 1997.

Burgess, P. "Why Don't We Have More Teamwork in Higher Education?" Paper presented at AAHE Forum: Faculty Roles and Rewards, New Orleans, Jan. 1994.

Bystrom, V. A. "Learning Communities in the Community College." In J. H. Levine (ed.), *Learning Communities: New Structures, New Partnerships for Learning.* Columbia, S.C.: National Center for the First-Year Experience and Students in Transition, 1999.

Callahan, B., and Colson, M. "Report on College Park Scholars Discovery Projects: Comparison of Student Pre- and Post-Essays." Unpublished report, University of Maryland, College Park, 1998.

Center for Research on Learning and Teaching. "The Pilot Program: A Residential Experiment for Underclassmen." Memo to faculty no. 47, University of Michigan, 1972.

Chickering, A. W., and Gamson, Z. F. *Seven Principles for Good Practice in Higher Education. AAHE Bulletin,* 1987, *39*(7), 3–7.

Coles, R. *The Call of Service: A Witness to Idealism.* Boston: Houghton Mifflin, 1993.

College Park Scholars Annual Report. College Park, Md.: University of Maryland, 1997.

Cross, K. P., and Steadman, M. H. *Classroom Research: Implementing the Scholarship of Teaching.* San Francisco: Jossey-Bass, 1996.

Dewey, J. *Democracy and Education.* New York: Macmillan, 1916.

Elliot, J., and Decker, E. "People, Structure, Funding and Context: Resources for Learning Communities." In J. H. Levine (ed.), *Learning Communities: New Structures, New Partnerships for Learning.* Columbia, S.C.: National Center for the First-Year Experience and Students in Transition, 1999.

Enos, S. L., and Troppe, M. L. "Service Learning in the Curriculum." In B. Jacoby (ed.), *Service-Learning in Higher Education.* San Francisco: Jossey-Bass, 1996.

Evenbeck, S., and Williams, G. "Learning Communities: An Instructional Team Approach." *Metropolitan Universities,* 1998, *9*(1), 35–46.

Ewell, P. "Organizing for Learning: A New Imperative." *AAHE Bulletin,* 1997, *50*(4), 3–6.

Ferren, A., and Slavings, R. "Quantitative Tools for Analyzing the Cost and Effectiveness of the Curriculum." Workshop presented at the 85th annual meeting of the Association of American Colleges and Universities, San Francisco, Jan. 30, 1999.

Flannery, T., and Snyder-Nepo, N. "College Park Scholars and President's Scholarships: Two Critical Factors in Improved Yield Rates." Unpublished report, University of Maryland, College Park, 1994.

Forgione, P. D. "Achievement in the United States: Are Students Performing Better?" National Center for Educational Statistics, Office of Educational Research and Improvement, U.S. Department of Education. [http://nces.ed.gov/Pressrelease/housetest2.html]. 1999.

Freire, P. *Pedagogy of the Oppressed*, New York: Continuum, 1974.

Gabelnick, F., MacGregor, J., Matthews, R. S., and Smith, B. L. (eds.). *Learning Communities: Creating Connections Among Students, Faculty, and Disciplines.* New Directions for Teaching and Learning, no. 41. San Francisco: Jossey-Bass, 1990.

Gaff, J. G. *General Education: The Changing Agenda.* Washington, D.C.: Association of American Colleges and Universities, 1999.

Gardner, J. N., and others. "A Natural Linkage—The First-Year Seminar and the Learning Community." In J. H. Levine (ed.), *Learning Communities: New Structures, New Partnerships for Learning.* Columbia, S.C.: National Center for the First-Year Experience and Students in Transition, 1999.

Gilligan, C. *In a Different Voice: Psychological Theory and Women's Development.* Cambridge, Mass.: Harvard University Press, 1982.

Goodsell Love, A. "What Are Learning Communities?" In J. H. Levine (ed.), *Learning Communities: New Structures, New Partnerships for Learning.* Columbia, S.C.: National Center for the First-Year Experience and Students in Transition, 1999.

Halfman, R. *Tactics for Change: Checklists for the Academic Innovator.* Cambridge, Mass.: MIT Press, 1972.

Harris, E. L., and Dillingham, A. E. "Student Characteristics and the Efficacy of Learning Communities." Paper presented at 1998 AAHE Assessment Conference, Cincinnati, June 1998.

Herrington, A. J. "Writing to Learn: Writing Across the Disciplines." *College English*, 1981, *41*, 379–387.

Herrington, A., and Moran, C. *Writing, Teaching, and Learning in the Disciplines.* New York: Modern Languages Association, 1992.

Hewlett Grant Assessment and Evaluation Committee. "Focus Group Study: Learning Communities—College of Engineering's IMPACT Program." Unpublished report, University of Miami, 1996a.

Hewlett Grant Assessment and Evaluation Committee. "Focus Group Study: Learning Communities—'Influences of Psychology and Public Relations on Cinema and Society' and 'Why Are Your Parents So Weird: The 1960s.'" Unpublished report, University of Miami, 1996b

Hill, P. J. "Inter-Generational Communities: Partnerships in Discovery." In R. M. Jones and B. L. Smith (eds.), *Against the Current.* Cambridge, Mass.: Schenkman Publishing, 1984.

Jacoby, B., and others (eds.). *Service-Learning in Higher Education.* San Francisco: Jossey-Bass, 1996.

Johnson, J. L., and King, S. G. "Russell Scholars Program: Evaluation of the Inaugural Year." Unpublished report, University of Southern Maine, 1997.

Johnson, R. T., and Johnson, D. W. *Cooperative Learning: Warm Ups, Grouping Strategies and Group Activities.* Edina, Minn.: Interaction Book Company, 1990.

Joint Task Force on Student Learning, American Association for Higher Education, American College Personnel Association, National Association of Student Personnel Administrators. *Powerful Partnerships: A Shared Responsibility for Learning.* Washington, D.C.: Joint Task Force on Student Learning, American Association for Higher Education, American College Personnel Association, National Association of Student Personnel Administrators, June 2, 1998.

Jones, B. B., Thompson, W. E., and Ketchum, W. E. "Which Way Is Up? An Integrated Learning Community and Rites of Passage for Men of Color." Paper presented at the Eleventh International Conference on the First-Year Experience, Dublin, Ireland, 1998.

Jones, R. M., and Smith, B. L. (eds.). *Against the Current.* Cambridge, Mass.: Schenkman Publishing, 1984.

Jundt, M., Etzkorn, K., and Johnson, J. N. "Planning the Production: Scheduling, Recruiting, and Registering Students in Learning Communities." In J. H. Levine (ed.), *Learning Communities: New Structures, New Partnerships for Learning.* Columbia, S.C.: National Resource Center for the First-Year Experience and Students in Transition, 1999.

Kellogg Commission on the Future of State and Land Grant Universities. *Returning to Our Roots: The Student Experience.* Washington, D.C.: National Association of State Universities and Land Grant Colleges, 1997.

Ketcheson, K., and Levine, J. H. "Evaluating and Assessing Learning Communities." In J. H. Levine (ed.), *Learning Communities: New Structures, New Partnerships for Learning.* Columbia, S.C.: National Resource Center for the First-Year Experience and Students in Transition, 1999.

Klein, J. T. *Mapping Interdisciplinary Studies.* Washington, D.C.: Association of American Colleges and Universities, 1999.

"Lessons Learned from Promoting Academic Agendas in the Residence Hall." ACUHO-I, *Talking Stick,* 1995, *12*(7), 20–22.

Levine, J. H. "Fall 1994 Focus Group Report." Unpublished report, Temple University, 1994.

Levine, J. H. "Building Learning Communities for Faculty." *About Campus,* 1998, *2*(6), 22–24.

Light, R. *Harvard Assessment Seminars, Second Report.* Cambridge, Mass.: Harvard University School of Education and Public Policy, 1992.

Love, A. G., Russo, P., and Tinto, V. "Assessment of Collaborative Learning Programs: The Promise of Collaborative Research." In Washington Center Evaluation Committee (ed.), *Assessment in and of Collaborative Learning: A Handbook of Strategies.* Olympia, Wash.: Washington Center for Improving the Quality of Undergraduate Education, 1995.

Love, A. G., and Tinto, V. "Academic Advising Through Learning Communities: Bridging the Academic and Social Divide." In M. L. Upcraft and G. L. Kramer (eds.), *First-Year Academic Advising: Patterns in the Present, Pathways to the Future.* Columbia, S.C.: National Resource Center for the First-Year Experience and Students in Transition, 1995.

Love, P. G., Kuh, G. D., MacKay, K. A., and Hardy, C. M. "Side by Side: Faculty and Student Affairs Cultures." In G. D. Kuh (ed.), *Cultural Perspectives in Student Affairs Work.* Washington, D.C.: American College Personnel Association, 1993.

Luberto, A. "College Park Scholars." Essay published in *The Sunspot: The Newsletter of the College Park Scholars Program,* University of Maryland, College Park, Fall 1998. p. 9.

MacGregor, J. *Intellectual Development of Students in Learning Community Programs 1986–1987.* Occasional Paper no. 1. Olympia, Wash.: Washington Center for Improving the Quality of Undergraduate Education, 1987.

MacGregor, J. "Collaborative Learning: Shared Inquiry as a Process of Reform." In M. D. Svinicki (ed.), *The Changing Face of College Teaching.* New Directions for Teaching and Learning, no. 12. San Francisco: Jossey-Bass, 1990.

MacGregor, J. "Going Public: How Collaborative Learning and Learning Communities Invite New Assessment Approaches." In Washington Center Evaluation Committee (eds.), *Assessment in and of Collaborative Learning: A Handbook of Strategies.* Olympia, Wash.: Washington Center for Improving the Quality of Undergraduate Education, 1995.

MacGregor, J., Smith, B. L., Matthews, R. S., and Gabelnick, F. "Learning Community Models." Paper presented at the National Conference on Higher Education, American Association of Higher Education, Washington, D.C., Mar. 1997.

MacGregor, J., Smith, B. L., Tinto, V., and Levine, J. H. "Learning About Learning Communities: Taking Student Learning Seriously." Materials prepared for the National Resource Center for the First-Year Experience and Students in Transition Teleconference, Columbia, South Carolina, Apr. 19, 1999.

Meiklejohn, A. *The Experimental College.* Edited and abridged by J. W. Powell. Cabin John, Md.: Seven Locks Press, 1981.

Mintz, S. D., and Hesser, G. W. "Principles of Good Practice in Service-Learning." In B. Jacoby (ed.), *Service-Learning in Higher Education.* San Francisco: Jossey-Bass, 1996.

National Institute of Education. *Involvement in Learning: Realizing the Potential of American Higher Education* (NIE 1984): *Study Group on the Conditions of Excellence in American Higher Education.* Washington, D.C.: National Institute of Education, Department of Education, 1984.

"New Century College Competency Base Program." [http://www.ncc.gmu.edu/new_century_collegecompetency_ba.html]. Sept. 1998.

Newcomb, T. "Student Peer-Group Influences." In N. Sanford (ed.), *The American College: A Psychological and Social Interpretation of the Higher Learning.* New York: Wiley, 1962.

Pascarella, E. T., and Terenzini, P. T. *How College Affects Students.* San Francisco: Jossey-Bass, 1991.

Patton, M. Q. *Practical Evaluation.* Thousand Oaks, Calif.: Sage, 1982.

Patton, M. Q. *Qualitative Evaluation and Research Methods.* (2nd ed.) Thousand Oaks, Calif.: Sage, 1990.

Perry, W. G. *Forms of Intellectual Development in the College Years.* New York: Harcourt Brace Jovanovich, 1970.

Pew Higher Education Roundtable. *Policy Perspectives,* 1993, *5*(2,2A).

Portland State Advisor's Guide to University Studies. Portland, Oreg.: Office of University Studies, Portland State University, Dec. 1997.

Rasmussen, G., and Skinner, E. "Learning Communities: Getting Started. A Maricopa Center for Learning and Instruction Monograph." [http://hakatai.mcli.dist.maricopa.edu/ilc/index.html]. May 1998.

Reumann-Moore, R., El-Haj, A., and Gold, E. *Friends for School Purposes: Learning Communities and Their Role in Building Community at a Large Urban University.* Philadelphia: Temple University, 1997.

Rohall, D., and Morrison, D. "College Park Scholars Focus Group Report." Unpublished report, University of Maryland, College Park, 1996.

Schneider, A. "When Revising Curriculum, Strategy May Trump Pedagogy." *Chronicle of Higher Education*, Feb. 19, 1999, pp. A14–16.

Schneider, C. G., and Shoenberg, R. *The Academy in Transition: Contemporary Understandings of Liberal Education*. Washington, D.C.: Association of American Colleges and Universities, 1998.

Scholnick, E. K. "A Two-Year Longitudinal Study of Science and Math Students in the College Park Scholars Program." Unpublished report, University of Maryland, College Park, 1996.

Schroeder, C. C. "Developing Learning Communities." In C. C. Schroeder and others (eds.), *Realizing the Educational Potential of Residence Halls*. San Francisco: Jossey-Bass, 1994.

Schroeder, C. C., Minor, F., and Tarkow, T. "Learning Communities: Partnerships Between Academic and Student Affairs." In J. H. Levine (ed.), *Learning Communities: New Structures, New Partnerships for Learning*. Columbia, S.C.: National Center for the First-Year Experience and Students in Transition, 1999.

Senge, P. M. *The Fifth Discipline*. New York: Doubleday Currency, 1990.

Shapiro, N. "Rhetorical Maturity, Context Independence and Cognitive Development in College Student Writing." Paper presented to the Penn State Conference on Rhetoric and Composition, University Park, Pa.; 1984.

Shapiro, N. "Rhetorical Maturity and Perry's Scheme of Cognitive Complexity." Paper presented at the annual conference on College Composition and Communication, Minneapolis, 1985. (ED 255 935)

Shapiro, N. "Discovery Projects: Contextualized Research Experiences for Second-Year Undergraduates." In S. P. McGraw and S. L. Newkirk (eds.), *Fund for the Improvement of Post Secondary Education Project Descriptions*. Washington, D.C.: Fund for the Improvement of Post Secondary Education, U.S. Department of Education, 1997.

Shapiro, N. "Learning Communities: Moving Beyond Classroom Walls." *Metropolitan Universities*, 1998, *9*(1), 25–34.

Shulman, L. S. "Disciplines of Inquiry in Education: An Overview." In R. M. Jaeger (ed.), *Complementary Methods for Research in Education*. Washington, D.C.: American Education Research Association, 1988.

Smith, B. L., and MacGregor, J. "Reflective Interviews with Learning Community Teaching Teams: Strengthening Dialogue About Teaching and Learning." *Washington Center News*, 1991, *6*(1), 26–28.

Smith, T. B. "Introduction: Why a Monograph About First-Year Residential Colleges?" In T. B. Smith (ed.), *Gateways: Residential Colleges and the First-Year Experience*. Columbia, S.C.: National Resource Center for the First-Year Experience and Students in Transition, 1993.

Srinivas, A. "Call to Community." Essay published in *The Sunsport: The Newsletter of the College Park Scholars Program*, University of Maryland, College Park, Fall 1998, p. 9.

Student Life Studies Abstracts. *A Student Success Story: Freshman Interest Groups at the University of Missouri-Columbia*. No. 1. Columbia, Mo.: University of Missouri, 1996.

Student Life Studies Abstracts. *Longer Term Effects of Freshman Interest Groups (FIGS) on Students' College Experience and Educational Outcomes*. No. 5. Columbia, Mo.: University of Missouri, 1997.

Tinto, V., and Goodsell, A. *A Longitudinal Study of Freshman Interest Groups at the University of*

Washington. University Park, Pa.: National Center for Postsecondary Teaching, Learning and Assessment, 1993.

Tinto, V., Love, A. G., and Russo, P. *Building Learning Communities for New College Students: A Summary of Research Findings of the Collaborative Learning Project.* University Park, Pa.: National Center on Postsecondary Teaching, Learning and Assessment, 1993.

Tompkins, D. P., and Mader, R. "Creating Learning Communities Among Teachers: Faculty Development in Learning Communities." *Metropolitan Universities,* 1998, *9*(1), 17–24.

Walvoord, B. E., and McCarthy, L. P. *Thinking and Writing in College: A Naturalistic Study of Students in Four Disciplines.* Urbana, Ill.: National Council of Teachers of English, 1991.

White, C. R. "Placing Community-Building at the Center of the Curriculum." *Metropolitan Universities,* 1998, *9*(1), 55–62.

William Rainey Harper Faculty Handbook. Palatine, Ill.: William Rainey Harper College, 1998.

Wingspread Group in Higher Education. *An American Imperative: Higher Expectations for Higher Education.* Racine, Wis.: Johnson Foundation, 1993.

Youtz, B. "The Evergreen State College: An Experiment Maturing." In R. M. Jones and B. L. Smith (eds.), *Against the Current.* Cambridge, Mass.: Schenkman Publishing, 1984.

Zeller, W. J. "The Evolution of the Learning Specialist: A Hybrid Emerges from the Clashing of Two Campus Cultures." Unpublished manuscript, 1997.

INDEX